Long Exposure

My Life In and Beyond the Copper Country

JOSEPH B. KIRKISH

Published by Mission Point Press
2554 Chandler Rd.
Traverse City, MI 49696
(231) 421-9513
www.MissionPointPress.com

Front cover: Lake Superior sunset from the cottage at Copper Harbor
Back cover: Joe Kirkish at Brockway Mountain Drive, 2021

Cover and book design by Sarah Meiers

ISBN: 978-1-954786-75-2

Library of Congress Control Number: 2022902348

Printed in the United States of America

Long Exposure

My Life In and Beyond the Copper Country

BY JOSEPH B. KIRKISH

Edited by Meg Ostrum

MISSION POINT PRESS

TABLE OF CONTENTS

Preface vii
Foreword by Meg Ostrum xi

PART 1: Roots, 1925–43

1: Transplanting the Old World to America 2
2: West Houghton Childhood 6
3: Navigating the Wider World of Houghton and Adolescence . . . 20
4: Detroit Interlude 28

PART 2: My Educational Odyssey, 1943–56

5: GI Postings and Perks 36
6: Three Midwestern Universities 47
7: Three Fateful Summers 71
8: Bohemian Years in New York 85
9: Return to Camp Nebagamon 109

PART 3: Careers in and beyond the Copper Country, 1956–88

10: Becoming a Humanities Teacher 120
11: New Horizons 138
12: Heartland Studies 145
13: Camp Nebagamon Connections 153
14: Students, Colleagues, and Friends 160
15: Zigzagging Toward My Doctorate 168
16: WGGL and NPR 193
17: Thriving in Academia 212
18: A Home and a Hostel on College Avenue 220
19: Becoming a Don 234

PART 4: Emeritus, 1988–99

20: Travels 246
21: Encores and New Creative Ventures 262
22: Another Inheritance 273
23: The Return of Lord Krishna and the Birth of Pastor Joe 279

PART 5: Elder, 2000–

24: Zigzagging through Aging 286
25: Long Exposure 296
List of Illustrations 310
Acknowledgments 313
About the Author 314

Self-portrait, 2006

PREFACE

Nearly the end of the line....

The luminous face on the radio beside the bed reads 1:07 a.m. A Debussy piece whispers from it, just audible to help me fall asleep ... undermined by the coldest night of the spring, May 12, 2020. Unwilling to cave in to Morpheus, I think about the fact that three times in my life—including in 1925 when I was born—my late May birthday has been ushered in with at least a foot of the white stuff, and now, with those new normal "climate change clouds" heavy with decades of outpourings of poisonous matter from we humans below, another unwelcome atmospheric debacle is even more possible.

It's uncommonly cold. Instead of turning on the electric blankets (two of them), I huddle into my typical fetal position—on my left side to avoid the tingling sciatic pain that would otherwise prevent slumber—as it has, off and on, for decades.

Finally, I give up on sleep and leave the semi-comfort of my bed to sit down at the computer and muse.

We, all, are sent into the world from that auspicious moment of birth as innocent creatures, developed and modified by inner and outer vicissitudes, by the places in which we lived, by nature or nurture—or both. It's been nearly 95 years since I lay as a newborn child on a bassinet where I almost ended my life by picking up a canister of zinc oxide, shaking it like a rattle, and leaving behind enough residue in my lungs to perform a lifelong battle inside me. And that's not all that followed me from that early tabula rasa to the present—the slate now crammed and before old age starts its erasure in subtle, insidious ways: a slight impression in the rear of my skull, where, as a youngster, my sister accidentally felled me with a baseball bat, or a permanent leg scar from falling off a low wall in my preteens. It seems miraculous that as a lung-polluted child I could outlive so many of the family.

With normal life arrested by the pandemic, the impetus to start working on a memoir took over, a project urged on by dear Meg Ostrum (née Geismer), with whom I've been fondly connected since I met her at the age of 11 (and I at least two decades older) and who wove in and out of my life as a perennial creative presence for 60 years. A published author and experienced editor, she insisted that I possessed an engaging style and a remarkable way of talking about things (likely, I suspect, from years of writing in the daily paper and in class lectures) and that such a memoir was, indeed, publishable.

I thank her even now, recalling this morning's hour-long conversation: she, making her usually sage editorial comments on the latest chunk of writing and I, so pleased to have that hour with her—caged as I have been for nearly two months, while the world outside is being modified by an insidious coronavirus that spread from murky birth somewhere in China across the earth.

It's so cold. I should retreat to my bed, cover up over my head, and fall asleep, but the writing project has taken on a life of its own. I think about the Romans, a Polish couple, through whose generosity I've inhabited this house for 40 years, and whose presence I still feel living here. I continue to ruminate over the legacy I might leave behind. What do I think about people in general? Some good, some not so good. What do I think about my life in general? Some parts good....

My mind sleepily wanders further, backward in time, filling in so many near-forgotten incidents that Meg inquisitively has helped excavate.

It's now the 14th month of lockdown during this seemingly endless pandemic. Month after month of volleying responses to Meg's queries through extended phone conversations and emails several times each week—we in a yin-yang creative collaboration. I had the information, the imagination, and to some degree, the ability to dredge up buried fragments of experience (sometimes colored more by imagination than actual verity) that I could encapsulate into episodes in the attempt to, as an Irish novelist once said, "Make them as interesting to others as they have been to you," while my keen-eyed collaborator has applied her natural talent for organizing material and probing for details—and able through her resourceful internet searching to flesh out my descriptions and sharpen their accuracy.

An adventure in its own right, yes! Surprisingly, I've come to find satisfaction in retracing the arc of my life. I've let my thoughts percolate during the day and then devoted the evening (often well past midnight) to writing them down. Meg's steady coaching has lifted me from the ongoing doldrums (which had grown into a boring, real-life version of the 1993 film *Groundhog Day*, as I became actor Bill Murray forced to unaccountably repeat each day over and over—forever?).

Occasional surprises have livened my long days and contributed to the work in progress—a call or message out of the blue from a former student, faraway friend or relative, and best of all, unexpected visitors. Serendipitously, a few days ago, just when I was starting to write the last section ("Long Exposure") to sum up my reflections, around 9 a.m., I was wakened by a team (Kevin Store, director of the Portage Health Foundation and a filmmaker) who had come to interview me about the roots of my philanthropic activities around Copper Country. (They came as planned, I had the days mixed up.) While they set up equipment in the living room, upstairs I leaped into yesterday's clothes, slapped water on my face, and then descended. The Q & A continued for two hours, and during that time, my life kept flashing in and out, with Kevin encouraging more tales from out of the past, building me up, and I tearing myself down. It was a remarkable morning of renewed insights. When they went off to edit and reshape the interview, I was left with a mess of information from out of the corners of my cobwebbed brain.

But it did fortify something I desperately needed and helped answer the question of my magnetic draw to this place of my birth and childhood years. I gave here, I received here, and have gained recognition here; what more could I seek?

And now I have a full memoir of my life in the Copper Country and beyond. So many to thank: those instructors who taught me to write well; people who beyond my parents touched me deeply—from abroad, at work and play, while in New York, and elsewhere;

oh, and the COVID-19 pandemic which finally prodded me with so much spare time on my hands to take the leap. A blanket apology as well for lapses in memory (particularly dates and names of people and places)—any mistakes are due to my inveterate absentmindedness and an aging brain that has compressed time and people. Nothing may come of this, but for better or worse, it has been accomplished. In summary, you have my word for it: I did my best.

FOREWORD

"**Aaahhh, Meg. I was hoping it was you,** and not 'Yvonne,' 'Janette,' 'Meredith,' or an anonymous robocaller who pester me on a daily basis." Over the past 16 months, this is how Joe frequently greeted my calls. With Joe having neither caller ID nor out of area phone-calling service (not to mention, a cell phone or Zoom), I would dial him up every three or four days and then spend a rich hour or two discussing revisions to the latest section of his memoir (sent as a 1000–2000 word email)—what was missing, extraneous, inaccurate, or could be used elsewhere, and topics to explore in the next batch of material. And always, the ups and downs of his daily life being "incarcerated" (his words) by the pandemic. When I hung up, I would regularly have to remind myself that he was in his mid-90s, not a peer; having interviewed many octogenarians and nonagenarians, I absorbed his in-depth storytelling, acute observations, along with his still fluent writing abilities, with amazement.

Despite not having the satisfaction of seeing him through video conversations, all I had to do was look around my study and Joe's presence was everywhere. On the wall, next to my desk hangs a 2021 calendar with his stunning panoramic and close-up color photos of the textures and light of Lake Superior and its surroundings. On display on various bookshelves are a few of his small, theatrical laser prints of exotic flowers bursting with plant energy amidst arrangements of his intimate and posed photos of family members. In one grouping, there's a candid shot of him beaming, dressed in a fancy, three-piece suit and tie at our Thanksgiving gathering. And, propped against a tabletop wooden file cabinet is a poster-like black and white portrait of me with a pensive expression that he shot during my college days. All of these are special keepsakes both from a dear family friend <u>and</u> a mentor who informally has guided my creative and professional development since childhood.

Meg by University Circle Lagoon, 1969

For me (and I suspect, too, his protégés at Michigan Tech and Camp Nebagamon), Joe was not just an accomplished photographer and prolific writer whose work elicited admiration, but equally gifted as a teacher whose trusted criticism could inspire confidence and continued exploration—and who was eager to track my progress over time and distance. Thirty years ago, I began sending him copies of documentary publications that I had edited, always receiving thoughtful commentaries. Then, in the late '90s, Joe was the first person to whom I wanted to show the first chapter of my book about a true, little-known WWII resistance story in the French Pyrenees that I had spent years researching. Getting his immediate and strong approval (not without some red marks) propelled me forward as a first-time author.

When the book (*The Surgeon and the Shepherd*) appeared in 2004, Joe eagerly volunteered to arrange an event at a local bookstore and help promote it through his weekly column. That was the third "pilgrimage" I'd made to Copper Country, with Joe acting as host and tour guide. The true highlight of the trip was a Club Indigo film screening of Alfred Hitchcock's *North by Northwest* at the Calumet Theatre, which he emceed; it was evident that, now nearly 80, he had lost none of his skills as a teacher and entertainer.

Regretfully, though, I have not seen him since. A health emergency prevented him from traveling to Cleveland to speak at my mother's memorial service in 2012, but emails, calls, and packages every now and then have kept us in touch.

My gratitude for Joe's generous tutelage over many decades made it easy to offer to help him produce a memoir when I learned, from a phone call a few weeks into the pandemic lockdown, that he had started churning out vignettes from his past. Impressed by the few samples that he sent me, I initially envisioned being just a reader who would provide periodic feedback and some research assistance. He lapped up my first batch of written notes and ideas generated by our follow-up discussion, deeply appreciative that my feedback about content and structure was exactly what was necessary to propel him forward with this unplanned writing project. So, quickly, my role enlarged into his coach-editor, or as he phrased it, "to help put together the jigsaw puzzle of my life."

Indeed, reconstructing Joe's long and full life into a coherent narrative entailed challenges for both of us. From our long association, I was well aware of his passions and some of his many persona—magician, photographer, professor, art critic, community volunteer, radio producer, and journalist. I was cognizant, too, of his overflowing kindness, modesty, deep curiosity matched by deep religious faith, boundless energy, and even his foibles. What I didn't know, and came to realize, was that he never had had a grand plan nor road map for his life. He was only determined not to replicate his father's fate as a small-town merchant. Instead, he had always lived day to day, concerned neither about the past nor the future. Luckily, he had a large, if disorganized, cache of articles, resumes, flyers, letters, awards, and other memorabilia to draw upon, and of course, thousands of photographs.

Joe's recollections were vivid, yet early on I recognized that his chronology was often scrambled: his memory had creatively overlaid impressions to yield a satisfying composite (much as he did with his manipulation of photographic images!). To separate these layers of experience required my investigation of a host of topics, through which I made all kinds of fascinating discoveries that helped make the puzzle pieces fit (for example, learning about the visionary Bob Gard, founder of the Wisconsin Idea Theatre, under whom Joe worked as a graduate student in speech and theater at the University of Wisconsin in the early 1950s). The fact-checking process also made me understand what an extraordinary life of serendipitous adventures Joe has led, one that affords glimpses into and insights about historic moments, important American institutions, and public figures from many spheres. How many small-town grocers' sons can claim association with both the co-pilot of the *Enola Gay* and the father of the H-bomb?

While writing came easily to Joe, having only one good eye, plus a string of other health challenges both chronic and acute (including a few trips to the emergency room), slowed or arrested the work in progress. An even greater frustration was his inability to master the process of drafting and saving text ("my computer hates me" was the subject of many emails), and after the loss of several extended passages well into the writing, he was ready to abandon the project. Over the months of collaboration, I had learned to write in Joe's style, but I did not want to become a ghostwriter. I convinced him that I could not finish it, and fortunately, he perse-vered ... a further reminder of his inspiring capacity to adapt and rebound.

The result is a complex self-portrait of the first-born son of an American immigrant family who fought to carve out his own identity, and then, return and thrive in the small town of his birth in Michigan's Copper Country. No matter the length of contact, Joe's radiant personality and prolific talents have always made an indel-ible impression; no doubt that the many hidden or lesser-known dimensions of his remarkable life that are revealed in this memoir will only expand understanding and deepen appreciation.

This project, too, was a first for both of us: I had never worked so intensively as an editor to shape a personal narrative, while Joe, always preferring to write solo, had always shied away from any kind of joint endeavor. Our marathon quest has produced a lasting legacy and given purpose to both of our lives through an uncertain and stressful period.

Aaahhh, Joe.

Portage Lake Bridge with view of Houghton

PART 1

Roots, 1925–43

1

Transplanting the Old World to America

"When you arrive in New York, take a train west as far as Chicago, then another train straight north. Get off at the end of the line."

T hese were the simple directions given to my father's family when they left Lebanon around 1912 and that brought them to their new land in the northernmost part of Michigan's Upper Peninsula (U.P.): the Copper Country. It was a region that had a century of boom-and-bust history of copper and iron mining and that had attracted successive waves of immigrants, initially from the British Isles (Ireland and Cornwall), then Northern and Western Europe (predominantly Finns, but also Croatians, Poles, and Italians). In the first decades of the 20th century came another influx, this time primarily from southern European and Mediterranean Basin countries.

The Kirkish family settled in Houghton, near the heart of the industrial boom, a small city along the Portage Canal with a twin city, Hancock, on the opposite (northern) bank. Aged 16 (more or less—families in Lebanon rarely recorded births officially, so all we knew was that he was born "a Monday after Easter"), my father was the youngest of the three sons. They plied the only trade they knew—peddling. They carted huge amounts of general home goods for sale around the area, eventually with a horse and lorry stuffed with everything from black stockings and mittens to pots and pans. The men of the Kirkish family claimed they learned Finnish well before they could converse in good English, thanks to the proliferation of Scandinavians who had settled on farms and in small surrounding communities.

Early on, Mike, the eldest of the three brothers, took his bride, Freda, and wisely headed for warmer climes, settling in Sunnyvale, California, to raise a family and to open what became a very successful clothing business. (He managed to outlive the others who stayed behind in Michigan's Upper Peninsula.)

That left my father, Azar, and his older brother, George, to fend for themselves and their parents. The peddling business boomed, enabling them to move into a grand old three-story building on West Houghton's main street—large enough to be divided into storage space on the top floors and, on the main floor, groceries on one side (run by my father) and farm clothing and housewares on the other (run by Uncle George).

As the manager of the grocery portion, my father was considered a "good catch" for a Lebanese girl (unthinkable that his wife should come from any other background). With only two candidates in the area, he set his eye on the one employed in his store: Anjool Brady (yes, a bona fide name from the old Arabic sod; we think it might be a corruption of the Arabic word for mailman: *brah-ah-dee*). She was the daughter of Shafeeha (Sofia) Brady—"Mama Fee" to me—a respected woman, well-known as a saleswoman of imported laces and tablecloths.

Shafeeha was happily married to Joseph Brady until a tragic streetcar accident took his life, just a few years after their two daughters were born. City-bred and well-educated, Shafeeha had been swept off her feet by Joseph, who wooed and brought her to the U.P., first to Iron Mountain, then to Houghton. Their courtship followed a very common pattern in those days: daughters would meet visiting Lebanese men from America who spun dreams of a promising future, then follow them back to the States, often to a less-than-promised life, but willing to accept their marital agreements without question. Then, as a young widow, but also a strong-willed woman with overseas connections, she recognized the needs of local families and became quite successful as a traveling

**Joe's grandmother, Shafeeha Brady,
with daughters Anjool and Nabeeha**

saleswoman. She would lug a huge suitcase from wealthy home to wealthy home on the Eastside boulevard and graciously display her fancy samples from Venice and other European textile centers for eager buyers, leaving with lucrative orders.

For Anjool and Azar, it was not important that their Arabic backgrounds were the only thing they had in common; at the time, it seemed enough. She was petite, a nice complement to Azar's short stature, shy, with huge olive eyes and nice features topped by wavy dark hair—always neatly and appropriately dressed. Then there was Azar, uneducated and barely able to speak English. He was a simple man, easygoing and liked by the men of the community, with whom he would join at the local tavern more for socializing than drinking. My father, in fact, rarely drank liquor at all, unless on some special occasion might sip a bit of *arak* (a strong licorice-tasting brew).

It wasn't necessary for my educated mother, with dreams of a prince of a man she'd always hoped for, to wrench him away from those nightly pleasures for something more elevated. He acquiesced, instead, congenially filling his evenings in an easy chair, smoking and listening to the radio.

Gradually, the differences emerged—he, from a rural area, she, from a more sophisticated milieu—with my mother nagging and trying to mold him into her royal image. Compromises were never enough; it usually left my father, who dreaded confrontations, to give in. When he didn't, their bedroom became a war zone, after which wife would punish husband with a Silent Treatment, something he dreaded, but accepted even when he never knew why.

It became obvious within their household that the disillusioned Anjool was not content. She married the man she had hoped to turn into something special; she wanted an orchid, got a daisy, and never really settled for it. Her gradual embitterment as the wife of a typical Arabic fellow (who expected to rule as head of the roost), led to conflicts, arguments, nagging, and a grinding of opposites, resulting in a bitter competition of "he wins, she wins"—endlessly, evident to us at home, but rarely in public.

Another serious, but typical, problem of the times resulted from this young, innocent girl marrying an innocent man ... but one who insisted on regular sexual rights, to which she felt forced to suffer, to fulfill a traditional obligation leading to childbearing, accepting it as her plight in married life.

With nothing in common but their backgrounds, they struggled through the early days, eventually delivering four children, in a compromising outward appearance as a happy family. Their differences developed into a love/hate relationship without recourse—until his death, at which time my mother, perhaps guiltily, fell into deep sorrow, painting him as her true and faithful husband, imagining (quite believably) a loving tribute for the rest of her life.

As I grew up, my mother would try her Silent Treatments on me for any possible reason, whether it involved my fault or hers. By that time, I was well aware of the system; I resolved never to follow my father's acquiescence. It led to one intractable situation after another with neither of us winning out. I tried to put them out of mind, but they continued to roil inside me.

2

West Houghton Childhood

It was late spring—May 23, 1925, to be exact—that I took my first breath of life ... during the blizzard of the year. From my parents' account, my father carted my mother carefully through a foot or more of the white stuff to a taxi waiting for us, a typically black Model A, that struggled with difficulty through the snow steadily piling up on the bridge over Portage Lake from Houghton to Hancock to the St. Joseph Hospital. Halfway across the bridge, we spun our tires in the steadily deepening snow with my father incoherently shouting in a mix of Arabic and broken English at the driver to hurry or I'd be born there on the bridge.

They did make it on time, and early that morning, I became a native son of the U.P. As the first-born, I was named for my grandfather—whom I never knew, and never knew much about, except for his tragic accident. My parents and I lived in a small, but nicely furnished home, one of three modest side-by-side houses on a hillside in West Houghton (a purchase aided by Uncle George, who, as expected in family tradition, hovered patiently over his younger brother's ongoing struggle with the grocery business). A fourth member of the family, my beloved spinster Aunt Muroon (a Brady relative), lived with us for a few years until her death. She was a quiet, unobtrusive woman who took to me from the start; I still feel the warmth of her holding me in her arms as if she were, indeed, substituting her open love for what never came from my mother— or, for that matter, my father.

To be fair, both mother and father fulfilled their familial duties as well as could be expected; they watched carefully and critically over me and the three siblings that followed, occasionally showering us with gifts and other unexpected niceties, but always seeming to do so as good parents should, yet without any real parental expressions of love.

As we grew up, it became obvious that my mother favored their second child, Celia (Cis), recognizing, perhaps, the inevitable fact that she might, like herself, fall into some marital trap. My father took instinctively to the next child, the naturally cuddly Barbara (Babe). If ever I felt left out, I had my Aunt Muroon as a very young child and, later, my grandmother Shafeeha, who lived alone and bestowed special treatment on me—even taking me on her sales junkets, which I found fascinating. She had small features in an oval face and could speak in a perfect unaccented voice. I liked how delicately she could carry herself and her hefty bag of samples; though she had a stocky body, she was not overweight. I remember, too, that she was a tough disciplinarian, but could soften at times as well.

Joe with his parents, Anjool and Azar Kirkish, 1925

We children were two years apart; that seemed to be the completion of our family, until one day on my tenth birthday, when our mother, with a shy, guilty smile, announced that there was to be the sound of little footsteps soon among us. It turned out to be brother James (Jimmy), a darkly brooding kid with a definite mind of his own—and a kid for my mother to "stick up for" all the way through his bad boy years in school. Right or wrong, she overlooked his devious mannerisms (catching flies and pleasurably pulling them apart or purposely breaking things around the house) as nothing but natural child's play. I always wondered if his odd ways had been caused by an accidental fall on his head onto the sidewalk while still a baby.

My parents raised us more as Arabs than Americans—the way, at the time, most immigrants, no matter from which nationality, did with their children. We ate healthy food with lamb (never mutton) as our main meat dish, along with plenty of soups and stews made of fruit and vegetable leftovers from the weekend (stores never stayed open on God's Day). Saturday evenings were a family delight. After the main meal (we called it "supper" then), we gathered in the kitchen while my mother separated, chopped, sliced, and piled everything into mounds, each to become a hearty meal for the rest of the week. And as we worked, we listened to *Amos & Andy* and soap operas on the radio.

When they didn't want us to understand a conversation—or argument—my parents spoke in Arabic. Their moral code was simple: do it the Lebanese way, i.e., regard ourselves as second, with everyone else first. Our ethnic background was much more evident than that of the children we played with—and later schooled with—something that haunted us well into our late teens. We were different, ate different food, mingled in communal proximity with one another, followed traditional values.

Our household was a stark contrast to our Uncle George's family, a more typical Arabic one in which the father ruled, while his wife proudly gave him five sons to raise in strict obedience. His paternal demands for perfection spread to include us four children as well ("What's a matter, no soap in your house?" "Where's your tie for church; you got no ties?"), which we accepted from him as sarcastically instructional.

Unlike my father, who made a decent living, but nothing more, Uncle George had prospered. Ambitious and eager to expand into the furniture market, he had first moved to the second floor and then, later, into a separate building as his rugs and furniture enterprise thrived. His motto, which he would repeat to me over and over in my teens, was simple but sincere: "Good quality, good price, good service." (It worked and resulted in a thriving business for the next three generations.) During my youth, I also witnessed this proud man become tragically subdued when gangrene took one leg; it was also pitiful to see him angrily drag his body along the rows of vegetables in his garden or have on occasion to ask (demand) some help from his wife.

Aunt Tamimi, meanwhile, spent her time proudly educating us children. She spoke with pride in perfect English on the beauty and importance of our national heritage, emphasizing how the Lebanese separated themselves from the "barbarian Syrians." Her favorite topic: the contrast between educated, inventive Lebanese who lived on the border of the Mediterranean as opposed to the crude inland Syrians. She would claim our ancestors' invention of the abacus, among other things, and their traveling as far as the British Isles to sell their precious artifacts and purple cloths (dyed from juices squeezed from sea creatures—favored by the rich across the seas, worn as a sign of greatness). We assumed these, plus so many other tales honoring our ancestry, to be true.

She was gracious in her storytelling, smiling broadly and revealing oversized false teeth which she displayed with pride. She was a direct contrast to her brother, the black sheep of her family who operated a second grocery story in a nearby town with the power and bravado of an empowering lord. Despite his notoriously foul breath and jabbing elbows, he would force himself on his help—particularly the young, unmarried girls—in the back room of the grocery store. He also fraternized with local politicians, sharing with them the results of shady legal deals. Most of this was never observed by others, but in front of me, when I'd be asked to help out at his store. I'd witness things that made me uncomfortable, even ashamed.

My Aunt Karma's family also played an important part in my early education. She had married out of the Kirkish clan back in

Lebanon to Uncle Charley Karam. Because of his occupation as a common laborer—a tall, amazingly powerful man who fit comfortably in his work among slabs of raw copper at the local smelting factory—the Kirkish brothers kept somewhat at a distance.

As in most Arabic families, without an argument, Uncle Charley ruled the roost. Uneducated, what he lacked in civil deportment he made up for with his native intelligence and huge presence—a giant of a man whose fierce features belied the gentleness of his demeanor among the family. His hands were so large they could encompass one's entire head between those rough palms.

I liked the Karams the most. As often as possible, I (usually with a sister) would trudge in pleasant anticipation up the footpath through saplings and wild brush to the last house on the west side of town. It was a rather plain wooden building, painted in a variety of colors, jerry-built by Uncle Charley and friends with additions as the family grew, that offered never-ending fascination in the backyard, including a chicken house filled with the creatures (one or another eventually fated for a supper meal), along with some ducks, geese, and other equally noisy critters, also doomed eventually to the kitchen. And beyond, the field of wildflowers, and berries when in season. How could any youngster not find this a plethora of things to do, to play with, or smell?

Each visit began the same; a ritualistic walk up the creaking steps to the second floor, where, next to the only bathroom in the house, was our grandmother's prim little space. She would be sitting in a worn easy chair next to the window, in ritual black out of deference to her recently departed husband, crocheting socks and mittens for all of us—originating from a huge ball of store wrapping string (the kind we used at our grocery/clothing store with which to wrap sales items; shopping bags and plastics were not yet invented).

She would hear us coming, put down the needles and string, and wait with open arms for us to greet her. It was an uncomfortable ritual because she knew no English and our Arabic was limited to *leck* (no) or *aye* (yes)—and if we used the wrong word, she would chuckle, pat us with a gentle slap, and send us on our way with one of her omnipresent perfume-flavored cookies.

Then we could play with the younger members of the Karam family—inside, when the weather was bad, out among the chickens or in the fields when it was not. Our playroom was the parlor with its slick wooden floor (covered as elsewhere by rugs homemade into ovals of tightly woven cloth strips). Or we might take turns operating underneath the foot-peddled sewing machine with our hands or helping Aunt Karma or one of the older daughters create various pieces of bedding (pillowcases from empty cotton flour sacks, to be stuffed with chicken and duck feathers—wonderfully comfortable, unlike the "regular" pillows we normally slept on at home).

The Karam children were a carnivalesque mixture of personalities. Marie and Joe had been born in Lebanon and were teenagers. She was a fun-loving, ambitious person who developed a sharp mind for business (eventually opening her own local grocery store in competition with my father!). Joe was like an older brother, who looked—and acted—like the cartoon character Popeye ... even to his occupation as a sailor in the local Coast Guard. He was my idol and, later in my teens, became my teacher in all things sexual with his wild stories about his "one-nighters" and what sailors did when at sea for weeks on end. Annie was somber and serious; Arthur was studious. ("Art" to us, "Arth" to the men of the family, was praised and admired by all of the Kirkish clan—graduating with a degree in chemical engineering from nearby Michigan College of Mining and Technology and then becoming a manager at GM in Flint.) Last, but not least, closest to my age, was gentle, playful Ginny. With our combined imaginations and a home full of possibilities, she and I invented and enjoyed all sorts of games together even long after we grew up.

On the best days we were given permission to stay for supper at the large table covered with unmatched dishes and silverware, to a meal of Lebanese food: lentils, thick homemade yogurt, salad from the garden enriched with exotic spices, homemade flatbread for butter and jam, succulent lamb in a variety of combinations, and the sweetest, richest dessert too good for royalty—all routinely made by Aunt Karma who reigned most of each day in her kitchen among an array of large, well-worn pots, pans, wooden spatulas, and more. From early morning to supper, savory odors permeated the entire house from that miraculous kitchen; I can smell it now, as I write. And I can recall with pleasure when I'd be given the task of taking a tray of samples up to our grandmother, who would move to her little table and, after a gesture of thanks, attack and scrape it, leaving nothing but a tray now emptied to the last crumb.

Then, the finale to a perfect day: undressing to our underwear to share the large spare bed. We would lie sideways down its length, girl, boy, girl, boy, until one day when it was decided we were too old for that—a new arrangement of girls down one side and boys the other. We would awaken next morning, fill our stomachs with creamy gruel and flatbread (and butter and jam), then head back down the path to our waiting mother, to return to the expected Kirkish-type ritual expected of us at home.

◆ ◆ ◆

When people would ask, "What do you want to be when you grow up?" I would say, "a priest or a magician." (As a kid, I was very taken with the hypnotic powers of the comic book character—and first superhero—Mandrake the Magician.)

I grew up faithfully following the Ten Commandments under the supervision of the nuns at school and the priests in church sermons—and, of course, at home. I became an altar boy at St. Ignatius Church, starting at age seven. Monsignor Reszek, the senior priest, was a highly educated man who had been ordered by his superiors in Austria to emigrate to our town. Though he came to this strange land with reluctance, he set to work, building a magnificent church with imported stained-glass windows and elegant statuary also purchased from Austria—and a spire that could be seen from nearly every part of the town. And though he regarded us as an ignorant, unsophisticated lot, he led us with some patience through the expected rituals of faith.

For me, a winter-long terror was walking on dark mornings to serve at daily Mass. Alone, I waded through the unplowed street for half a mile, hearing the roar of plows in the distance and dreading what might happen should I come face to face with it. Then I had to brave climbing up a series of church steps from basement to sacristy, with only the flickering of light from the blazing furnace as a guide. However, all was made good at the end of each week's Masses: along with the other boys, I would wait at the sacristy door for our beloved Father Reszek, hand in cassock pocket, jingling dimes, pulling a shiny one out one at a time and ceremoniously dropping it into each awaiting hand—followed by his roar, "*Rous mit der Doich*" (or something like that). We would "*rous*" off to the nearby favorite candy store to happily conclude that week. And then the routine would begin again....

We attended St. Ignatius Catholic School, operated by the nuns who lived next door. They were a motley group of shiny-faced ladies of unknowable age, each in control of us in one classroom or another, each to be obediently respected as spectacularly mysterious, yet eagle-eyed, religious teachers in concern for our time spent with them. For some reason, most of the nuns favored me, would comment to others about my lunches (which included flatbread filled with a Lebanese concoction and lettuce), and would show appreciation when I'd volunteer to perform tasks for them. They always referred to me politely as "Jozeph" with a *z*.

A most profound experience occurred when the young nun who was my third grade teacher was flummoxed by a question for which I needed spiritual guidance: in my neighborhood, dominated by Protestant families, I felt my religion at times created a distance between my friends and me. She enrolled the help of the youthful assistant priest, who was easy to talk to, played ball with us, and was forever enthusiastic and patient, so I asked him: "How could I bring my chums into the Catholic faith?" "Why?" he asked. My innocent response: "Because, Father, when I die and go to heaven, I want them to go there, too." And his response, rocking me gently on his knee, "Ah, Jozeph" (always with a *z*), "if they feel as true to their faith as you do, you'll see them in heaven, too." I didn't know the word "ecumenical" at the time, but his response kindled my becoming a Catholic with an ecumenical spirit.

Growing up during the Great Depression on the working-class side of town, I never actually realized it until I accompanied my grandmother on her sales calls. For the first time, I was exposed to the lifestyles of the wealthy inhabitants of the grand, beautiful, 19th-century homes built by the mining barons along tree-lined East Houghton Boulevard. However, in the midst of the 1930s, our family had other things to worry about than trying to keep up with the Joneses.

We accepted the processions of begging men (most of whom lived in abject poverty in shacks constructed in the "Hoover Hotels" along the West End's garbage heaps) who took advantage of our mother as a relatively well-off wife of a relatively well-off grocery store owner—for a free lunch traded for some work around the house. That was fine until she caught one of them making a chalk mark on the sidewalk in front of the house—a signal that this was a place ripe for begging. She continued helping them but always more cautiously after that.

We were proud that my father could afford the first car on the block—a Nash, which neighbors admired, commenting with unconcealed envy that he had paid almost a thousand dollars for that object of beauty. The Nash was never thought of as a luxury; it was used constantly for business—regularly delivering orders of food out of town to organizations like the Conservation Corps Camps. (My father would carry a rifle in the back seat, hoping to get a little extra food for the table along the forested way.)

My father would fill the car with special baskets for his poorer customers on special occasions like Christmas, Easter, and Thanksgiving. At the store, we all participated the day before those holidays. Space was made on the counters for a lineup of baskets, which were filled with fruit, candy, produce, and some special items to match each special occasion: a pork loin for Christmas, turkey for Thanksgiving, ham for Easter. For the delivery run, I would sit in the front seat, barely tall enough to see out of the side window, observing a delightful sight: a knock at the door of a ramshackle house, a lit kerosene lantern coming to the door, youngsters behind the mother or father attending in shy anticipation, the giving of a basket, thank-yous, my father returning back to the car and driving away, slowing growing from his 5'6" height into the giant of a man I hoped to imitate in some distant years.

All this activity was perceived through the eyes of a silent, obedient son not yet in his teens, who saw and believed in what he'd been taught about honesty, generosity, and love of people regardless of circumstances, from his dad and uncle, who with all their superiority as heads of families taught us, both by actions and direct edicts, the goodness of selflessness, love of others first, and honesty. At least, from this elder son's vantage point, so it seemed and, I still believe, so it is.

Azar Kirkish with Joe, Babe, and Cis

❖ ❖ ❖

Strangely, as children, we never actually thought of ourselves as deprived or under-privileged. Along with our parents, we adjusted creatively to the times. My sisters and I put on occasional shows, usually on weekends, rain or shine, for the neighbors on our side porch, for the price of a safety pin. We acted out short plays of our making, singing and dancing. Sometimes we just sat in front of the audience devising dramatic stories—fairy tales, historical reenactments, etc.

Our house on the hill was just a few blocks from where the large lake ships would dock. They carried tourists from Detroit to Duluth and back, pausing at key stops along the way—a getaway cruise for those who could afford it. When they'd roll up to the dock, they'd announce their presence with a blast from their powerful horns—a signal to my neighborhood pals and me. We'd head for the docks, leaping and shouting, "Money! Money!" to the people watching us from above; eventually, they'd throw pennies to us, amused by the excitement it caused in our scrapping over them.

Being much smaller than most of the boys who attended with regularity all summer, and not just a little embarrassed at my reticence, I'd back away while the gangs would yell, then leap for the coins. As the penny flow stopped, they'd return home via the local candy store, leaving me to scavenge the dock for a few missed coins. Over the years, the money scramble became de rigueur; at each boat's landing, the bags of coins came out, the kids ran to the docks, and the competition began. Now and then, to heighten the fun, someone would drop a dollar bill from the deck, to watch the older boys strip and leap into the water to retrieve the floating treasure.

I remained the scavenger but still enjoyed the entire routine. The scene at the ship inspired a new special giveaway event at our house. When our parents would return from out-of-town trips, they'd arrive with bundles of surprise gifts—dolls, mechanical toys, and even nice new clothing; we kept the playthings in a big chest upstairs. One Saturday, while Mom and Dad were off on one of their weekend trips, my sisters and I had an idea. We gathered up some of the well-worn treasures, opened the upstairs window, and shouted to the youngsters playing in the street below: "Toys, toys, toys!" and would toss the prizes to the clamoring groups below—a lot of fun for them and for us, who had been taught about "sharing" years earlier. Fun, until one day we were caught in the act, and that was that. Still, for years after, we kept finding ways to share with kids far poorer than we, always with the same sense of joy in doing so.

Wading waist deep into wild thimbleberry patches to pick and eat the raspberry-like fruit was a regular activity (we just had to be on the lookout for hornets' nests hidden beneath the leaves). But our favorite summer pastime was walking down a footpath through a tree- and bush-filled square leading along a creek below and a few blocks up to the Karam family. Among the trees of that as yet unoccupied area were saplings, which we would dare each other to climb to the top; we would hold tightly onto the supple crown, dropping our legs away from the tree and sailing slowly, gently until our feet touched the ground. Somehow we never got caught doing this fun but dangerous game.

For a child, Houghton's severe winters were less difficult than for our parents, who had to walk or drive through huge snow drifts. We used the drifts for fun, carving out their interiors and creating caves. Winter fun also consisted of taking advantage of the heavy snowfalls by leaping from second-floor windows or roofs into the snow below. A near calamity once happened when my little sister walked out from under a porch eave just as I leaped and hit her, sinking her up to shoulders in deep snow, eventually pulling her out with the help of friends.

There were secret games with my neighborhood pals, most of whom were the children of parents who had immigrated from the coal regions of Cornwall. We did things in our garage which we thought were not wrong, just harmless secret pleasures—stripping, applying grease here and there, then dressing again. For us it was great exploratory fun, and, again, if ever our parents suspected it, nothing was done to end it. I felt more comfortable with them than the girls (who played with my sisters), though it was fun to be around them, too, teaching me to dance the popular steps, etc. The idea of sex had not yet entered our heads, though I did notice odd gestures, giggles, and whispers among the girls as they looked at me … and felt uneasy.

One summer—when I was still young—we visited my mother's cousins in Brooklyn, New York, during our summer vacation. My mother and her brood of three spent several weeks with great Aunt Zakeeye and family in Bay Ridge, living as part of their household (she, Uncle Mike, and a daughter, Eleanor, and son, Ted, who were close in age to us). It was a huge mansion sitting above the street on a high lump of a hillock, with seemingly dozens of rooms and closets, from two basements (one a bowling alley) and the upper three floors—broad stairways leading everywhere, sometimes lit by stained glass windows alongside them. What fun we had had as children, playing hide and seek, free to inspect every floor, every room, every closet. After that, in alternating summers, they would stay with us at Grandmother Shafeeha's summer home on Portage Lake, not far from our house.

My father loved being outdoors, and though hardly an ace in business, capitalized on a real estate opportunity that turned into a treasured family summer place. One year our mother took my two younger sisters to a Copper Harbor vacation resort for a change from summers at our grandmother's cottage. My father and I would drive up after closing shop late Saturday afternoon to spend an overnight with them, but never found them at the resort. Instead, they would go a few miles down the Lake Superior shore road to a deer path leading through a dense outcropping of trees—and play on one of the most picturesque beaches along that drive. Because it could not be seen from the road, it was the only stretch of shore property yet unsold. When my father found that he could buy all 660 feet of it (with 800 feet back across the road) for $7 a foot, he leapt at it.

What to do with the property? He encouraged his store help to come up for a Sunday each week, bring the family, and make a day of it—the men clearing space for a cottage, the kids carrying the branches to the beach for a grand bonfire, and the wives setting up a makeshift table on which a feast from the store rewarded them all.

Then came the carpenters who set a foundation, 30' × 30', topped it with a half basement and main floor, a guest bedroom, bathroom, and kitchen, plus family sleeping quarters above. I was given a small middle room between our parents' bedroom and a back bunk bed bedroom. At my mother's insistence, there were big windows looking out to the lake in the living room. Errors in measurement were made and repaired, and before we knew it, we had a summer cottage fit for up to 20 people (most of them store families whom my father felt deserved weekends for their summer of help).

At the store, it would be like this: one clerk to another, asking, "What are you planning for the weekend?" "Oh, I thought we'd take the kids to Azar's place on the lake." "Good idea; I think we'll do it, too." It was fun, at first, a communal picnic from Friday night to Sunday night—my father continuing to supply the food and drinks, while my mother spent all her daytime in the little kitchen fixing meals to be served on the lengthy table along one side of the living room. But when the number reached 32 one weekend, both parents decided it was time to pull the plug, stayed home for a few weekends until the message connected, then to return to quieter weekends after that.

When construction was complete, my parents could now invite guests as they wished, including a covey of nuns from the Catholic school, who, romping around in their habits and laughing, entertained themselves and us. Of course, there were relatives from downstate who became regulars, half a dozen at a time, and being of the clan, capable to share and share alike. We looked forward to them—my father with the husbands renting a fishing boat to bring home Lake Superior trout for a copious evening meal, my mother with the other mothers fussing about the house, cooking together, sewing curtains or sofa covers, chattering in a mix of English and Arabic as they pleased. And we youngsters ... well, it was an endless enjoyment of excursions into the wilds across the road or swimming and diving from the rocks into the cove in front of the broad beach of water that extended the full 660 feet of shoreline.

Then, as a preteen, it was decided that I should be part of the fishing expeditions, though I detested it, with nothing to do for an entire day but sit and stare at the endless shoreline while the men enjoyed the privacy and pleasure of "man talk" punctuated with "Yeah, sures" and "Damned if I knows" as they drank quarts of Bosch beer. For me, 12 oz. bottles of cola. As the boat chugged on and the sun rose in the sky, we would strip to our summer union suits and enjoy the fresh coolness of summer breezes, while six fishing lines dangling from the boat would offer up their largesse to waiting hands. My only enjoyment would arrive as the sun arrived directly overhead and a large box offered us egg salad sandwiches, more beer (and pop), and huge chunks of homemade apple pie. Then the dreary wait for me until the sun would approach the horizon and we'd head back, clothed and arms heavy with the day's trout catch. At least I could rejoin my cousins afterwards, and sleep among them in the crowded room of bunk beds.

3

Navigating the Wider World of Houghton and Adolescence

From grade school to high school graduation, I was educated most rigorously by my father, since I worked under his jurisdiction after school and all Saturdays. For my father, life after 10 was preparation for a future in business.

My job? At first, dusting, sweeping, weighing up and packaging bulk foods for the shelves, then serving customers from the array of stacked bulk cookie cases, and later, waiting on customers as well. Most humiliating of all: making the rounds of customers' homes on College Boulevard trying to collect overdue charges from mothers who made promises never kept about taking care of it right away, while daughters or sons I knew from school would snicker at the farcical visits. Of course, I knew full well that they'd be back fawning to my father for the pennies he'd make off their sales.

Odd, how clearly those days at the store still impress in detail even now—that large three-floored boxy building on the west end of Main Street. The facade faced north, directly across from the massive wooden edifice that held sawdust-covered blocks of ice (cut from the lake during the winter) to be sold from a horse-drawn dray to homes on the streets above us. The store was just a few blocks from where we lived, making it easy for me when, on Sundays, a desperate phone call from a customer fresh out of cigarettes or beer would send me, key in hand, to the rescue.

Memories flood in of standing with my father and uncle outside the building and examining the facade and the red Kirkish

Brothers sign above, trying to figure out how to make it more successfully compelling among other shops on either side of us—a rival tobacco, liquor, and sundry food shop to the west and on the east side, Apple Mary's luncheonette and candy store. A proud, full-blooded American Indian, Mary would tell wild stories including about being jailed for selling bathtub gin during Prohibition. She taught me how to lie straight-faced, as she did: just believe what you say.

❖ ❖ ❖

When I turned 10, my father made another great real estate decision. He offered a small price for a nearby grand home in East Houghton and half a block of property and won out. It was a three-floored mansion just a block away, owned by a former Michigan governor who'd contracted TB, making the home something difficult to sell. Thanks to a doctor friend's explanation that a good cleaning and the burning of special disinfecting camphor candles would solve the contagion problem, the deal was made, and we moved in.

My father, of course, always pleased with making a good financial deal, bragged about it, while my mother, who'd occasionally played cards with the governor's wife and some of her female friends in their expansive living room, was thrilled. She even joined in with helpers to scrub the house down with disinfectant. When we children walked in for the first time, we were in awe.

Huge changes were made in our lives, including the fact that my sisters had their own bedroom with two double beds and I had my own bedroom. And when baby Jimmy came along, he was kept in a baby bed in a small room adjoining the master bedroom. An alcove on the first floor, separated from the rest of the house, provided room for a live-in maid (very popular at the time for anyone with the space and inclination to share in a family-like compatibility). Rosa (Rosie to us), the Italian teen who became our mother-surrogate and helper with daily house-keeping, was another bonus, filling our waking lives with exciting tales, fun and games, and a certain amount of instructive training.

As I grew into my teens, I was assigned various seasonal chores:

in the fall, fearfully climbing a ladder to put up three floors of storm windows, then taking them down in spring; in winter, shoveling the front steps which included seven stone steps leading to five porch steps—a seemingly endless occupation. It was also my responsibility to tend to the filling of the coalbin that led into the furnace in our huge dungeon of a basement (fine in the summer, great for a Halloween horror house, but in winter, perpetual dread). If I forgot or was tardy, the fire would be extinguished and the entire upstairs chilled, and I would suffer a punishment for it.

My room was on the third floor and nicely separated from family below. The room was expansive, compared to what I had in the other house, with its large bed, a desk, a closet, and (unfortunately in winter) surrounded on two sides by drafty windows. Since the windows faced north and west, it was often unbearably cold. Out of necessity on the worst nights, I adjusted by changing in bed under the covers—shoes and all.

My room was adjacent to an adjoining apartment for rental to newly married couples or college students, which opened up interesting eavesdropping opportunities that could last well into the night. I might explain that the east end of town was the site of the steadily expanding Michigan College of Mining and Technology, which was growing too rapidly to house all the incoming students. Gradually, as the dormitories and external housing were completed, however, the need for rentals diminished.

When relatives came for an extended visit, it was automatic that one or another of us shared a bed for a single guest or, for couples, my parents relinquished their room and slept on a downstairs sofa, something we accepted by rote. I usually enjoyed sharing with uncles (all older Lebanese men were uncles to us) but could never understand why they always shoved a pillow between us. (Later, when I was older and shared the bed with a youngster, I knew why: kids in bed are all sharp elbows and active legs.)

The first public use of the huge living room occurred with the tragic death of Grandma Fee. She'd been visiting her sister and family in Brooklyn and drove with them to Florida for a bit of a vacation. On the way, Uncle Mike, who occasionally would fall asleep at the wheel, drove and fell asleep during a heavy rainstorm near Atlanta. He crashed the car, sending our grandmother through the front windshield, killing her instantly. (This was learned from a police officer who'd witnessed the results of the accident and, at the request of my mother, later exposed the details. The Brooklyn relatives had remained hushed about it, fearing a lawsuit.)

As was the custom, the open coffin was displayed in the living room for friends and relatives to pay their respects. My mother and her sister remained upstairs, mourning in silence. Some of the downstairs mourners included an elderly Lebanese woman who, shocked by the apparent lack of respect for the dead, rushed to the coffin and in accustomed Old Country tradition lifted my grandmother into her arms, loudly wailing, "Shafeeha! Shafeeha!" and then, satisfied, lay the body back in place and with proper satisfaction returned to her chair among the shocked American friends. Not quite understanding, we children watched in silent fascination from the doorway of the room, retaining the memory of the experience for the rest of our lives.

On occasion, we also shared the entire house with Greek families (wives and kids) who fled Chicago's heat and allergies to enjoy a late summer month with us—for small rental payments. Smelling the exotic odors from their kitchen space in their two connected rooms on the second floor, listening to their chatter in a foreign language, enjoying the company of the children of our age—those definitely were benefits of temporary cohabitation.

Alisa, a Greek girl, was my first model. With a quantity of hundreds of Jefferson nickels earned from the grocery store, I had purchased an Argus C3, my first 35mm camera (having owned a cheap Brownie camera before), and found a willing photographic subject in the teenaged daughter who had arrived with her mother as summer vacationers. Alisa proudly showed off clothes she had designed, and we spent hours together, indoors or out, while she modeled her wardrobe for me. To my great thrill, one photograph of her atop a diving board in a daring swimsuit won me a $5 prize from a photo magazine. We splurged and spent it at a local soda shop.

Winning the prize also impressed my father (who probably saw financial benefits in my hobby), and I was permitted to create a simple darkroom in our cave-like basement. Besides the multitude of closets in the house, the basement with its open spaces and closeted rooms was always a place of mystery, and with a mix of curiosity and trepidation, I would explore its abundance of dark corners. I created a small, windowless darkroom underneath the front porch (connected to the furnace room with a wooden door that made it light tight). And with that darkroom, my pursuit of photography grew.

One day, working in the darkroom with two of my cousins, Uncle George overheard us laughing, pounded on the door to question our actions. The more we protested, the angrier he became and shoved the door open, which ruined the film we were developing. They gave up darkroom work after that. I continued but played it safe and had the 35mm film developed at our local photo shop. The owner, Mr. Wilcox, became interested in me, would examine the processed film and make helpful comments, which I would follow as I printed the photos and which I stored away in my mind for future shoots. At his encouragement, I also started a camera club when I later entered high school and, with his further help, built it into a popular one for interested camera buffs. He even went so far as to allow us the use of his portrait studio after hours, hovering over us and giving more helpful instructions.

As a teenager, being invited to be part of the Calumet Camera Club was a special form of recognition. I would accompany a small group of amateur photographers from Houghton to meetings organized by Ray Forster (Calumet's postmaster); his photographs of Lake Superior were prized possessions, making him the "photographer laureate" of the Copper Country. His home was not far from my parents' cottage, and he even took me on a few photo shoots, teaching me about the importance of waiting to capture cloud formations.

Photography was becoming my great pleasure, opening up a whole new reality seen in the rectangle of a camera's "eye," not only as seen accurately, but inventively with creative manipulation. I saw a new world in a rectangle, and, eventually, by photographing and printing photos of school friends, gained acceptance where, usually, I was considered just a shy loner with foreign ways. And, still later, when I developed a passion for ink printing, my popularity shot up as I designed pamphlets and posters for school events.

❖ ❖ ❖

As I entered my teens, I did search out friends beyond those from St. Ignatius and our relatives. I had attended Catholic school through its final eighth grade and then went on to public high school. What a difference! After spending all those developing years among students who came from French, Polish, Italian, and Yugoslavian Catholic heritages, there I was, suddenly thrown into a mix of Brits, Finns, and other Protestant Scandinavians. It was like moving to another world. Some, especially those who moved here from other parts of the United States, were, as newcomers, easier to bond with.

Among my new friends were a pair of brothers slightly older than I, boys from Detroit, teaching me the city "facts of life"—envying them for their metropolitan ways and their fashionable clothes, including new white brief underwear (in contrast to my drab shorts). We did little but sit on the lawn and talk, with me listening attentively to their city experiences at their original home, in school, and around the metropolis. I never found out whether or not the tales were exaggerated or false; I simply listened with great awe. They became the bridge with which I gradually melded as much as possible with our local high school students.

Movies were a passion for me; I was permitted to attend whenever a film was deemed proper for youngsters. I would sit in the front row and gaze up at that distorted rectangle as if I were included in the action. When *Gone With the Wind* appeared in 1939 at the country's movie theaters, our local Kerridge Theatre was to show it for a one-night, advance ticket performance. So, when I heard about the one-night showing for so famous a feature, I leaned heavily enough on my parents to obtain, not only the expensive ticket, but a seat right there, in the front row, basking in the glory of witnessing a film in wide screen and vibrant Technicolor from that vantage point! Being the only teenager on the block who'd done it, I stood in the street outside our home the next night, in the dark, giving a grand performance, a reenactment of that glorious three and a half hours of a blissful, otherworldly experience. I was Lord Krishna to my entranced friends that evening and I savored it.

I found plenty to do by myself. Besides photography and printing, there was the public library to fascinate me—a treasure chest of everything an eager kid could want. Through my youth, it became my favorite place in town, because books and boys' magazines took me everywhere. I'd be sitting at the children's table and the phone would ring. The librarian would pick it up and, smiling, would look in my direction, saying, "Yes, he is." And, reluctantly, I'd have to head home. We did have books on the expansive shelves on either side of the living room's fireplace, my father's books in Arabic and my mother's Book-of-the-Month selections, but nothing to excite my attention. Even in my preteens I preferred books of travel and adventure—and, later, anything oversized, like *Les Miserables* or historic tales from ancient Greece or Rome.

I tried to fit in to high school ways, rarely succeeding. I was no athlete, no outstanding pupil, showing no signs of knowing how to deal with my Americanized peers. My sisters—especially bubbly Babe—fared better than I, and only when I could become involved with their groups could I feel "at home." I took to writing plays, one for Babe's friends—a three-act comedy, which they liked enough to produce as a high school project. Prompted by that success, I wrote a religious play for Holy Week, called *The Three Eyes of Buddha*, which I directed and toured around from one school to another, in nearby Hancock and all the way up to Calumet, 13 miles distant. It had a melodramatic plot about a poor beggar in search of a Buddha which would grant him sight of a heavenly child coming to the area, with Tchaikovsky's recorded music backing the exuberant acting. I lavished every device I could muster to make it work, and, surprisingly, it did. One teacher from another school thought I should go into drama for my future. Nice to hear but I dropped it in search of less demanding pleasures.

My social (and sexual) activity through to the end of my teens was paved with mixed successes and failures. I did discover the enjoyment in mingling with the opposite sex, though always shy about singling one girl out for fear of being rejected. There were the usual experiments—in the back seat of a car, at the prom, at school dances—but always with mixed feelings. Then in late high school days, my sister Celia introduced me to Martina, a charming, very popular girl of Italian descent. If there's such a thing as love at first sight, I was a victim of it. We group dated at first, then double dated, and finally we discovered we had so much enjoyment together, we did all the usual things high school kids did together. I couldn't believe my luck—the girl of my dreams—and kept wondering when she'd tire of me and search for better bets. She never did.

Lacking self-confidence, I never pushed our relationship beyond casual "petting." It was a familial event that ended the romance: one day she announced they were moving south. I stood at her door, held hands, and wished her luck. Impetuously, she threw her arms around me, pulled me to her, and gave me a kiss I will to this day never forget. Afterwards, I felt stunned and confused, wondering how and whether I had dropped the ball ... with no one to talk to about this experience.

4

Detroit Interlude

I was sixteen when the bombing of Pearl Harbor occurred. It was as much a blow to our community as to the rest of the nation, and it changed the future of us boys as we grew old enough to either enlist or be inducted into military service. As each of us fellows would graduate from high school, we could count on a "welcome message" from the draft board and, singly or in groups, leave for a stint in the military. My father had been grooming me to take over in his store, and he tried his best with the board to keep me at home. It worked for a brief time, but one day I received my "welcome letter," giving me eight weeks to prepare.

With a phone call from my Aunt Nabeeha (my mother's sister) and her husband, I was encouraged not to waste the waiting, instead to come live with them in Detroit. With the help of Uncle Nick, they were sure I could get a job because the factories were hiring.

How easily I can flash back to Aunt Bea driving into town in her flaming red coupe, swooping me up, her 11-year-old admirer, and dropping me into the front seat, saying with genuine excitement, "Today we're going to have an Uncle Wiggily adventure." (Uncle Wiggily Longears was the main character of a popular children's book series filled with his fun and humorous escapades.) Off we'd drive to any one of the many foreign restaurants for a Chinese, Italian, Bohemian—or any other—wonderful experience in learning about food and nationalities beyond our Middle Eastern milieu.

I loved my aunt dearly and could never understand why she

surprised us by marrying the least likely immigrant available. Nicholas Hydar was uneducated, unsophisticated, unattractive—a scowling fellow with a speech impediment that kids would mimic behind his back, and with few prospects for work during the coming Depression. Possibly for spite, to prove her independence from a domineering mother? I was too young to fathom anything save the fact that our days of Uncle Wiggily adventures were over.

Aunt Bea had convinced my father to hire Nick, putting him in charge of the produce section of the store. As it turned out, he was a bull in a china shop. To entertain our customers one day, he brought in an album of Syrian music, exchanged the light pop music normally played, and in less than 10 minutes, an uproar closed that episode out. He couldn't last, so my aunt found a way to bring in a salary by going door to door, giving away free gifts—little metal bottle openers for the wall—from the Coca-Cola Company. Eventually, the two moved to Detroit, and as the war approached, he found a job as a janitor at Budd Wheel, a factory turning out parts for tanks.

Their residence in that booming city became, over the years, a second home for me. From my childhood, we would drive in our Nash the 600-plus miles down US 41 to Woodward Avenue, to Gratiot Avenue, to secluded, tree-lined Garland Street, to a modest home typical of others dotting what was once the eastern outskirts of the city, now a quiet suburb.

I visited them as often as possible, enjoying the company of my aunt and their two children, and I learned to accept Nick for her sake. He remained adamantly opposed to any of our family, fully aware of their resentment of him. But on one such visit, I was met by him at the door and, according to tradition, made known my regrets for the death of a close relative. He was visibly touched. After that, I became the sole positive connection between him and our family.

So, when Uncle Nick and Aunt Bea invited me to stay with them for that indeterminate period, I immediately accepted. True to his word, Nick found an opening for me at the plant. "Don't tell them," he warned, "that you have a high school education; they'll put you in an office. Just tell them you're willing to do anything, and you'll get a regular laborer's job and make twice as much." He was right.

My time in Detroit was my first introduction to life away from family and home. Being a part of the blue-collar workforce was a growing-up experience I'll never forget: changing into coveralls at work each morning, pushing a wooden flatbed with nails, etc. off to my rounds to noisy machines, room to room, as needed. And always observing, listening, my eyes and ears open to the wonders of this larger world I'd entered.

The best part for me was meeting an American Scot who worked as a welder and was a magician, very accomplished at doing sleight-of-hand tricks. He reignited my childhood dream about becoming another elegant Mandrake the Magician with his hypnotic powers. After I told him that story, and with considerable delight, he guided me through one intricate trick after another.

I was working with people I found vastly different than those from my sheltered life in Houghton, where different ethnic groups cohabited, more or less in harmony. I met a trio of Black people who introduced me to their lifestyle. But I also encountered several white people from the South who brought their racial prejudices with them and made life miserable for my friends and me.

My uncle, working among bigoted men, developed similar prejudices, especially toward Blacks and Jews. He taught his son a poem in which a Black person was killed by a soldier; they would laugh heartily each time the boy repeated it. He would also repeat it for family friends, one of whom dropped in at the end of Saturday night after closing his neighborhood grocery store—joyous, because, he claimed, he had early sold out all the bread and milk, so, "Now all those other Americans won't have any for the weekend."

I began to contrast the depth of prejudice my uncle and his friends felt toward anyone outside their own Arabic upbringing with my father's less overt, less aggressive attitude, particularly to Jews. With my father, I began to realize, it was less anger or hostility; among family or friends he simply went with the flow of anti-Semitic comments, while his attitude toward produce wholesaler Sam Cohodas, for example, was actually in a manner of business bantering and never an open resentment so popular with Uncle Nick and his compatriots—something new that startled and disappointed me.

Beyond Uncle Nick's bigotry, he was a responsible, caring father and husband. He favored his son, especially, but also gave attention to his daughter. Curiously, I never noticed any open affection for my aunt, nor she for him; they simply took their marital obligations for granted—no arguments over issues like management of the children or finances.

He would take Saturday nights off for a ritual poker game with friends, return home long after we were all asleep and, if he'd won, would leave the winnings on the dining room table. If not—well, that was life. My aunt never complained; it was "his way."

I learned more during our weekly trip to the local Syrian church. She and I would get up early (leaving behind my snoring uncle) each Sunday for a two-hour-long service which was almost entirely in Arabic. One day, as we climbed the stairs to the entrance, my aunt pointed out a dapper, impeccably dressed man going up ahead—gloves and cane in hand. Aunt Bea leaned over to me and, with the slightest hint of regret, said, "That's the man I could have married once." Chapter closed; for better or worse, she had made her choice and lived by it. I actually think she grew to share a mutual kind of tacit love for Uncle Nick and, of course, her children.

With rare free time, my curiosity took me by trolley to the city center. There I would walk the streets like the hick that I was, staring up at skyscrapers on both sides with marvelous high-rise stores and, tucked in, an ice cream and homemade chocolate shop where I could satisfy dreams for any young fellow. An odd thing happened on one such excursion. I noticed a narrow, crooked street winding away from Woodward Avenue, wondered where it went—I started down but suddenly stopped. Somehow, I knew that just around the corner I'd find a shop, windows aged with dust, that housed Chinese articles. I could imagine some brilliantly colored garments on headless mannequins there, surrounded by brass drinking vessels on small inlaid tables. Almost urgently, I made my way around the corner, and to my amazement, there it was—dirty window, costumes, and all. The experience always remained a mystery to me.

By contrast, returning to the avenue, I would be drawn to its shabby street of quick food restaurants and—almost magnetically, to the three burlesque theaters, each blatantly hinting at the plums inside. Once, trying to look of legal age, I purchased a ticket, found myself in the dreary atmosphere smelling of stale food, occupied by what appeared to be elderly men with passive faces, waiting for what?

A man in a wrinkled tuxedo stood at one side of the stage, singing some sort of romantic song. Watching the writhing and twisting of the tired, middle-aged strippers was a big disappointment from the seductive pleasures described by my cousin Joe Karam.

So then at the eighth week, the date for military enlistment came in the mail. I returned home to Houghton with a box full of magic tricks from my friend, packed, and headed off, first to a nearby military base in the U.P. for a very thorough physical and mental ("Do you like girls?") examination, then on a train to a naval camp located between Milwaukee and Chicago for basic training.

What was I thinking along the way? A jumble of thoughts, a patriotic acceptance to what was to follow (without the faintest idea of what that would be), a farewell to home and family for an unknown period of time, life's little mysteries (what I had to offer, Mandrake moments, what unexpected and unknown Uncle Wiggily experiences I might encounter)—questions that finally lulled me into a light sleep before they were to be answered.

First self-portrait

PART 2

My Educational
Odyssey,
1943–56

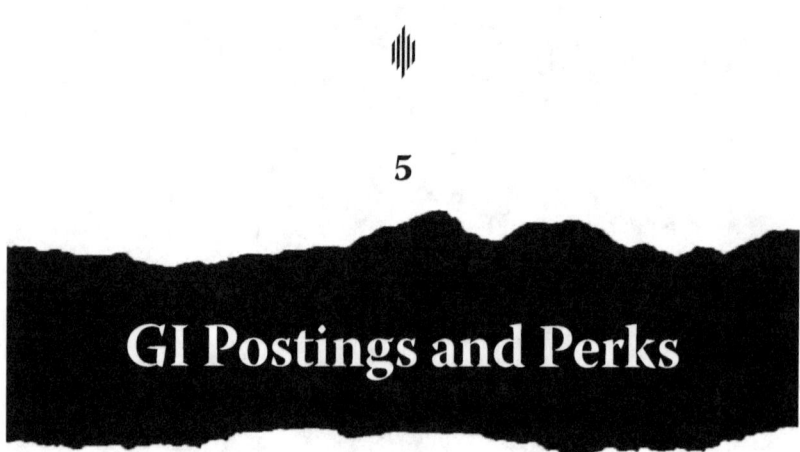

5

GI Postings and Perks

Cleaning up piles of memorabilia, I came across a long-forgotten charcoal sketch of me in formal military dress, looking proud for all my 18 years—a souvenir from my days at the San Antonio Air Corps base in 1944. I answered the call like any normal fellow of my age, ready to follow other previous Houghton High youths who preceded me. But my service in WWII was hardly what I'd expected. Much is hazy from that time, but some experiences were vivid and long-lasting.

After passing my physical and mental exam in Marquette, I moved on to Fort Sheridan, Wisconsin, for basic training to become a full-fledged soldier ... sort of. Basic training, I soon learned, was a carefully planned endeavor to bend us as individuals into soldiers, and it began the evening we entered the base. Much like a fraternity hazing, we were kept up and busy for the entire night, on the verge of mental and physical exhaustion, performing what seemed like useless labor—moving crates from place to place in a huge hangar, lifting and piling containers, climbing up and down stairs—all in double time, without pause. As the sun came up in the morning, we were herded into a barracks, provided with a bed and blankets, and slept until awakened for the first day of "normal" routine: meals in the rec hall, orientation classes, some marching drills—anything, it seemed, to mold us into the military automatons we were destined to become.

After two weeks, still uncomfortable in our new uniforms,

those of us with a particular IQ went to Indianapolis, deposited in what appeared to have been a school dormitory, now headquarters for a two-week program in learning the intricacies of high "Fi-nance." They divided us into two groups: those who calculated monthly salaries for military cadre and those who calibrated final salaries for men being discharged. I became trained for the latter.

As Thanksgiving rolled around, and we were given a free holiday, I bussed to Milwaukee to spend the time with relatives. After enjoying the break tremendously, two aunts ushered me to the bus station, and with hugs and kisses, I boarded the bus for Indianapolis. It was getting dark. I noticed strange smiles on my fellow passengers' faces. One fellow asked jovially, with a wink, "Enjoy your vacation, soldier?" Yes, I replied, wondering why the special notice I was getting. Not until I returned to the school, undressed, and went to the washroom to clean up that I saw in the mirror what had caused the knowing looks: lipstick all around my face! Some of the fellows from our quarters had been on the same bus and had in silence observed the incident. From that day on, I was looked upon not as the loner of the company, but someone far more interesting.

My only other free weekend was spent in Detroit with the Hydars. They invited me to attend a little lunch; how could I refuse? I left Indianapolis too early for breakfast, picked up some cold doughnuts at a bus stop on the way, and by the time I left the Detroit bus station for a streetcar trip to their home, my stomach rebelled. Twice along the way, I had to leap from the car to vomit heartily. Then, at their home, as they opened the door to hug me, I rushed past them to empty myself once again in the bathroom.

Whether the ailment stemmed from the doughnuts on an empty stomach or, more likely, a flu bug, didn't matter. By the next day, weak and not terribly hungry, with the TLC I needed from my favorite mother surrogate, I sat with the family at their banquet, ate simply, enjoying being among them again, and went back to Indianapolis on a lighter stomach, but very much contented.

❖ ❖ ❖

Finally, my school time was up and I was on my way to my next destination. While my papers mysteriously went elsewhere, I arrived by train in San Antonio. There, without proof of the original experience, I was forced to repeat basic training, only this time as a bona fide rank private in the Air Corps.

Unfortunately, without my papers, I was in military limbo, eight hours daily performing KP (kitchen police) duty—sweating over a steaming tub, scraping unending stacks of crusted pots and pans. Eventually, I exchanged the pots and pans for a typewriter in an office that included civilians, on an eight-hour, five-day shift of duty. So, I spent weekends delightfully touring the city, the Alamo, and even some of the great Texas expanse surrounding us—sometimes mingling with locals and even an invitation to visit a Texas ranch. It almost made up for the misery of KP days.

My quarters were on the second floor of our barracks—a bunk at the far end. I was grateful for that. On the first floor resided a fellow from New York—a soldier with deep hostilities, especially toward Jews. He had me pegged as Jewish; even the crucifix I wore around my neck could not convince him otherwise. Usually, I was able to evade him, thanks to an Italian brute of a fellow who'd taken to the likes of me (better educated, good magic card tricks). He was the only person in the barracks able to bout with the other fellow with mutual respect; so as long as he was present, I was safe.

But one night, the New Yorker came into the barracks, wobbling drunk and searching for a fight. He saw me climbing the stairs from the washroom, shot up after me and, as I walked to my bunk, whirled me around, ripped my T-shirt off my back, held onto me with a violent grip, and all I could see at the moment was a balled-up fist heading straight for my face. And then, suddenly, his fist froze. Behind him, my Italian friend, as if by *deus ex machina*, leaped in to whip him around and in a few seconds played a challenge game of tossing footlockers at one another. They continued their byplay down the stairs, while I, along with the rest of the awakened fellows, went back to our beds—they to sleep, I to tremble long enough to shake myself finally into something resembling light sleep. The next day I requested a change of barracks, got it, and even then the fear of "what next?" hovered over me until orders came, sending me off again.

Despite that unpleasant incident, I hated to leave San Antonio with its historical character and curious residents, but it had to be.

Before I knew it, new papers arrived and I was at another air base, stationed near Salt Lake City. There, replying to the general's wife's search for volunteers to help in entertaining the base's children, I revealed I could perform stage magic, complete with light patter and a rabbit—well, not a real one, but Harvey, a lovingly troublesome glove rabbit. With an Edgar Bergen routine, I became successful enough to be a volunteer adjunct to the USO shows traveling from base to base. Of course, in those days a typist was something of a rarity, so I also continued office work as my primary job.

One day I was called to base headquarters and notified that my father's store had burned nearly to the ground. Thanks to the Red Cross agency, I was given a two-week pass to return to help him with the necessary follow-up. It was not an easy journey. The top two floors of the building were destroyed, leaving a badly burned-out main floor and basement. My father was in emotional straits, made worse when his insurance company gave a very minimal settlement of his claim. When time was up, I left guiltily in a vacant sort of blankness, not knowing what to do. Rebuilding seemed out of the question at his age, and the insurance provided only enough money to live on. A proud man who had spent his life in business, he then was forced to spend the rest of it in unsuccessful attempts at trying new things.

I returned to my base, tried to put the present in focus, but I felt remiss. Neither office duty nor free days exploring the Great Salt Lake and Mormon attractions seemed an aid to winning the war, now winding down without me. I was sent from one air base to another—typing—but each time only after my records were again recovered. They still vanished with each successive trip, thus being reassigned to KP or guard duty or ditch digging or whatever until the records returned. It became an on-again, off-again bumpy existence.

At one western base, without papers, I was assigned to the worst job ever: doing guard duty. I would leave my regular quarters for a tawdry cabin miles into the desert, where—away from harm— on a hillock stood an ammunition bunker. I had to stay at the cabin for two sweltering days at a time: two hours on duty, marching around the ammunition building, loaded rifle in hand and four off, day and night. It was hot, sleeping on a well-used mattress, with no one else around, and became a monotonous drudge. I would march around that building, rehearsing new magic tricks with one hand while shouldering the rifle with the other. To lighten things, I'd sing hit songs from popular musicals at the top of my voice.

Near the end of one stint, diversions exhausted, I sat down against the rear of the bunker. Before I knew it, I fell fast asleep. How long, I never knew; but suddenly I awoke, the sound of an approaching jeep coming slowly into my head. Wide awake now, I shouldered the rifle and, as the jeep came around from the left, marched around the right to meet at the appropriate spot; I was exchanged for the next guard and rode back, fully realizing that had I been caught, it would have resulted in a court martial and possibly even death. My goose was nearly cooked!

❖ ❖ ❖

Though the war was now officially over, I was given what appeared to be great new orders: to fly with a dozen other specially selected men to the Philippines for an unspecified position. However, once again, my records flew across the Pacific and I wound up at an air base just north of San Francisco … performing guard duty (eight hours on, four off). Finally, I was assigned to apply my acquired knowledge in "Fi-nance," unfortunately not in the category I studied—discharging men—but on monthly salaries for the permanent cadre. While this type of clerical work was entirely unfamiliar to me, in true military fashion, when ordered, I performed, fully realizing that each day resulted in an accumulation of errors. For a month.

Since we were less than an hour's bus trip from San Francisco, weekends often included trips to explore its magnificent Golden Gate Bridge, trolley cars, Nob Hill, the Presidio, art galleries, and restaurants famous for exotic seafood plus the luscious Ghirardelli chocolate center along the waterfront. But most exciting of all, for a small-town-bred Yooper like me, was the introduction to live theater—Broadway shows, ballets, opera—with a few comrades who, like me, soaked up the culture with never-ending pleasure.

The routine was generally the same: leave Hamilton Field with light jackets (it was always cooler on the Bay); head for our favorite restaurant, The Fior del Italio (always received by the mama of the place with a hug and a free bottle of red wine), and enjoy a good meal; then attend any one of the theater offerings.

Afterwards, we would buy some liquor (de rigueur among visiting military men) and go to our favorite hotel where we could get a reasonable room with a pair of double beds for up to four of us at a shot. We would finish off the drinks, get a good night's rest, and head back to the base the next day feeling well-entertained and ready for more-of-the-same drill in the base office. One night, bored with the other three fellows languishing over bottles of liquor, I wanted to sleep. In desperation, I took the last bottle still half full of Southern Comfort from the table, chug-a-lugged it, dropped the empty into the astonished group, rolled over, and fell blissfully asleep. I was well respected as a good buddy after that.

One day, before the month was up, I found I had the choice of remaining still as a private in an impossible situation or escaping with an honorable discharge. After a hasty route through the separation process, I spent one final night on base, performed in a USO production as emcee and magician, and—before the financial horrors back in the office were discovered—fled with mixed memories and a duffel bag filled with various remains of my military life.

I spent the next few weeks with Uncle Mike, Aunt Freda, and their family living in Centerville, just south of San Francisco. While there, I joined up with three military buddies and headed for Los Angeles. The city was another hallowed place in any serviceman's dream, where we spent four fun-filled days that began rather seriously but ended in fond memories of the Land of the Stars.

It began as we headed for the USO headquarters, registered for the four-day stay, showered and were about to head out for new adventures when over the loudspeaker system we heard of a desperate need for volunteers: a child in the area had been badly burned, needed blood immediately. Two of us hopped a bus to the hospital; the date was Friday the 13th, which caused a bit of anxiety, exacerbated by a gigantic street side sign advertising a new movie *You Can't Live Forever*. Still, we went to the hospital, learned that my buddy was too anemic to be of help, leaving me as the sole volunteer. We left with the stern warning to me, "No liquor for the next three days, soldier." Partly joking, I said, "Put it back!" But it did put a damper on my expectations and I still joined the other three fellows at bars—with 7-Up, Pepsi, and colas.

Joe with Army pals in California, 1945

The four days were a classic tourist whirlwind of Tinseltown and environs, including an evening in one of the many fancy nightclubs. My buddies went home; I returned to my relatives and, thanks to their clothing shop, transformed myself into a colorful, Levi-jacketed civilian. And I got an education climbing trees in an almond orchard. After a disappointing hot, rainy Christmas, I headed back to snowy Copper Country.

Even the train ride had its moments. Halfway through Montana, we were delayed by a rock avalanche and sat for a few hours as the tracks were cleared. What to do? I resorted to an old trick of mine: palm-reading. I used deceptive tricks of the trade with sly generalities based on careful perception of the person being "read." After playing the game with some other ex-soldiers, I was accosted—yes, accosted—by civilian passengers for their sessions. Apparently with enough guesswork I actually convinced them that I had a "talent" and this made the time go by.

I was amused by the way the strangers had me pegged as a fellow with strong mystic powers until I began to think about amazing, unexplained incidents in my past such as the premonition of the Chinese shop in Detroit. From time to time such unexplained incidents would occur, generally when under some sort of stress, but not of late, until the fortune-telling. Coincidences, explainable situations—what? For the moment, such thoughts were replaced by thoughts of home.

We arrived in Chicago and then, as if following the earlier route of my ancestors, went straight north until the train stopped.

❖❖❖

Now in the postwar period, what to do next? Having sampled city life, I wanted to see if I could land a job outside of the Copper Country ... and away from my father's grocery store.

My mother cooked for me, washed my laundry, but failed to talk with me about my future. Aware that I was no longer her little boy, she was confused, and disturbed when one day, while washing a pair of khaki pants, she found a pack of condoms in the pocket and confronted me—quite embarrassed. I had to laugh (to myself); a soldier could not leave the base without them, and now I had forgotten this souvenir of my military service.

My father said very little as well, though it was obvious his hopes were set on my returning to manage his store ... for me, a fate worse than death. I didn't want to spend my life working hard, eking out an existence for pittance as he had. So where could I escape? I convinced my parents that New York held out all kinds of future opportunities for me. And, of course, best of all was that I could live in Brooklyn, where a bed and breakfast always awaited me with the best of relatives. I waited until after my 21st birthday, then packed up, borrowed my father's old Chrysler, and was off.

That trip in late spring 1946 ended up being an Uncle Wiggily experience. First, an overnight with my relatives in Detroit, followed by a visit with friends in Toledo, then an overnight at a motel and Sunday Mass in Pittsburgh. And that's where a curious event occurred. I didn't want to return to the motel to change from suit to casuals, so I drove on, a T-shirt and slacks sitting on the seat beside me, just in case an occasion for a change popped up.

The day heated up. It was not only hot but sweltering, and that Dacron suit was becoming clingy and insufferable. Traffic was heavy; I was doing well in the long line of cars heading out for the day, so I hated to pull aside to change. A thought occurred to me: I was a good driver, and even at top speed, why not change as I drove? With cooling relief, I got out of jacket, tie, and shirt and into the light T-shirt. Slipping off the clinging trousers proved something of a problem. Patience. I weaved a bit as I worked at it and then, pants down to the pedals, caught sight of a police car trailing me, red lights flashing.

Nothing to do but pull out of the traffic to the side of the road and wait. A young cop approached my window and looked in and, ignoring the unusual sight, blandly asked why I was weaving at high speed. I explained, trying to be casual about it, that I was changing my clothes. With no change of expression, he looked into the window, reviewed the situation, and said, "Follow me."

We drove off the highway onto a narrow, unpaved road that led through a forest to a lone house sitting up above on a hill. By that time, I was really getting nervous. The officer came up to me and told me to follow him into the house. I was getting more nervous. Dressed by then, I stepped out of the car and, with fearful trepidation, did as he ordered.

Inside the house was an elderly man and his wife, preparing for lunch. The officer approached, addressed the man as a judge, and explained our presence. I was told to sit in the next room, which looked like an office, then sat down and waited.

Eventually, the judge entered, sat at his desk, gave me the Lionel Barrymore look, saying, "Young man, you realize you were speeding, driving recklessly in heavy traffic?" It was a question, not a statement, so I replied in agreement, explaining my rush to get to New York before the endless line of late Sunday traffic would hold me up at the tunnel. "And you were leaning down, apparently putting out a cigarette at the same time?" "No, sir, I was trying to pull up my pants." A snicker from the table behind us.

He showed no change of expression, simply continued educating me to the dangers I'd faced, then said, "Son, this is a serious crime you committed. I'm going to ask a stiff penalty." (I was suffering; he saw the fancy car I was driving, imagined I had money to burn.) He said, "Son, this is going to cost you $20."

I hid my relief, returned with, "That much, sir?" "Yes," he said, "it has to hurt enough to teach you a lesson."

I forked over the money, returned to the car and the highway (which was now increasing in traffic) and got to the tunnel to New York in time to face, as I'd feared, maximum traffic. By the time I crossed through and over to Brooklyn, darkness was settling in. Climbing the stone stairs to the Sahadis, being met by them with armloads of hugs and kisses, I shoved the day's incident out. I was "home" again. I never divulged the reason for my tardiness.

My aunt (actually my great aunt) was delighted to have me, treating me like a second son. As expected, she directed me up to my room, the one adjoining my cousin Ted's on the third floor. He'd just returned from the Navy and I from the Air Corps; we had much to talk about.

Cousin Ellie was delighted to see me, but her older two brothers seemed a bit dubious. With no definite plans, I was an additional extended burden financially. When we discussed it discreetly, I explained that I was receiving a weekly ($20) subsistence check from the government and, like Ted, would pay my share. Unlike me, as I was to learn, Ted was spending his time and money on a girlfriend while in his spare time brushing up on what he hoped would become his future as a cartoonist. It didn't take me long to realize he had no talent, and I suspected he also realized it—a difficult situation. He was wasting time instead of searching out for a paying occupation.

To make matters worse, Ted would spend hours on the phone talking with his girlfriend Mariana, who lived in the Bronx. In those days, it was a long-distance call. The brothers hinted that I was increasing the phone bill. Instead of explaining, I simply stopped using the phone entirely, going to the corner drugstore to make any necessary calls. But the bill kept increasing. So, I would leave the house and spend my days wandering in Manhattan— sightseeing, window shopping, attending double features of foreign films. It was a pleasant pastime but getting me nowhere. I would indulge in such carefree activities between paying my weekly visit to the government office to collect my subsistence check and inquiring about employment. Truthfully, I didn't really know what it was I wanted to do and, just like so many other ex-GIs, made up satisfying stories to keep the checks coming.

My conscience weighed heavily on me; eventually, after some

months, as my GI unemployment compensation was about to give out, I decided to find some excuse to return home and did. Soon after I arrived back there in early 1947, I made another escape decision: I took advantage of the GI Bill and applied for entrance to the only school of higher education I was familiar with: Ferris Institute in Big Rapids. My plans? To take business courses.

6

Three Midwestern Universities

M y father knew as little about advanced education as I, but he gave his blessings to my plan to use the government stipend to take bookkeeping and other business courses at Ferris. It also helped that my cousin Larry was going to be attending the school in Big Rapids, a secluded little town (not far from Detroit) populated almost entirely by a large community of religious fundamentalists. So off we went in his second-hand, 1930s Hupmobile to start a new page in our lives.

Regardless of our home's proximity to academic life at the local technical college, I was a rank novice, not even knowing what a "degree" was. With the help of a rather officious academic guide in severe dress and gold-rimmed glasses, I enrolled in typing, various math classes, and bookkeeping. To balance out my studies, she also arranged for me to take a basic course in psychology, some literature courses, and speech—none of which sounded spectacular, but at least they put me on full steam toward a bachelor's degree.

Larry took to the double entry bookkeeping class with ease, while I suffered through it, refusing to agonize over solving each step in office management. In fact, at the end of the course in bookkeeping, I found I was three cents short, so to balance it, I simply taped three pennies to the final page. But when the instructor saw what I'd done, he furiously lifted the book as if to throttle me with it. I knew at once that I was not cut out to be a bookkeeper.

The lit courses proved, well, interesting, with each covering various European authors. The teacher? Magda Bloom, the wife of the psychology professor, somehow accepted as proficient in literature from her days in a German *gymnasium*. She read her lectures from a sheaf of handwritten notes, would pause at times and, with a knowing smile, lean back against the blackboard to reward us with some scatological gossip about one famous writer or another. She relished the revealing of dark secrets as much as we did and then would continue back to her notes. In later years I found that she may not always have been accurate, but at least she kept us entertained.

Her husband, Professor Jacob Bloom, on the other hand, was the complete embodiment of a learned scholar; he soberly took us by hand from Freud to Adler to any number of other followers of the psychoanalytical theory of id, ego, and super ego. Like his wife, he spoke English with a thinly disguised German accent, as he heaped prodigious amounts of detailed information, excitingly new to me and prompting me to explore further the mysteries of the mind. I decided I might even minor in that remarkably informative subject.

His wife also introduced us to another side of her personality: a passion for theater. She volunteered to produce a play by some Italian author which was rich in conflicts, violence, political corruption, and hints of good over evil. Recognizing the restrictions placed on any production that might be seen by the local community, she had gone with the script to the dean, discussed it with him, then returned to us with an elated announcement: "I haff saved for you, three hells and four damns!" I was impressed by her fervor, not only attending her rehearsals but volunteering to take on a small role if needed. I was no actor, but if effort had any merit, I developed into a worthy player. Prompted by her, I even went so far as to write short dramas that smacked heavily of the European dramatists she'd presented to us in class.

Thanks to her taking notice of my efforts in both hers and her husband's classes, I was invited to their home for a traditional German dinner. Nervous but excited, I ate with them—formally dressed and formally conversing, as I supposed was customary. The meal was tasty but came in small quantities; obviously, they were unaccustomed to American table abundance. So, I ate sparingly, refusing seconds, claiming to be stuffed by strudel's end. As I left, I thanked them for the bountiful repast and then headed for the downtown apothecary/soda shop and ordered the largest ice cream soda possible. I was slurping it down when the professor entered to get his evening paper. In gentlemanly silence, he purchased the paper and left without any sign of acknowledgement; I was left in utter humiliation.

So much for My Most Embarrassing Moment—the first of many. (I used to joke half seriously that I was born with a silver foot in my mouth.) Though I smarted from the unfortunate experience, it seemed to go unnoticed by the Blooms, and we still remained in cordial contact. In the speech classes, which included writing as well as acting exercises, I discovered my niche. I could write: trite dialogues held together by equally trite plots, but gradually improving to compose a one-act play, *Miracle In Uganda*.

On the side, I also exercised my writing skills by joining up with two fellow students talented in improvisational comedy and wrote scenarios for them. By grouping some of the episodes, we created an evening of comedy and put on a show open to the public. A disaster! We were denounced by the general community as vile and sinful for including such lines as, "I was assigned to a ship called *The USS Constipation*: we never moved." Word reached the administrative office at the college and only by the skin of our teeth and a dozen mea culpas were we permitted to continue on as students— with the promise to never again peddle publicly what had been labeled as unacceptable smut.

Not a week later, ironically, the local paper announced with great fanfare that I had won a national prize with my *Miracle in Uganda*. This announcement was almost immediately followed up by the dean of students, who apparently had forgotten the outcry over our little show. With a hearty handshake, he congratulated me and invited me to be honored at a formal dinner at his home! Of course, I accepted but reluctantly, and endured a meal of under-cooked chicken, suffering in confusion over the accolades from the dean and others from his office who just days before considered my expulsion. In retrospect, this was my first lesson in the vagaries of college administration politics.

❖ ❖ ❖

Before departing Houghton, I'd learned from a friend about a Big Rapids family who lived in one of those typical old-fashioned homes in a typically standard conservative community, who had a room to rent. It was small but inexpensive and clean and neatly furnished with a kitchenette, a study space, and a double bed, the latter shared by cousin Larry and me. This sleeping arrangement was difficult, since my gargantuan football hero cousin dominated more than his half of the bed, snored, and had the habit of turning over and painfully plopping his leg-of-lamb arm across my face. (That latter problem was solved when I learned how to sleep with my head underneath a pillow and got used to the soft thud of his bulk on top.)

However, Larry, who had high hopes of becoming a member of the institute's football team, failed to impress the coach with his small-town proficiency. Before the semester was over, he tossed in the towel, took his ancient Hupmobile, and chugged home—leaving me without transportation nor the supplier of half the room rent. I soon learned that walking a dozen blocks was no big deal even in the winter, when snow was far less threatening than the sub-zero cold. As for long-distance traveling, since student cars were a rarity at the time, owners of cars advertised for riders at a cent per mile, permitting me easy access to rides home and back at a cost of $5 each way. I also learned how to slim down on meals, again no big problem since I ate with the habits of a frugal grocer's son.

For social entertainment, there were young girls living in the neighborhood, eager to become friendly with any of those equally abundant college men. At an ice cream social, I found Rita, daughter of a Baptist minister, who shared my interest in the dramatic arts and joined me frequently in bus trips to nearby Central Michigan University for theater entertainment. It was on those trips that I learned something else: that pretty, sloe-eyed daughters of ministers could smolder with passionate abandon and (up to a point) could offer unexpected thrills. Innocently, I learned from her the excitement and pleasures of commingling arms, legs and lips in the rear of the bus on those all-too-short trips—and once, during a lengthy farewell on the dark porch of her home, was sent reeling into a barbed wire fence, severing a brand new pair of pants at the thigh. (Though it cost me a new pair, it was, I concluded, well worth the experience.)

A contrast to the ongoing relationship with Rita, the pastor's daughter, occurred during one weekend spent in nearby Grand Rapids, where I often sought cultural pleasures not found at a school specializing in creating secretaries, bookkeepers, and dentists. A bus ride would take me to the YMCA, where I would register for two nights, then scour the papers for something interesting to attend. An all Brahms concert at the Music Hall drew me in one Saturday; the local orchestra, while hardly of Juilliard standards, satisfied me well. That evening I found myself sitting next to an attractive girl in a plain black outfit, wearing no jewelry or makeup—and certainly not needing any. She sat, program in hand, rapt in attention, applauding heartily after the violin concerto (also my favorite of the program). We chatted comfortably during intermission. Laura, seventeen, came from a Dutch Reform family, and was studying the violin at their local church college; she was radiant in her thrilled discussion of the concerto.

Concert over, still early, I braved asking if she would like some ice cream at a soda fountain; yes, she would. So, we headed out together. Her ease in simple conversation was surprising and definitely pleasing to me. I pushed further; could I walk her home? With a gentle smile, she said yes. It was a warm late fall night; the world opened up as we walked to her neighborhood and parted at her doorstep, leaving me overjoyed at the unexpected turn of events, from a solo musical entertainment to something warmly promising.

I returned each weekend after that, with her postcards suggesting cultural things on the docket. More musical concerts, a Shakespearean play, an art exhibit—anything but movies, which she admitted were banned by her parents as vulgar and irreligious. No matter, until I discovered a new Hollywood film based on the life of Chopin currently showing at a downtown movie house; would she like to go? She could close her eyes and just enjoy the music. She said she would.

Each visit with Laura increased what seemed to be a mutual attraction, which felt close, almost ethereal. I met her parents and her grandmother in their home, felt comfortable with them, like an old friend of the family. And for the first time in my adult life, I was in love!

I called her from the YMCA about the movie, letting her know that I'd see her after I first went to confession at the Catholic church, a regular monthly routine for me. She seemed confused by it. Okay, no big deal; I'd explain when I saw her.

But something went awry at her home. I was met at the door by her father, who spoke in austere monosyllables, ushered me into the parlor, where we sat in silence while I heard whispering behind the drapes leading to the next room. First thought: the aging grandmother turned ill? Laura came from behind the drapes, alone, her eyes rimmed red. Yes, she'd been crying; definitely, her aging grandmother.

We sat through the lavishly produced musical, a lush skimming through the composer's life with just enough verity to back up the dramatic plot that took him from his Polish home to early death on the Mediterranean. We left, headed for home in relative silence, the sensuous music clinging heavily. I was floating. At her doorstep she asked if we could take a little walk together. I was in ecstasy. Puffy white flakes floated gently from a dark sky. It was idyllic. And then she lowered the boom.

I had no previous knowledge of a traditional bitterness that had divided the city: Catholic Poles to the South; Dutch Reformers to the North. And never the twain to meet. We corresponded on postcards a few times after that, then nothing. So, for the second time (at least less scary than my experience in the Army), I sadly discovered how religious prejudice could be blinding and personally injurious—and a true roadblock to fulfillment.

Despite this big disappointment, by the end of the first year at college, I felt charged up and intellectually transformed. Knowledge poured from every classroom, from every textbook, from every new educational incident. I wanted more. My visits with Rita to Central Michigan University had excited dreams of growing "upward and onward," so it was not difficult to shut off memories of a lesser life in a disliked occupation. Career assessment tests (administered by the student guidance officer) confirmed that business was not the right vocation for me, and that a more liberal education was more appropriate. I applied to Central and was accepted as a second year liberal arts student. I left Big Rapids behind to face my father with my change of plans. We ended in a kind of "we'll see" truce.

Course catalogue in hand, I mapped out the years that it would take me to obtain a bachelor's degree, now majoring in speech and theater, minoring in psychology and writing. My future was being writ in stone, under the tutelage of some passionate scholar/educators.

Studying drama was a snap. I spent a great deal of time trying, with more energy than talent, to prove I had some acting ability. A helpful drama teacher named Dr. Throckman worked patiently to turn me into Baptista, father of Kate in a *Taming of the Shrew* production, which resulted in a tour to the schools surrounding Central. I never rose above that role as a catchy old geezer and decided instead to trade acting for directing. Dr. Throckman was truly a nurturing professor, in and out of the classroom, often bringing me with his entire family to interesting theater productions in Detroit (an hour's drive away). Those trips added tremendously to my interpretation and appreciation of teachers and teaching.

At the same time, writing was ever fulfilling, never work. I caught the attention of an English professor who took me under her wing and encouraged experimental writing—from serious nonfiction to my favorite form, satire. She was patient, detailed with her instructions, and generally most encouraging. She preferred that we refer to her not as "Dr." but as Mrs. Luke—I think, just to prove that she'd once sampled marriage. As a divorcee, I believe she missed family life and, particularly, her son, and gave me kind attention by proxy to him.

A third influential figure was Dr. Drummond, the head of the Speech Department, who had fallen seriously for a developing theory just emerging on academic fringes, called "non-Aristotelian Logic." Briefly, it was a new way of thinking, replacing "either/or" in the great Greek's manner, to a broader scale from black to white. Sadly, as interesting and logical as it seemed, the theory never burgeoned in the academic world, but it remained tremendously effective for my professor and me, on the ready cusp of accepting differences by degrees. And, thanks to him, I still do.

Psychology? Another explosion of knowledge supplied by Professor Gerhardt Stein, who, like my freshman professor and his wife, had escaped Nazi Germany by the skin of his teeth, now to grace our classrooms. Through class lectures and informal discussions, he would impart his optimistically humanitarian way of thinking. A committed follower of Freud, he also introduced me to the use of "projective techniques"—the study of Thematic Apperception Testing (TAT), in which a series of pictures produced insights to a person under study and to which I seemed easily responsive. In fact, one TAT study I did of a teenaged girl proved successful enough for him to request it for permanent use in future classes. Of course, I obliged. I was impressed with his insights, some of which I already suspected about myself, that brought me to an introspection that would never have been possible without his help.

Professor Stein had come to the United States with an Aryan wife, and a teen son and daughter. However, Mrs. Stein divorced her husband shortly after they arrived (never knew why) and took their son, leaving the daughter to him. A dedicated culture vulture, Professor Stein often invited me, along with his daughter, to attend the performances and programs imported to Central—each time, enriched by his extraordinary extracurricular instruction. I listened raptly to him as he explained everything from the 12-tone system to his theories of modern art. I also once heard him turn around and curse "*schwein*" at two women who were whispering loudly during a performance of a well-known operatic soprano (my first introduction to the beauty of that singular talent and to his short tolerance for idiocy).

During my second semester, I took a chance with a course in stage design, though I'd never had a class in art of any sort. It began with the instructor asking us to find three colors that might prove interesting together. While others were trying out everything very subtle, I went for red, blue, white. The teacher wandered among us, commenting on interesting groupings and then, when she saw mine, looked puzzled. "Well, that's an obvious trio, Joe; why don't you try something more exciting?" I knew I was in trouble.

Fortunately, I was paired with a sensitively bright partner; when the next assignment called for creating a stage setting, her drawing talent and my understanding of stage implementation worked out well. I had a head full of ideas for each set but had to rely on her for the final sketches. The Drama Department was planning a production of *Waiting for Godot*, a favorite Theater of the Absurd play, well familiar to me. I outlined the simple set: a spindly tree off center against a nondescript background, everywhere yet nowhere. My partner immediately picked up on the concept and came up with more than I could have imagined. We continued to work together as a team, learning from one another as we progressed. The results were amazing, awarding us an A rating for the course.

My burgeoning interest in stage writing and directing was rewarded when I learned that there was a homegrown, lighthearted musical held each year as a charity event. Curious, I applied to create the next show and was accepted. I called it the *Seven Lively Arts (In Seven Lively Scenes)*. I put my heart into it, created each of the seven scenes with something of a comic spoof of each art, then ending each with a surprisingly dramatic climax. My script was amply fortified by a music student with a knack for turning Tchaikovsky melodies into usable tunes and by my art partner who could work creatively at the hint of any suggestion for each cartoon-like setting. With high spirits and plenty of aid from a few students equally interested in doing something light and original, I labored week after week until the production was nearly up to my expectations. It brought in record audiences and a record amount of money. For the first time, too, family members attended a show I'd created: even my cousin Art Karam (then living in Detroit) brought his wife to see it.

Joe directing a play at Central Michigan University

Of course, since it was my opus, they applauded heavily after each scene but, to my happy surprise, so did everyone else in that packed auditorium. Even months later, the university's president claimed that it was the greatest show he ever saw on that stage. It was my first big success, and I began to dream bigger prospects for a future in the theater.

Writing for the school newspaper was another creative outlet. The small newspaper hut not far from my dorm room became my favored office, where I could feel comfortable among a small band of students who weekly performed a variety of publication tasks. I wrote reviews on everything from stage productions to visiting personalities; on the side I worked on my personal writing (and even won a prize for an essay on the difficulty of remembering names, called "A Rose by Any Other Name," in an academic trade publication).

My favorite assignments were the touring dance and theatrical performances, and I enjoyed meeting with the casts offstage. Martha Graham arrived with her group of modern dancers—new to me, and truly impressive. In an interview after the performance, I asked her why so often she or members of her troupe would writhe on the floor or perform a confusion of gestures about the head. She smiled, explained that in dance you "talk" with your body; leaping in the air to telegraph pleasure or happiness, while groveling on the floor, just the opposite. Aha! She was an amazing woman, looking quite grotesque close-up in her stage makeup and far shorter in person than onstage, where she'd dominated with her dynamic power among a carefully selected group of properly sized partners … a program and an interview I still recall with nostalgia. (Little did I dream that I was to meet some of her dancers in my later life in New York.)

Another talented person, Donald Gregg, a master of the classical accordion on a national tour, also impressed me. At his suggestion, I followed him to his room to ask the usual questions for the paper. While I sat, pen and notebook in hand, he slipped out of his stage clothes and into a steaming tub, to carry on our conversation as he "came down" from his performance. We talked for what seemed like hours; after he'd dressed in a robe, he walked me to the door, shook hands, and left me with pages of material to edit. Once more, I was impressed with the contrast between onstage performances and offstage reality.

❖❖❖

During my three years at Central, I lived on campus. Dorm life interested me—the mingling of fellows from every walk of life, from the studious to the party boys, the almost invisible ones to the noisy intruders down the halls. Like me, most of the students at Central were from small towns in Michigan. Occasionally, there were unpleasant discoveries, though: it turned out that Dan, one of my roommates, was a kleptomaniac—unknown to us, until a school official came to our room, opened the door to his locker, and exposed a load of scarves. From then on, this seeming extrovert became very reclusive.

Another friendship ended in shock and confusion. Our French class offered extra rewards for volunteering little episodes in French to the class, to prove ourselves capable of using the language informally, but also, for me, to show off my dabbling in the art of magic. I selected a fellow student to perform as my helper—a shy young loner, who lived down the hall from me in a singles room overlooking a path leading to the girls' dorm. We would practice on little French magic shows ("*Voici le sac, voici le mouchoir*," etc.). It was great fun; we created a series of short routines, generally practicing in his quiet room before returning weekly to entertain our professor and the class.

Then one night, he was gone. A shocking scandal erupted around the entire campus. My friend was caught by coeds one night as he exposed himself nakedly in his window as they passed; when one girl screamed, he leaped from the window, clothes in hand, and disappeared into the night, never to be seen or heard from again. I was stunned, and nothing was ever officially explained. Some questions in life, I learned, could never have an answer.

A certain number of men were slightly older, like me, having been in service. I developed a friendship with one whose sad history stays with me.

Entrance to our dorm rooms was by a single outer door that led to side-by-side rooms, each with its own door. One night, groans could be heard coming from the adjacent room; my roommates sighed, "Oh, Matthew, drunk again." The groans continued; I felt compelled to check. On the floor of the room was a fellow in a ragged bathrobe, twisting in agony, his head lying in a foul-smelling mix of stomach upheaval and blood. I was shocked.

Disregarding my fellow roommates, I took a towel, cleaned up as much of the mess as possible, then lifted the still moaning, slight, and limp body to his bunk. As he calmed, I left the room. The next day, in a reasonably better frame of mind, he introduced himself to me with thanks and went on to explain: he had concluded his service in the Air Force, where he'd been teaching flying to cadets (considering it a discouraging occupation) and, for some reason, decided to enroll instead in a psychology program at Central.

The more he talked, the more amazed I was: this diminutive fellow with huge eyes and dark curly hair, looking far younger than his mid-twenties, with the perpetually agonized expression of an age-weary man. He wanted change and hoped to eradicate his conception of a world of decay and degradation. He also wanted to be free of his rural Kentucky heritage, where he'd been raised by God-fearing parents, whose preaching, he noted as he grew into adulthood, was to him pure rubbish. It didn't take him long to realize his demons had followed him. He took to drinking, more and more heavily until he developed a serious stomach problem. But still he drank and suffered the results that I'd just witnessed.

All this touched me curiously and deeply; as we continued into the semester, taking similar courses in psychology, we became friends. One Saturday, after a grueling final examination given by a particularly difficult professor, we left the campus for a walk to town. He told me he would rent a plane for us, to clear our minds, if I liked.

Why not? We were near the Catholic church I normally attended; I asked if he'd mind waiting while I made my monthly confession. He did, after which without much conversation we made our way to the airport, where he rented a small two-seat Cessna 150, and up we went. High above the campus, the building in which we'd just suffered looked like an insignificant dot; I understood the relaxed smile of contentment on his usually disturbed face. He asked if I'd like to do some "tricks." Sure, I thought it would be fun. So, he took me up high and away from the campus site, dove into a series of twists and turns, then cut the engine; the plane sputtered into silence and with a whine we fell into a nose dive.

I recalled one of our earlier, more serious discussions when he'd admitted he would like to end his life dramatically with a plane loaded with explosives and smash into a populated area, to take as many people as possible with him. I looked at his face, staring straight ahead, grinning. What could I do? Nothing. I knew that after confession I was now in the state of grace ... let it happen. As we were now spinning well in sight of the campus grounds, going ever lower, he suddenly switched on the ignition, replacing the whine with a grinding roar, and we shot up into the air once again.

Neither of us spoke. We left the field, walked back to the dorm in silence, and parted at our divided rooms. It was days later that he explained something to me: A determined atheist, he'd tested other so-called religious people with his tailspin to set them in screaming panic; that convinced him about the weakness of faith. But I had disappointed him. I told him that, yes, I was sure of impending death, but being in the state of grace, I had nothing to fear, so I'd simply folded my hands in my lap and waited.

That puzzled him but made him feel somehow closer to me. When he suddenly quit school to rejoin the military, again to teach flying, he wrote openly, pages of things he could never bring himself to discuss when we were together. His comments slowly turned sour on the pages to follow, destructively depressed. After the last one, particularly and fatally negative, I never heard from him again.

My life at Central became filled with all things cultural—writing, working on dramas, even singing in the church choir on Sundays. I was never a great singer, but by listening carefully to the tenor on either side of me, could fake a fairly good addition to the choir. Why did I join? Almost ashamed, I admit, I was drawn to the rehearsals and the Sunday Mass because of a secret crush on the conductor: Elaine, who majored in music, who sang as a soprano in musical productions, and who could send me into heavenly flight each time I heard her sing "O Mio Babbino Caro" with heartrending feeling. Her final degree concert was held, unfortunately, at the same time I had a bit part in an important production on our main theater stage. On impulse, in between my scenes, I dashed from the theater to the music hall in full makeup and costume, opened the door and, to my wonderful surprise, stood in the back just as Elaine broke into that aria. She told me later that she recognized my silhouette in the doorway and sang her finest, "just for you, Joe." It left me elated. I knew she was seriously dating an older student, but that evening she was mine.

Quite the opposite experience occurred with a girl named Claire. She was a local girl, attending classes as a drama major. We often worked together on sets or lighting. She was not particularly bright, but she was pretty and she owned a little red sports car; one night she offered to drive us to town for a soda, and afterwards, to park. She knew I was taking a class in French, asked me to say something sweet to her in French. Looking deeply into her eyes, I whispered, "*Un, deux, trois,*" etc. to 10. It shook her up; she asked what I'd said, and when I told her, well, the evening closed shut on me and never did I ever have another pleasure of a ride in that little red car.

I did date, usually students from our Speech and Theater Department, but never seriously—just often enough to enjoy the pleasure of a young woman on a casual movie date now and then.

I received my bachelor's degree in spring 1951, but skipped the graduation ceremony (never being one for grand, ceremonial events, and recognizing the fact that my parents, always nervous around anything academic, would not wish to attend). Over those three years, I had grown comfortable—even thrived—being on a mid-sized academic campus, and I was now on my way to a large, impressive university that had, until then, frightened me away. Without notifying me until it was assured, the dean had arranged a partial scholarship for me to pursue a master's degree in speech and theater at the University of Wisconsin.

As nervous as I was to test myself at a large university, it turned out that my earlier experience had already familiarized me with life in the groves of academe, so the university and the surrounding city weren't too intimidating to me by then. Regardless of age, style of architecture, or location, there was a kind of familiar aura: the spread of imposing academic buildings connected by broad sidewalks, animated by students crossing and crisscrossing on them on their way to or from classes.

For me, finding a place to stay was easier than I thought. Running down a sheet listing dorms and private homes, I saw one that looked promising: a home just off State Street, with second and third floors for rent exclusively to grad students. It proved exactly as I'd hoped, in a mixed environment on a street of Madison families and university rentals—mine tucked in between an all-coed residence and a Jewish fraternity. As time went on, it turned out to be a delightful new environ for me, with friends easily made in a sort of Wisconsin, casually friendly manner.

Spread through the two floors of our house were grad students ranging in age from 16 (an awkward but brilliant kid from New York's Delancey Street not yet old enough to know much about personal cleanliness nor socializing with strangers, but astoundingly capable with anything mathematical) to near 30 (teachers from America, India, China, Japan, and Sweden, struggling to complete their degrees ASAP)—all amazingly comfortable in this salad mix and almost instantly blending like a big, easygoing family.

Even before classes began, I headed for the huge union building at the foot of State Street, where I knew we would be eating our meals. Options were the cafeteria on the first floor or, on the floor below, the Rathskeller (the "Rat")—another tribute to the state's Germanic heritage—complete with man-sized sausage sandwiches and large mugs of foamy, dark beer from the bar.

But there was more to explore in that multi-floored building with its maze-like stairs leading to everything from a classical music room for relaxing to a miniature movie theater that played a broad array of foreign films from early morning until night. Over the course of my two years as a student, I spent hours in this filmic hive (where I was introduced to the works of foreign filmmakers such as Truffaut, Bergman, Kurosawa, all previously unknown to me, but who rose to the level of my greatest appreciation). On the top floor of the building was a ceramics studio, where I even tried my hand in crafting some clay pieces for Christmas gifts.

◆◆◆

Classes? Find your degree topic, check out the "must" courses and the "ecstasy" courses, then spread them across the two expected years for completion. I was majoring in speech and theater, but within that area, there were plenty of choices. The courses were an appealing combination of traditional classroom lectures on history and philosophy related to the theatrical stage, and others that relied on actual, hands-on learning: TV and radio production, stage acting, and directing. Though I hadn't intended to lean in that direction, I did take a series of courses in radio, including script writing, voice training, and more. For the writing course, I even transcribed short stories by William Faulkner or Eudora Welty, whose rich regional dialogues were magic when adapted as radio plays. For additional work in the creation of radio advertising, I amused the instructor by taking advantage of special sound effects, like blowing bubbles in a glass of water to suggest amplified sounds of perspiration. It wasn't work. It was fun—creative fun.

In theater classes we produced scenes and later complete acts of plays. For the final project, I selected an emotionally charged moment from *Our Town* in which the heroine, now dead, is permitted to experience a memorable day of her former life. It worked so well, I accepted a request from a Madison church group and produced the entire play for them, using eager Presbyterians of all ages as the cast on a stamp-sized stage in the church's basement, spending the meager budget on lights, which I used creatively, negating the need for a regular set. Thornton Wilder might not have approved, but the church community called it a winner.

Enthused with some departure from class regimen, I also volunteered a magic show to various homes for the elderly and even went to one for mentally handicapped persons (a real experience). I developed a half-hour show, performed in a lighthearted manner (pretending the tricks wouldn't work but always did), winding up with my old faithful, Harvey; even if the tricks didn't entertain, Harvey was guaranteed to do so.

What a contrast this university provided from the two previous ones, which were, in retrospect, my scholastic building blocks!

Joe performing a magic show

❖ ❖ ❖

Camera in hand, my favorite pastime was to ask some of our thespians-in-training to pose for me. One girl in particular—delicate, sensitive Heather—who seemed always to be playing her roles in real life, would give a vast number of character changes as I asked for them. (I later sold one of these photos in New York to Columbia Records for the album cover of *Percy Faith Plays Romantic Music*!)

At other times, I photographed dancers in rehearsal or in performance. There were also theatrical "hams" who relished devising roles for me to shoot, sometimes backstage, others in field trips to the Wisconsin Dells and other of the state's natural wonders. Sometimes the photo shoots bordered on the scatological, but most of them were serious explorations of characters in experimental situations.

I also volunteered to help with backstage chores for shows both locally produced and from traveling Broadway companies. Uta Hagen, after her Tony-winning role in *The Country Girl*, was playing a lead in a national touring production of *The Deep Blue Sea*. Standing in the wings, I caught her body and face in a moment

**Joe shooting a Univ. of Wisconsin theater student
at the Wisconsin Dells**

of preparation for her entrance onstage. The result was a perfect dramatic portrait and I knew exactly what I was going to do with it.

Uta's father, Dr. Otto von Hagen, a theater art historian, taught classes in our department. I sat in on one called "History of Theatrical Design." He would stride heavily to the podium, a thick heap of aging sheets under his arm, set it on the lectern, and in the stentorian tones of a man trained in a German *gymnasium*, would read to us. His delivery was terrible, almost soporific, but the substance was so valuable, we would sit in silence, scribbling away as he lectured. One day, after he'd described a Renaissance production utilizing people dressed as fish and dead ducks, he paused, looked out at us, and exclaimed dryly, "Zat was a funny joke; vie aren't you laughing?" We American-bred students were confused by his attitude. At the final lecture, when in Germany it would have been proper to show appreciation by stomping or applauding, we simply waited for him to leave and then silently we left as well.

I felt remiss for that ending and knew this was the moment to deliver the photo. I made an enlargement of the actress's portrait, toned it in sepia, slipped it into a frame, and left it in his office with a note of thanks for the lectures. Not two days later I received a handwritten note, thanking me and telling me that he and his wife thought it the nicest portrait of Uta they ever owned, which was now on display on their grand piano.

The von Hagens' passion, I learned, was classical music. For their pastime pleasure, he played the violin, his wife the piano. And they attended every concert held in the Music Department's little auditorium. I attended one, a performance by the Wisconsin String Quartet, with the combination of Beethoven and Shostakovich on the program. The couple sat a few seats in front of me, she in stately silence, he following the music with a folder containing the full Beethoven score. During the applause, he closed the portfolio and began to rise—obviously not about to sit through the dissonant, modern piece to follow. Then an amazing thing happened. As he was rising, his wife reached up and with one finger gently touched his elbow. As if by cue, Dr. von Hagen froze in midair, then slowly, obediently, dropped to his seat, folded his arms, and stared with stony discontent. It occurred to me, this was a lesson concerning unspoken communication between two people who, over many years of marriage, knew precisely how to react with private signals in public.

Meanwhile, there was the work requirement of my scholarship, which turned out to be field assignments through the university's unique Wisconsin Idea Theatre. It was the brainchild of Robert Gard, an Abraham Lincoln-looking man (without the beard). His ambition to bring theater away from Broadway and to the general population propelled him to design a plan that he eventually "sold" to both a state representative and the university's head, whose visionary jurisdiction almost immediately turned his dream into a jewel in the state's crown. (Only much later would I come to fully realize the national impact of the Wisconsin Idea Theatre and Bob's pioneering role in the development of community arts throughout the United States.)

The Idea Theatre offices were in a rather nondescript building slightly separated from the rest of the campus. Inside, the main room was a jumble of desks, chairs, and plenty of theatrical posters spread around on the walls. The atmosphere was casual—no sense of academic formality. At the secretary's desk, I was given a form to fill out, including background information regarding past academic training, focusing on subjects theatrical, along with a copy of my dates and days of free time for assignments. At one of the free desks, I filled out the form and returned it to the secretary, who looked it over, kept a copy, and handed me the original. "In a moment Dr. Gard will see you; give this to him."

When I was requested to follow her, she opened a door and ushered me into a small office, also decorated with things theatrical. He surprised me. In a dark suit, white shirt, and rather plain tie, he scanned the sheet, then stood and put out a friendly hand to shake. He smiled, asked me to sit down, and threw several questions at me: my hometown (Houghton), my interest in theater (much appreciated with its fascinating literary history and as a way to bring people to enjoy it as much as I), and why I was at the university (my hope to write professionally for radio or theater). As I responded, he sat back in his chair, his small eyes seriously intent on me, with an occasional slight smile. He set me instantly at ease as I rambled with details concerning my theatrical bailiwick, until with his Lincoln smile, he said he was satisfied, felt I would fit in, and ushered me out.

I rarely saw him after that, became accustomed to his relaxed administrative style and his trust in our contributions. Almost daily each week, I would drop in early at the Idea Theatre's office, enjoying the rather freewheeling, easygoing mood set by Gard (whom we referred to informally as "Bob") and would check in for an assignment. It might be a trip to nearby Oconomowoc to judge an amateur play production or a longer trip to Appleton for a lecture and demonstration in theatrical makeup. (Obviously Bob recalled my interest in that subject and gave me repeated assignments for it.) While in the office, I would meet other students, with one thing in common: a commitment to the department's unwritten attitude that we were doing something remarkable and would approach each assignment with dedicated eagerness.

Probably the most memorable of the field assignments occurred in a rural community not far from Oshkosh to critique the dress rehearsal of an upcoming one-night production. As usual, I hopped into the state car, map in hand, and found a dairy farm where the amateur director of the play lived. By arrangement, I was to have dinner with her, her husband, and son, critique the dress rehearsal in the role of the "State Man," then stay on overnight as the family guest. What an experience it turned out to be!

Dinner included an inch-thick steak (perfectly regular at a farm table but barely tolerable to a near vegetarian like me) and sleep that night in the son's bed—clean but still retaining some of the natural farm odors in the pillow—while the son, I found in the morning, had slept on the living room floor. No problem ... he enjoyed it. His mother, I also discovered, was the sole teacher in the area's little one-room red schoolhouse. I was curious. I had the time to attend morning classes with her as she wandered around the dozen or so students of various ages, giving appropriate assignments, then later drawing them together for a waltz lesson, little boy paired with older girl, etc. as they stumbled through the "Missouri Waltz." I hated to leave, but was expected back by noon, so, reluctantly, I bade them a thank-you and farewell, humming the waltz tune off and on all the way back to Madison, where I would check in.

And it was through the Idea Theatre that I would get to know Tallie Handler, whom I'd seen flitting in and about with drama students in their customary café or backstage gatherings. Boisterous, confident Tallie—always appearing in her large owl-like glasses, never wearing makeup, and in anything but the latest styles, hair frizzed as if blown by a heavy wind, rarely remaining in the out- skirts of a conversation, always diving in with a know-it-all atti- tude that offended no one and was actually enlightening. She was respected for a splendid knowledge of things theatrical, from the early religious traveling shows of the Middle Ages to Shakespeare and beyond. Obviously, theater was her reason for existence.

I took to her instantly and, like the neophyte that I was, enjoyed every moment I spent with her. I never knew what her duties were at the Idea Theatre; that was entirely irrelevant. She was also any- where and everywhere theater was present. And she was quick on the draw; when once someone asked her what she'd look like as a Shakespearean actor, she tossed back, "Like a seventeen-year-old boy." That was Tallie.

◆ ◆ ◆

My two years at the university overflowed in many directions, and I rarely hesitated for a new creative opportunity. One day, noticing in the cafeteria a poster announcing a contest to name the university's new product, a soft ice cream dish topped with a variety of choices of goo, I knew what could win and it did: "Freezee." For the prize I was to have all I could eat in one sitting. I chose a very hot spring day, selected no less than 13 varieties, and with cameras snapping, I ate them all—enjoyed them so much I went back to the counter for seconds. Refused. Why? "You already sat."

I also took on regular assignments from the campus humor magazine. It was great fun photographing and writing, ranging from the story of a fraternity man, "from insemination to birth" and another about life in the "Rat" that included the eponymous creature on a plate. Any academic subject was grist for the mill, sometimes straying a bit too far into questionable areas and resulting in near expulsion. Once we did a mock-up of *Life* magazine that caught censure from the *Life* publishers; it bordered on a libel suit. I got to work with a staff of clever writers, artists, and others like me who enjoyed the ribbing we gave out, month by month. Some of the staff went on to professional publications, while I simply enjoyed it as a great sideline to my regular schoolwork.

Meanwhile, I continued to grow in photography, even won awards in the school's annual exhibition, something that almost ended in defeat. I had been permitted to attend the judging by three men: a professor from the Art Department, a writer for the *Milwaukee Journal*, and a commercial printer. My submission was a uniquely treated portrait of Mrs. Ayoub, an elderly Lebanese lady (from Houghton) which was immediately appreciated by the first two, but the businessman strode up to it and examined it closely. Then, pointing with the stub of his cigar, in a professional voice said, "This photo is a phony—obviously copied from a newspaper." Shocked silence before the art professor asked, "Are you sure?" (I held my breath.) When he said positively it was so, I raised my hand and timidly said, "Excuse me, but I happen to know that it's not a copy but made with a special double printing." "How do you know?" "I was there when it was printed." After a rather embarrassing moment of silence, the businessman stubbed at the photo again and in triumph said, "The fellow that made this photo is a genius." And so, I took the prize.

Mrs. Ayoub

❖❖❖

In truth, my extracurricular activities not only fed my scholastic requirements, but as it turned out, also opened doors to my post-graduate life.

Part of my dabbling in extracurricular theater included creating makeup and costuming for one of the university's treasured traditions: the annual all-male satirical musical. It was a serious, laborious production, involving a chorus line selected from the toughest fellows in sports (football, rowing, etc.) and directed with more serious care by one of the department's most respected faculty members. At first it did not impress me as worth exploring but was persuaded when I learned that alumni from those shows included Hollywood stars like Fredric March. I dove right in, learning the trick of dressing and making up the least likely of men into gorgeous women. The shows would be tested by performances on the campus stage, then traveled to one theater after another around the area including, finally, SRO performances at a theater in downtown Milwaukee and another in Chicago. These were so successful that after each show, it became natural to expect lines of men outside the stage entrance, bouquets of flowers in hand, for the stars. And, tongue planted firmly in rouged cheek, the guys loved it!

At the time, I had been searching for a subject for a thesis, something that would be of value in my major field, yet not simply a dull obligatory task. The topic I selected was perfect: "A Theoretical Approach to Theatrical Makeup," involving a history of the subject all the way back to ancient societies using it for magical/religious purposes to the present. I did it almost effortlessly and I succeeded easily, passing the approval of three professors whose lives were once spent in some aspect of commercial theater.

I also had discovered that the little movie theater in the union was occasionally used for amateur productions. With the backing of our professor in play production, I received permission to test my playwriting with a one-act drama similar to a popular Arthur Miller play, *The Crucible*. Titled *Thunder in the Hills*, it was set in the rural South with a familiar witchcraft focus. A press release in the campus daily paper caught the eye of a Madison theater reviewer; he attended opening night and wrote in his news column the next day about the "rousing play worthy of a larger audience." Apparently Bob Gard also appreciated it. Unknown to me, he sent the script to a national playwriting contest and it not only took second place (with a $25 cash prize), but also resulted months later in an invitation to a prestigious summer stock company in Massachusetts—a stepping stone to a stint in New York.

I left Madison in 1953 with my MS degree—and the results of a Rorschach test. On impulse, partly out of curiosity but with the hope that it might help me better situate myself as an adult, I took the test from a professor in the Psychology Department. There was nothing startlingly new to me: that I was "exceptionally intelligent and creative," that I had "issues" with my father and mother during childhood, that I struggled to leave my Lebanese traits behind in an effort to "belong," and that to please I was "exceptionally conscientious in all my endeavors with others." Armed with such assurances, I headed back home for a brief stay, then out to the East Coast, like so many of my classmates, eager to test their stage talents in the world of professional theater.

7

Three Fateful Summers

The summer between undergraduate and graduate school, I got an unexpected first taste of teaching. By this time, I'd convinced my father that his grocery business, now diminished, was not for me; with the destruction of his store, he resigned himself to struggling with substitutes, none of which lasted, so he left me to find my own way in an academic profession.

An opportunity to test a new career came fortuitously when I learned about an experiment developing at the local technical college: the creation of weekly summer classes for high school students, permitting them to sample higher education in search of their future careers. Since one of the listed possibilities aimed at theater and radio, I applied, concentrating on radio production, which seemed to interest a group of seven high school students from Grand Rapids. I felt confident about the material involved but found myself facing teenagers, away from home restraints, who were not quite ready to accept discipline. Among my pupils were three students sponsored by an academic group to provide them with a growing experience outside their urban ghetto. I later learned that the boys had chosen this subject haphazardly, with little interest in it at all. Two of them were wonderfully eager and adaptive, while the third one became the bane of the course, from the start doing anything purposely to distract. Finally, I took him from the room, told him it would be simple to send him back home if he continued in his recalcitrant ways ("What I do? I ain't doin' nuthin.") As it turned out, he was equally disruptive in other ways as well, was finally sent back to Grand Rapids, along with a few other disappointing students. Things improved with his absence, but I felt a failure for not quite knowing how to handle such a difficult situation. It was my first good/bad immersion in formal teaching.

◆ ◆ ◆

At the U of W, along with classes, experimental productions, and the Idea Theatre, I still had found time to work in the union's complete darkroom. It was there that I found the tantalizing offer for a "vacation with pay" as a photographer at a boys' camp in northern Wisconsin. Though I could have stayed on campus that summer to cram for my master's degree, I took a chance. That summer job in 1952 would lead to a long association with Camp Nebagamon.

I did not realize that I would be employed at a nationally renowned boys' camp, one that would prompt a former camper to reminisce (as I would agree many years later), "I enter these gates, I gaze at Paul Bunyan and the Big House, I inhale the air, and I know deep down in my bones that no matter how many years have passed, I am home again."

Without a car at the time, I took a train to a station in Superior, was met by a middle-aged fellow who immediately reminded me of a portly Al Jolson (the winning smile, especially)—a greeting, a firm handshake, and I was in his car as he drove me from shop to shop for general camping supplies. We headed to the camp (less than an hour's drive east), and on entry to its grounds, I took in the gigantic, painted wooden Paul Bunyan figure and the large white foursquare building with Palladian windows beyond. (The property was originally the home of the Weyerhaeuser lumber company founders, and their family house was now the camp's headquarters.) Inside, I was led to an office in the Big House, where the director pulled out a contract and handed it to me to sign. "But aren't you going to interview me first?" He gave me that marvelous Jolson smile, "We already did."

I signed, as he explained one thing about the camp: "I don't know what your feelings are about Jewish people, but if they're negative, keep them to yourself, because my family is of Jewish descent and this camp is populated almost entirely by boys of the same religious background." I gave him a weak smile and replied, "Well, you should know that I'm of Arabic descent," and quickly added, "but I have little reason to be prejudiced; after all, we have a great deal in common." His reply: "Yes, indeed, including a border." I was in.

The director was Max J. Lorber, commonly referred to as Muggs. His office was a small room on the first floor of the Big House, part of a grand reminder of the original owners, who could appreciate the view of the rolling pine-covered hills, the lengthy beach below, and a beautiful view of the *H*-shaped Lake Nebagamon beyond. The main floor was a mix of wood-paneled kitchen, dining room, sitting room, and the office—with a sign over Muggs's desk with the succinct reminder that, "I may not always be right, but I'm always the boss."

The Camp Nebagamon property, purchased in 1929 from the Weyerhaeusers, covered 77 acres of hilly, forested land rolling down to the lake, not far from the primarily summer resort village of Lake Nebagamon. The camp had grown to host 210 boys, ages 8 to 15, who came from all over the U.S.; the majority were from big cities in the Midwest, and many of them were the sons of previous campers and counselors. The campers resided in the four "villages" spread among the trees, for the Swampers (youngest) to Loggers to Axemen to Lumberjacks. Each village was under the supervision of a director, known as a "push" in camp jargon. Under Muggs's visionary plan, facilities had expanded as needed; when I arrived in 1952, it was a remarkably arranged and managed site that I would come to roam endlessly and photograph.

Part of my job, I discovered, was that I would double as a cabin counselor, assigned to a cabin across from the Rec Hall, which was just below the Big House. Logger Seven was a double bungalow attached back-to-back with Logger Eight. Each was roomy enough for eight campers with a space for the counselor in charge. Photography I knew well; counseling a group of kids 11 or 12 years of age—that was something else. I felt not just slightly uneasy about the prospects.

A week before the campers' arrival, we were made familiar with the property (reverently referred to by returning staff and counselors as the "hallowed grounds") and given an orientation to the spirit and aims of the camp. Muggs joined us for an informal introduction to his dos and don'ts, while stressing that this was a strictly democratic camp. I found out later, at times to my embarrassment, it was so, but only up to a point; there were many rules involving traditions, safety, handling of the campers, etc., that were to be diligently followed—and, I also found, with good reasons.

I returned to my cabin, unpacked, and the huge bell behind the Rec Hall rang out at precisely the right time for the evening meal—my initiation into the sound that governed not just meals, but the daily routine from morning until evening. Campers and staff were fed in the Rec Hall, a long, open-screened wooden building, which also doubled for group activities: music programs, stage presentations, etc. The walls attracted me immediately, almost completely covered with camp pictures and mementos of every sort, some obviously from decades past.

I quickly realized that meals also had a prescribed sequence: find a seat at one of the round tables spread around the room and scattered onto the long porches north and south, stand for a note of wisdom read by a different camper at each meal ("He who hesitates is lost" or "I complained about having no new shoes until I met a man without feet"), selected from a trove of such messages in a box next to the dining room's microphone. After a pause for the command, "Be seated," the noisy meal would begin.

Eating, serving, cleaning—all rituals that one would pick up after the first meal; they rarely changed, nor should they, and that included just about anything done while at camp. A ritual for when and how to take a shower in what was called in camp jargon "the Jop" (which at the time doubled as the group bathroom as well), when to remain as a group in the cabin together, when to leave, how to arrange to see the nurses or doctor at the Waldorf Castoria for whatever reason.

The days were spelled out—morning ritual, breakfast, cleanup, morning activities, lunch, rest, afternoon activities, etc.—with something special on Tuesdays ("Cruiser Days" for groups) and on certain evenings, plus secular Sunday all-camp sessions at an outdoor shrine, involving some hymns, nature observations, capped by a volunteered lecture.

There was some touch-up work to do in Logger Seven before

the campers arrived. With a good broom, I swept the place, made sure the bunks were nicely placed, then visited with Don, the counselor in Logger Eight.

That was serendipity. Don had been a camper for years, returned as a CIT (counselor in training) and was finally raised to the level of counselor with a cabin of his own. I listened to his almost rapturous ramblings about the camp, his delight as both camper and staff, even a brief history from his point of view. He asked to see my roster, and as he looked down through it, clouded. "Wow, that's a tough group from Swamper Seven last summer." He sighed. He obviously wanted to say more, but when taps shut down the evening, he said, simply, "Be strict; make them like and obey you."

I didn't sleep too well that night, but the sweet smell and soft sighing of the pines soon lulled me off and I didn't awaken until I heard the pounding of rain on the cabin roof in early morning. I leaped from bed, dressed, and rushed up to the Big House, where we were supposed to meet our groups and lead them to their cabins.

Big change: the bus had taken the campers to their cabins to avoid the soggy mess surrounding the Big House. Someone shouted through the rain, "Go back to your cabin; they'll be waiting for you there." I shot back down the hill, slipping and sliding through the torrent, to hear noises coming from my cabin. Threw open the door to find utter chaos—piles of wet bundles all over the place, eight kids leaping on bunks, shouting, throwing things at one another, ignoring me until I slammed the screen door and just stood there in shock.

I took advantage of the momentary halt, and gave them my prepared "little talk," filling them in about me, adding I hoped we would soon get to know each other and become friends. They sat, hands folded or akimbo, listening patiently to my conclusion and then went into action, preparing their bunks and spaces around them as if I no longer existed. When the breakfast bell sounded— rain still a downpour, the cabin floor a wet dirty mess—we marched to our meal as a soggy group.

The next morning as I pretended to remain asleep, listening to the boys falling into the awakening ritual, someone whispered, "Should we tie him up now?" followed by, "No, not the first morning." What had I to look forward to?

Day One had been far too hectic to worry about small issues. As the next morning lightened, we dressed in clothes appropriate for the weather: long sleeve shirts, jeans, work shoes, and ponchos for our trek to the Jop for morning washup, back to do a makeshift job on the dirty floor before the bell called us to breakfast. Another exercise in supervision—from appointing volunteers to get the food, then collect and return the remains, to controlling the volume of conversation, to sweeping around our upturned chairs before group departure back to the cabin to tidy up before morning activities.

All this structured order, automatically that first morning at breakfast and through the two months that followed, I came to realize, was the conscious design of our director, who, over decades of critical dedication to his thousands of campers, created a community so admired by the rest of the camping organizations. A democracy ruled with professional autocratic know-how was Muggs's secret to success, that along with his creed, that "Nebagamon is a place where we welcome and accept differences." I also compared Muggs's thoughtful approach to daily activities to that of the over-scheduled youth camp I had once attended (and disliked) years ago—his routine definitely had a point to it and made sense to me.

I even learned to follow and respect his public gestures—for example, to stop at the water fountain between the Rec Hall and the Big House for a healthy sip as he did, or to take a moment for a tête-à-tête with a camper when it seemed appropriate. Anxious to become an ideal CN counselor and used to adapting, I tried to mimic the "old timers," to become a CN regular overnight. Usually, especially with my group, I failed.

It was the second day when I awoke, roped and strapped like Gulliver from head to toe, that I realized a neophyte's helplessness. The more I squirmed, the more my young trappers cavorted and yelled with pleasure around my bunk until, after what seemed like hours of hopeless struggling and squirming, I was released. What to do about it? With thespian effort, I laughed it off, praised the group for their success, and then with a gentle threat, closed the book on that chapter.

Did it work? Did they gradually fall under my supervisions as all the other campers might? Hardly. This was a cabin of eight leaders with one helpless follower.

My lack of control over the group did not go unnoticed. The eagle-eyed "pushes" observed the strain between the campers and me and reported it to Muggs. After less than a week, they determined my inability to meld with the boys, and I was tactfully removed to a residency in one of the Lumberjack cabins, where the 13- and 14-year-olds accepted me with amiable curiosity. I was not their "boss;" I was a novel big brother.

I plunged into the photography project full force. Six days a week, I would publish the day's special: a photo hike around camp, a lesson in film developing and printing, a hands-on experiment in various photographic amusements (printing objects without film, etc.). Since this was, after all, a camp in a beautiful setting surrounded by some of the most luxurious examples of nature, it was easy to turn a camera walk into a lecture on how to "see" pictures everywhere. My "pupil" would raise his expensive camera (usually a new gift from his parents) to his eye, look through the viewfinder, and follow my directions. I did this often, and with mutually pleasurable results.

Occasionally, I'd find a loner looking for a project less strenuous than tennis or boating, who would come my way timidly to observe and then, at my encouragement, to take part in my projects. I would find things for them to do for me, to make them feel useful—special photo assignments like helping me mix chemicals in the darkroom (in the basement of the Big House). I recall one little fellow with a great comedic personality who would dip his entire hand into a gallon jar, mixing strenuously as he would say, "This hypo has been untouched by human hands; that's because I'm a little monster!" and let out a hideous laugh. I really got to like that kid, and kids like him, and did my best to give them special attention. We were, in a way, birds of a feather....

As I slowly adjusted to the CN way, I began to enjoy it. I looked forward to each day's activities around the grounds, on the shore, even when we required the camp bus to take us somewhere. I would perform a mix of show-and-tell, give little personal photographic secrets in composition, lighting, and endless more. Sorry to say, the darkroom/photo projects were hardly outstanding in popularity. Swampers and Loggers were my most frequent guests, with an occasional older camper with photographic interests.

The basement darkroom at Camp Nebagamon

Early in the season, Muggs handed me his ancient Graflex camera (complete with packets of film to be inserted for single shots at a time); he was proud of it, said he bought it especially for our professional use. I tried to get used to it, but thought its bulkiness made it nigh impossible for anything but setup shots and never mastered its tricky shutter mechanism. So, eventually, I'd leave it behind and substitute instead my handy 35mm cameras to do candid work. He rebelled at first but, after seeing the results, gave in. I always wondered what he did with that old relic after that.

Meanwhile, anxious to contribute to the camp's "Good Time Get-Together" nights, I timidly offered to entertain with my glove rabbit Harvey; he had been a hit during my USO shows, so I thought it might be fun to try him with the campers. Did it work? Harvey turned out to be the success of the get-togethers after that; he even intervened at other entertainments, became the friend not only of the group programs, but even more so when he would show up on the nights I would be in charge of a cabin subbing for a counselor's night off. But wouldn't you know, even with this successful friend of campers and staff alike, I made a terrible goof-up one night as the group gathered for a political session.

It went like this: while the country was going through the routine of selecting a new president, Muggs decided it would be good to have a similar election here at camp. Two older fellows were selected to run as candidates; they took it seriously, and so did the rest of the camp. They set up posters around the Rec Hall area and were given opportunities to give speeches. The excitement worked to a pitch at a final presentation, with members of the camp coming to the mike to give reason for their choice. Well, I didn't want to butt in, but when asked, I brought Harvey to the stand and asked him his choice. There was a roar of approval, 100 percent in favor of that choice. The room went wild, Harvey waved them on, and it was a monumental win ... until we all realized, suddenly, that thanks to the rabbit's presentation, the election was prematurely over even before others had a chance to express their approval of the alternate candidate. I saw Muggs's face cloud over; instantly, I realized I had ruined the climactic moment (supposed to come later) with a premature unanimous vote. The evening concluded with a win by Harvey's surprise entry into the event. As the campers left for their cabins, no member of the staff, nor Muggs himself, brought it up to censure me afterwards. They didn't have to.

Actually, despite such moments, I began to fit in, to enjoy getting to know all the campers, individually and collectively; they were sons of affluent families, accustomed to far more material things than I, and they lived a way of life quite different from mine. Still, during those two summer months, Muggs saw to it that we were democratically alike. Nor did I ever feel the need to face the fact that we came from different religions; rarely would the subject come up, and when it did on their part, it was simply curious questioning: "Why do you go to church on Sundays?" "Same as why you go to the High Holidays at the temple." As for me, whenever the occasion demanded a brief comment, say, at a meal, I'd usually toss in a Jewish word or phrase ("Oy, vey!") to a roll of the eyes or a snicker.

It impressed me that the campers were always eager to learn something new (also part of Muggs's personal growth agenda). That same year, Bendt Rorsted came from Denmark to begin a new project in orienteering. Muggs set up a platform tent for him in the midst of the cabins to be a living demonstration of wilderness existence. Bendt was eager to share his Danish way of life with the campers, either with a straight face but often with a wink or a slight smile. He had a remarkable sense of humor. Once, on a combined photo and orienteering trip along a Lake Superior beach, Bendt picked up a forked twig, examined it studiously, and said in his sober sing-song voice, "Look here, boys; this is what you call the horns of a dilemma!"

Since I was not strapped with counselor responsibilities, I was frequently called upon, or volunteered for, varied activities, but regardless my enthusiasm and eagerness to please, I was ever the klutz. For that reason, I never expected to return for another year, and when I went to Muggs's office to collect my salary at the end of the summer, I expected the check, a hand shake, and nothing more.

So, I was surprised—no, astonished—when he thrust a contract toward me and said, "This is for next year; I've raised you to permanent specialist with a fine increase in pay."

"But, Muggs, what have I done to deserve this? Hard as I tried, I was not cut out for what you hired me to do."

He gave me that smile and admitted, "Yes, you've made a lot of mistakes, more my fault than yours. But once you hit your stride, you became a valuable person to me. I noticed something unique in you, for example, your attitude toward the less successful campers. You helped more than anyone else to make their camping here a pleasant one. Just sign on the dotted line ..." I did, still amazed that somehow I had passed my novitiate under this legendary leader.

❖ ❖ ❖

Thanks to Bob Gard—and thanks to Muggs's patience for allowing me to defer my return for a year—I spent the summer after my graduation from the U of Wisconsin (in 1953) at another prestigious summer institution: Priscilla Beach Theatre, one of the first "barn" summer stock programs in Plymouth, Massachusetts.

A total of 40 college students from across the country—a curious assemblage including budding actors, writers, dancers, directors, designers—were there as summer apprentices. We were settled into little white cottages that bordered farm fields on one side and the Atlantic Ocean on the other. We rarely saw Dr. Franklin Trask and his wife, Agnes (founder/directors of the institution), and though they kept a keen eye on us and would occasionally show up at morning training sessions, we rarely interacted with them.

Mornings were spent in lecture on dramatics, often based on the experiences of our teachers—men and women who once possessed hopes and aspirations similar to ours, who had achieved a certain amount of professional success, now retired from the stage to nurture the next generation. Miss Madrich, teacher of movement, sat before us, one elephantine ankle hidden tastefully behind the other—a gracious example of bodily beauty despite the unexplained deformation, using arms, torso, and head with almost voluptuous additions to her lectures. Her aim: body articulation, the expressive control over the body. Her device: first, while seated, consider each part of the body as singular, to control and to keep it under control at all times. Example: an outstretched arm made capable of swanlike undulations from shoulder to wrist, a ripple of the torso as if it were comprised of four distinct parts. And, finally, putting it all together, she would have us create a great circle around her in the field and leap, performing with any number of rhythmic combinations, all the while counting aloud, "One-two-three, one-two-three" as we did so. We worked assiduously despite the awareness of the neighboring field hands' amusement.

Miss Archer, on the other hand, worked with us in small groups around her as she lifted little scenarios from her text and with both facial expressions and full command of her voice, thrilled us with the possibilities of visual and vocal controls. She could utter, "Yes, John," with dozens of variations. She was a wonder.

Then there was Mr. Windsor, not an actor but a director. With a slight sense of grandiosity, he would present a capsule of a scene, underline its psychological implications to the whole, and then smugly direct the scene, moment by moment, to achieve what he perceived to be the scene's importance to the entire play. He seemed a good prospect for helping us to Broadway, but rumors spread among us, especially among the male students, when we discovered his wandering fingers and his taste for handsome young men. He was, it was true, exceptionally gifted with comedies; ingenious funny bits would be developed from nowhere, turning his plays into audience favorites. (The teachers, incidentally, doubled in directing us in a new play each week.) When serving as his assistant on a play, I couldn't resist the insertion of a comic bit—which he appreciated and eventually requested my assistance on each of his productions. I was pleased, of course, but kept a safe distance between us during rehearsals, much to the amusement of my cottage roommates who well knew of his tastes.

A routine developed: morning classes, afternoon rehearsals of each new weekly show, and nightly performances the following week. There was tremendous talent among our group; I felt small and inept among them—definitely left out when the "sides" were handed out for each production. (A side, I learned, was the professional script, incomplete, but with the individual's lines proceeded by a phrase or action to be followed. I was given small roles and became known as "five-side Kirkish.")

Well, after all, acting was not what brought me to the place. Still, I was learning a great deal by osmosis. From a fellow from Los Angeles, I learned something about putting my words into professional-looking scripts. From a ballet dancer, I discovered, with some practice, I could do a reasonably good petit jeté. From a lithe charmer from Brooklyn, I found that dancing the waltz was actually fun when you had a good partner. From my Alabama roommate, I learned how to fake a realistic Southern accent.

Bringing in Broadway or Hollywood stars as leads helped fill the barn theater performances. It was a win/win situation; they filled their usually slow showtime during the hot New York summers, and we had a rare opportunity to work with them professionally. Of course, we all emulated our favorites, hoping to replace them on Broadway or the screen; few ever did. Pat Carroll was an obvious shoo-in, with her all-out talent for comedy; though she never planned to continue in what she referred to as the "Gotham Cattle-run," she did, almost easily, make it to the top, not only in comedies, but in serious roles as well. But I doubted if she would ever return to summer stock again.

A Priscilla Beach Theatre production

When not in a performance, we had the evenings off—spent on the sandy beach below our area—a wonderful way to divest of the day's labors, enjoy a dip in the salt water of the bay, and relax around a fire afterwards. Ever feeling shy and inadequate, I generally joined around the fire but without ever trying to live up to "one of them." As luck would have it, though, perhaps because the females well outnumbered us and, I assumed, also because many of the men were disinterested in them, the women surprisingly gravitated in my direction. One night, when my competition dwindled, I took four of them back to their quarters, spending an inordinate amount of time with each one, saying goodnight. I returned to my place after that, smugly pleased, and ready for come what may on future nights. Small town Joe Kirkish from the U.P. Styx—I was somebody!

The climax of the season included the presentation of *Good News*, a light musical comedy about coming of age in college, to be played in Boston. With most of our group heading for home or with hopes at making it in Gotham, I was talked into a part in the chorus. I took it, even knowing that I got the part not because of my musical talents, but because I was given an amply attractive partner guaranteed to draw attention away from me and my ineptness in singing and dancing.

So, Brattle Hall Theatre (in Cambridge) became my stomping grounds for two additional weeks. Despite its age, the theater's traditional fame drew audiences regularly. I learned how to dance comfortably on a raked (downward-sloping) stage, fake singing the tunes, and even took on the semblance of a pro. The smell of greasepaint became familiar, though destructive to my white shirts, resulting in trips to Filene's bargain basement, where prices dropped 25 percent weekly and where I discovered the dangers of competition among savagely competitive Bostonian female buyers.

I had been earlier warned about the frigid nature of Bostonians to outsiders (partly from a line in a play in which a father cries out in dismay, "My God, our daughter wants to marry a man from New York—a foreigner!") and was privy to it one Sunday when I stopped a woman on the street to inquire as to the location of a Catholic church. She drew herself up, folded her collar around her neck, said, "I really cawn't tell you," and stalked away, leaving me in a mix of amazement and wonder.

As our stint was drawing to a close, I needed to make a decision about my next professional move: follow the lead of others and head for Broadway, while anchored by residence with my relatives in Brooklyn?

A seeming alternative came in the guise of Charles, an exception to the chilly Bostonian, who played the piano for our show and who regaled us regularly with amusing stories about living in that New England city. When he learned that I was working on a new play, he showed interest, saying he was in the early stages of writing a modern opera and in need of a good writer for the libretto. Would I like to stay behind, live with him in his flat, and work with him? In a rush, I accepted. We became friends, would sit on the outside steps of the playhouse during intermissions, and arrange our future with high hopes. My lucky star was in the offing—until one warm evening, while we sat in the dark, expanding on plans, his hand slipped gently over to my leg, began massaging it, and moving steadily toward … well, the intention was obvious. I was stunned. So, it was in uptight Boston that I experienced what was rumored to be standard in show biz. The trip to Brooklyn suddenly became a more desirable alternative.

8

Bohemian Years in New York

The Sahadi home in Bay Ridge was easy to find: take the BMT subway line from Pennsylvania Station to its end on 86th Street in Brooklyn, walk a few blocks, and I was there, climbing the curving stone stairway that led up to the front door.

I felt comfortably familiar—walked in without bothering to ring, straight to the kitchen where I knew Aunt Zakeeye would be preparing, as usual, another grand meal for her family. Her reputation as a master chef with both American and Lebanese cooking was ubiquitous among friends and neighbors, who knew she would display her prowess once each season by preparing for three days a meal, beginning with *arak* (that delicious licorice-tasting drink with a kick to it) and appetizers sufficient for a full meal by themselves to multicourse dishes both American and ethnic, fit for royalty, capped by no less than three desserts. Everyone sought a place at her table for the occasion, but only 12 plus her family made it—and happily gained half an inch around the waist for it. I know … I sat through one myself.

We hugged, my overjoyed, short, and grossly oversized great aunt and I, spoke traditional greetings in Arabic, and was off to my old quarters on the third floor to settle in. The only thing different was that Uncle Mike had died, and the two older sons (now in their 30s) had become the reigning males.

That first evening with the family at dinner, we discussed my plans. First, to make contact with friends from the University of

Wisconsin who, like me and thousands of others, were seeking their futures in Manhattan. My great aunt was pleased, her sons less so. Invite your friends over for a meal so we could meet them. Fine. Good start.

But before introducing my friends to my extended family, I was eager to rediscover Manhattan ("the City" to Brooklynites). I even took in live TV/radio broadcasts—the kind that gave free tickets to fill seats for audience reactions, most especially the quiz and game shows. It was great fun. You called in for a ticket, picked it up before the show, then were given a form to fill out about yourself (ideal, I found out, for finding interesting people for future shows), watch the show, and sometimes even became part of the show, like me ... once.

On my form for "Double or Nothing," where it asked if I was married, I wrote, "No, but I'm here in New York to find Dianne." After the half hour was over, I was called, along with a handful of others, to remain behind, and was asked about the "Dianne thing." I explained that she had been a student at the University of Wisconsin as I was, that we both worked on theatrical productions there through which we became friends—and I pulled out a photo I'd taken of her from my wallet to help. The fellow's eyes lit up, he smiled, and said, "I think we can help you find her; what's her last name?" I didn't know but did recall that her home was somewhere on Long Island. He smiled again. "We'll look into this and call you."

The call came less than a week later; I was to arrive at noon before the show to be instructed for that afternoon's 3:00 p.m. performance. Excited but nervous, I arrived at the theater, joined three other people who would also be on the show that afternoon. A pretty, business-like secretary met with us, explained that we'd be given tickets to use, sit in diverse areas so as not to arouse suspicion, would go onstage when someone would call for six or seven possible contestants—we four among them. She did a brief Q & A with each of us, which she then turned over to the emcee, Bert Parks (later of Miss America fame), which would provide information as if he were ad-libbing with us, thus being sure to bring out whatever special interest we had for him.

We rehearsed, went out for a sandwich, more nervous than ever, returned to walk in as instructed, take diverse seats, and wait for our names to be called (along with bona fide members of the day's audience). A woman in front of me, filling out her form, gushed, "I don't know what I'll do if they call on me!" Hah! Her name wasn't called, but mine was.

We sat backstage, waiting our turns. I was second after a sailor returning home with a mustache that he knew he'd have to shave off (audience loved it). I was next, led to the side entrance to the stage, name called by the emcee, and suddenly I stood under bright lights, with Bert "ad-libbing" what he read on the info sheet: "Ah, I see you're in New York looking for a girl. Isn't everyone?"

Big laughs. "Now, tell me what this is all about." And I went into the prearranged explanation as he listened with a mix of surprise and amusement. As planned, I pulled out Dianne's sexy portrait for him to see. His eyebrows went up. He held the photo up to one of the cameras and said, pleadingly, "Dianne, honey, come home to Joe!" The audience cracked up.

Leaving the theater at show's end, I bumped into a group of ladies. One of them cried out, "There's the fellow looking for his girl!" "Yes," I said, "and I've been given a partial list of phone numbers to call; they've been pouring in." "You mean it's on the level?" "Oh, yes, ma'am; I'm really looking for her." "God-a bless you, honey, I hope you find her!" And she threw her huge arms around me for a huge hug.

The phone kept ringing off the hook with all sorts of women claiming to be Dianne. The secretary weeded through them and brought me back on air, still looking for Dianne—Wednesday, Friday, the following Monday for cameo appearances. The ladies in ever larger groups would surround me, begging for my autograph. I began to enjoy it.

I did call many people, including one mother at the other end of the line, berating me for playing around with her precious daughter—not "my" Dianne's mother. Finally, "my" curly, redheaded Dianne called in, indicating that she was now continuing with graduate work at Columbia University, not far from the CBS radio studio. She was thrilled to hear the news and promised to meet with me at the station the next day to plan ahead what we'd say.

From backstage, at the proper moment, when Bert announced, "Remember Joe Kirkish, looking for his Dianne? Well, folks, here he is—with Dianne!" Huge applause as we walked onstage, looking sheepishly like a pair of shy lovers. We knew the emcee would ask, "Now that you've been brought together again, how do you feel ... still in love?" Our pre-planned reply: "Well, Bert, we haven't had much chance to get reacquainted again, but it seems as though we still feel exactly as we did before." Ahhhhs from the audience. And that was that, I thought.

Though I was relatively free, Dianne's academic life prevented more than an occasional lunch together. Until one day, when I ran into her at an off-Broadway play that we were both attending, she rushed to tell me a coda to our story.

It seems the CBS people were impressed with her looks, demeanor, and personality; they called her in, said, "I think we've got something for you. We're doing a series of fashion shows soon; how would you like to model fur coats for us?" She nearly fainted but was revived when the man continued: "Of course, we like to give pretty girls a chance for the big time, but we also like to do something for the businessmen who come to our offices, spend a few days, lonely, at the hotel, and would appreciate treating some nice girl like you ..."

Dianne was stopped in her tracks. She walked firmly to the door, turned, and said, "Thanks, but no thanks," and left. For her—and for me—a firsthand experience of *Mad Men*-style manipulation.

❖ ❖ ❖

Eventually, I followed up on my great aunt's suggestion to invite some nice friends over for dinner sometime. The results were disastrous.

First, there was Faudi from Istanbul, trained actor and artist, making an alternative living by volunteering on TV shows and purposely making a fool of himself to the amusement of the audience. His uncommonly wild and unconventional persona hardly fit into the conservative members of the Sahadi home.

Then Magda, a talented dancer who had modeled for my camera frequently in Madison. Beautiful, sensuous, a willowy person of easy grace. But she was Black.

Finally, the *coup de grace*, Edgar, a blonde fellow with a Doris

Day pompadour and the demeanor of wispy delicacy. After he left, one of my older cousins asked suspiciously, "Isn't there something odd about him?" What did he mean, "odd?" "Well, didn't he seem a little bit effeminate to you?" A little bit? He couldn't have been more so without being a woman. "But why do you work with him, writing scripts?" "Why not? It's purely business; we work well together." Edgar joined the others beyond the Brooklyn Bridge.

It was obvious, my friends were never going to mesh with my parochial relatives.

When I lived with the Sahadis in Brooklyn, I would spend time in Manhattan photographing friends for the obligatory "composite"—an 8 × 10 sheet with photos illustrating specific talent and, on the back, previous credits. It was a combination of work and pleasure: seeing their places, setting up a simple three-light arrangement, and photographing a range of talents from acting to dance to, in one case, just hands. I had found a YMCA darkroom near Brooklyn Heights where I could do the printing (for a $12 membership). I relished doing this work, and at $5 to $10 per photo shoot, I could make enough to have pocket money and still put some aside.

I would return to that massive, impressive Brooklyn home in dark shadow against the sky, let myself quietly in with my own key, and climb the stairs to the third floor, where I shared rooms with cousin Ted. More often than not, I'd find Ted sleeping in my bed, would slip in beside him, and sink into a long accustomed easy sleep.

Since childhood, we'd slept together in a double bed, at first just slept, but gradually, with toys and flashlights, would create fantasy scenarios among the pillows, zooming in and out and under the sheets—great fun until a voice from outside the door would admonish us with, "It's late; get to sleep." As we grew older, we forsook the games for "boy-talk," as our conversations turned to girls, then women, forever attempting to unravel the mysteries of life with them, to differentiate one from another and, eventually, to imagine specific engagements and marriage. Nothing serious, certainly nothing vulgar or obscene, just boy-to-boy speculations.

Even as a kid, Ted enjoyed making sketches of the women of

his dreams while I photographed prospective models, using samples from movie magazines as a guide. Visits together to ever-crowded Coney Island beaches provided plenty of subject matter for us. My camera ever ready, inevitably returning to the YMCA darkroom with rolls of film: black and white photos of wet, fleshy bodies taking in the sun or busily engaged on sandy blankets— images that still please me when I go through my box labeled "Coney Island" to enjoy.

As days passed into weeks, it became further obvious that I would never achieve any talent exploration while living in ultra-conservative Brooklyn. I found (through friends) a small basement apartment in downtown Manhattan that I could comfortably afford with money from a variety of photo opportunities. I explained to my relatives the need to be nearer to what a creative future might hold for me. So, we parted on friendly terms, with the door ever open for me to stop by, even stay for a few days in my old room.

❖ ❖ ❖

My life in Manhattan bounced from place to place, situation to situation—a naif becoming used to being sold the Brooklyn Bridge in one way after another, gradually wising up. Examples ranged from guys blocking my walk along Broadway with expensive things to sell, supposedly "found" in hotel rooms, to volunteering work on a musical in Jersey with a professional couple, that turned into a huge sucker job that ended up with no pay, no rewards.

Still a small-town hick at heart, I never tired of the amazing big city aura, mixing in with tourists, gawking up at the huge signs around Times Square in their endless motion, down to the movie houses and the live theaters prominently displaying famous names on both the side streets, along where Broadway and 7th Avenue crisscrossed, to the gaudy 42nd Street and its sleazy movie houses and cheap souvenir shops. The noisy, glitzy feel of it all; over and over I took it in, my heart fluttering. I was in New York!

As I grew accustomed to the crowded mélange of old and new buildings, the streets and their environs, I developed at least the acquaintance of a variety of people, types never known to me in Michigan or Wisconsin: drunks asleep in doorways; young men with heavily painted faces, carrying piles of women's clothing, coming home from some all-night party; Jewish women off to shop early in kosher delis that dotted the area, or one pushing the other in a wheelchair; men or women walking their dogs to the nearest shrubs.

Manhattan wondrously manages (then and now) to handle the free flow of humanity, people scurrying from block to block, always in a rush, up and down ever-crammed sidewalks. Lost in the push to their next destination, people would sprint *en masse* through the crowd moving in the opposite direction, never touching, never paying attention. In time, one adjusts to the routine of crowded anonymity, finding friendships elsewhere.

I did develop my own special cast of friends, and among the closest, was Tallie Handler. She had recently left Madison to return to her native New York, though trying to keep as much distance as possible from her family in Brooklyn. Through all three years in various places where I would live, our friendship rarely changed. Tallie was my lodestone, and I was hers. There was never a romantic relationship between us, more of a brother/sister one, based, I think, on my lack of closeness to my sisters who blended more easily than I into high school friendships and to Tallie's often difficulty in being the youngest of three sisters with no brother in her family. We had our own lives when apart, but when together, we fit like a comfortable glove. It was, perhaps, an odd relationship, but for Tallie and me, it was perfect and ongoing.

With Tallie (who had Wednesday afternoons off from her part-time job in an office just off Broadway), I would check the papers for alternate things to do, things that cost no more than bus fare (or on rainy days, the subway), and we would "See New York." It might be to a Spanish art museum up in the 90s, a car museum a little farther north, or, if we had the money, a double feature classic film (foreign or American) in little art houses on side streets everywhere. Manhattan, we soon discovered, overflowed with interesting free or almost-free museums, parks, and curious sites that neither tourists nor even native New Yorkers would ever visit.

Exotic and everyday foods (and in a range of prices) were readily available and not just in obvious areas. Tallie discovered a little hole-in-the-wall restaurant near where she worked, managed by a

French family. It was a real find: reasonable prices, authentic cuisine served with an atmosphere that seemed transplanted from Paris. While uncle and husband worked the kitchen, a hefty wife with typically austere (even haughty) French attitude waited on the tables. We would pool our cash to begin our Manhattan tour there.

And the live theater productions, dozens of them. There was a not-so-secretly known system enjoyed by the thousands of us who lived for the lively arts but couldn't afford the extravagant theater tickets. The trick was simple but took some nerve at first: find the hours for a show to attend; arrange to arrive nicely dressed at the theater in time for a break in the acts; mingle casually with the smokers outside, a playbill in hand; then walk in behind the legitimate audience, slipping into any free seat to enjoy at least the last two-thirds of the show. Better than not seeing it at all.

◆◆◆

My portrait work grew and gave me some opportunities to experiment. I had traded my cheap Argus 35mm camera for a new Rolleiflex, which provided more advantages, especially in photographing candidly, looking unobtrusively down into it rather than having to hold it up to my eye. My photography also landed me in some unexpected places.

For instance, I used it for a whole new project at the Y where I did my darkroom work. I had met the fellow who supervised the sports area, including a section reserved for "muscle men"—men whose way of life consisted of not only developing the perfect "bod," but of assuring themselves of its continuing improvement with ongoing photos. With my friend's approval, I brought in my three lights and set up a temporary studio in one of the shower rooms, with plenty of space for shooting full-length photos against its plain background. It was amusing to see the pleasure I gave them by actually improving their individual physique with tricky lighting and angles; it wasn't long before the lineup of volunteers grew and so did the subsidy from them that helped pay for film and paper.

Just for fun one night, on my way to the BMT line to see my relatives in Brooklyn, I stopped to visit a friend I knew to be living in the area. Sherrie worked as a layout secretary for a popular movie magazine; she was capable of finding unexpected work for us freelancers (once directing me to an astute Japanese fellow who designed album covers and who bought the photo of Heather, which I'd taken back in Wisconsin). Sherrie shared an apartment with two other young, equally attractive girls, also waiting for their Big Chance. Out came my lighting bag and we wound up creating near pornographic photos of all of them in bikinis, lolling seductively in a lounge chair. One of the particularly arresting shots (purchased for a tidy sum) ended up in the pages of *Playboy* magazine!

On another occasion, returning to the BMT line to Brooklyn, in a seedy downtown neighborhood, I came across a man, obviously drunk and passed out in a doorway. A streetlight dramatically illuminated him. I pulled out the camera, set it on the sidewalk, and was in the process of taking a time exposure, when a voice behind me said, "Hmmm. Nice shot." I couldn't see his face until the fellow pulled out a cigarette and lit it … a guy, in his 20s perhaps. I thanked him, then went on my way to the subway station. He seemed to be following me as I got into the subway car headed over the Brooklyn Bridge toward my destination. One more stop, from the express train to a local; I climbed the stairs over the tracks to the opposite side. The fellow, suddenly realizing a mistake had been made, swore, turned, and took the next car back to Manhattan.

Confused, I told my cousins about the incident the next day at breakfast. They exploded in laughter. "Don't you realize, dummy? One guy throws out a hook. If you grab it, well, a date has been made." They laughed again. George said, "Joe, you hick, you just made a hopeful guy very disappointed."

Then, one time while Tallie and I were roaming under the Brooklyn Bridge for possible photo subjects, I found a group of nearly naked kids leaping from boulders into the frigid spring water. Tallie held back, pushed me on to get photos for possible sale to a daily newspaper. Turned out, these Lower East Side kids played a spring game, taunting first one, then another, to "break the ice"— to be the first in for the season. Good salable subject matter for the papers and they paid well for each one-time use. What I didn't notice was that two very cautious police officers saw me with the camera and moved in on me with a suspicious, "What's going on here, bud?" I explained, while indicating Tallie waiting for me. One

(Above) Boys jumping into the icy East River; Manhattan street scene; Tallie Handler on the Brooklyn Bridge

(Center) "5th Avenue High Fashion"

(Below) Boardwalk at Coney Island

cop saw her and said, gruffly, "OK, now get outta here and don't come back if you don't want a night in the clink." Tallie thought it was hilarious. I wasn't laughing, but it did add to my cautions about cameras and street kids.

During those years, I returned to the Wisconsin boys' camp each summer for two refreshingly invigorating months among the pines, alongside the lake—and came back with enough money to continue my creative writing quest. I was anxious to try work on short dramas and perhaps a novel. But leaving Manhattan meant finding a new place to stay when I returned. Brooklyn was out, though I often spent wonderful times with the Sahadis when an occasion would arise. I contacted Tallie for possible quarters; she came up with a friend of ours from Madison: a serious, up-and-coming dancer who needed a roommate to help pay the rent on his five-flight, walk-up, cold-water flat on W. 43rd Street, not far from Grand Central Station.

The place was small, divided into equally small rooms including two bedrooms, a sitting room, a kitchenette, and a diminutive bathroom. At first, it took great stamina to climb the stairs, but I was relieved to find that it did have hot water, but no heat, and that meant the use of a portable electric heating unit to be moved from place to place as needed.

Don Redlich was a quiet fellow rarely given to prima donna emotions, yet brilliantly capable of expressing himself through modern dance, which from his days of training with the dance company at the University of Wisconsin had become, body and spirit, his *raison d'être*. Now, in New York, he worked his way from one dance group to another, slowly building a reputation as a man of talent. Like his girlfriend, Rose (also a product of the Wisconsin group), he practiced dance exercises for up to eight hours a day, taking time off only for excursions to the various dance productions that dotted the city.

Though we had very little in common except for our U of W background (and the fact that I often photographed many of the dancers, most of whom were promising and willing subjects), our lives in that little apartment became a comfortable, if diffident, relationship. Only when Rose or any of his growing parade of friends from the dance world came to visit, would he come to life and prove himself an intelligent, eager conversationalist. I would remain mostly in the wings, willing to attach myself to the groups and their artistic milieu, enjoying like a fly on the ceiling their singular focus on a spectacular life in dance.

Rose reminded me (as if I could ever forget it) of the time when I was photographing a rehearsal for a performance in Madison, beginning with some basic movements concentrating on interactions. Divided into two groups, one at each end of the studio, they would in turn run toward one another, meet and, without touching, meld into a single shape, then move on. They needed one more person. Rose called to me, "Put down your camera, Joe, and join us." Well, why not? I was among friends. Clumsily, I situated myself at one end of the studio, watched a girl at the other end start toward me, and, resorting to a kind of Arabic movement recalled from family days, pranced and leaped, suddenly realizing that I was wearing loose jeans without a belt, and with each twist or leap, they inched downward. My upraised hands would drop and grasp, until one of the participants cried out, "What the hell, Joe, let 'em drop." That ended my singular participation as a dancer; I returned to becoming a cameraman once again.

A person didn't need to perform, I began to realize, to appreciate the subtle intricacies of modern dance; so much could be gained simply through observation. It wasn't long before I became a part of Don's group of friends and joined them for every professional performance possible.

In the apartment, our relationship remained casual; I learned to appreciate his hypersensitivity to colors, for example, and would never invade the sitting room in a green sweater over blue jeans, nor would I type while he was around, discovering that the repetitious clacking seemed to vibrate hideously through his mind and body. At the same time, he grew to accept, and even enjoy, my limited Lebanese cooking, and he would quietly move to his room when I entertained guests not of his liking.

❖ ❖ ❖

The typing problem increased as I pounded away on dramatic scripts, my novel, and anything else that might someday bring in money. Serendipity: at one of our occasional Wisconsin parties, I heard of a literary agent who was willing to trade using her typewriter in her outer office for buffering her against writers who would waste her time.

Don Redlich

Miss Hanchett proved a perfect solution. At an interview, she pried into my aspirations as a writer (liked what I was currently doing), my ambitions, and even my religious background. She accepted me based almost entirely on the fact that I was a practicing Catholic. "I like Catholics," she admitted. "I can usually count on them doing the right thing." She often, I was to learn, made spurious decisions like that.

She set a ritual for us: I would sit in her outer office from 8:00 a.m. until anytime into the evening, typing to my heart's content, and whenever someone arrived with script in hand, I would check it over, then according to her prescribed rules would either send the applicant into her inner office or tactfully but firmly dismiss him as useless.

Meanwhile, Miss Hanchett would sit at her desk appraising manuscripts sent to her for possible publication. Dressed always in well-tailored black, prim and proper in demeanor and language, she would also drop in on my interviews, to discuss ways I might help her. One day she dropped a foot-high stack of scripts on my desk, suggesting I look them over and write brief critiques for each of them. "Don't be too critical," she admonished; "they're paying for the service, so find something nice to say, even when I must reject them." In return, she paid me $5 for each critique, a nice, unexpected bonus.

One day, while I was writing at Miss Hanchett's offices, a pair of men walked in and asked to speak with her; interested, she invited them into her office, where they spent about an hour in serious discussion about a proposed new project for radio and TV (at the time not all homes had TV sets, so it was expected that a script written for television would also be reduced to half its length as a radio production). The men were privy to a secret society of crime busters who worked internationally when protocol might make capture and conviction difficult; no one would ever know who they were, but they would recognize one another by a special ring worn on the right hand. What a series it could make! At their request, Miss Hanchett would scour for the best talented writers possible. When they left, she went into action, notifying everyone she had in her files and even asked me to try my hand at it.

Thrilled, my imagination in full gear, I dashed off not only a TV script, but included a half-hour version for radio. As the results rolled in and were turned over to the men, she was more than pleased to announce that they wanted two writers to alternate: one certain Hollywood writer (who'd just won an Oscar for his script for a lavish drama about life behind the scenes in a circus) and me! Of course, stunned but thrilled, I rushed to Don's apartment to tell him the good news. He took it with customary restraint, but one of his friends said, "That's great, Joe. With the salary you'll make, now you can find a new apartment all to yourself." I took that as a hint that Don would very likely appreciate having his place all to himself again, so I started thinking about alternatives.

The good news proved premature. The next day, two men in dark suits and sober expressions arrived to speak with Miss Hanchett. They spent the entire afternoon with her, and when they left, she stood in the doorway of her office, face as white as paste. The men were from the FBI, checking up on her two men from Tennessee who had stayed at a posh hotel on Fifth Avenue and left without paying the bill. They never told her why the men were wanted by the FBI, simply said she should, under no circumstances, ever communicate with them again. And that was that.

While my big break didn't happen, working for Miss Hanchett did open doors. At her suggestion, I set a few of the more promising scripts aside and, with her approval, would follow up with favorable correspondence to the authors. One, a sophisticated three-act comedy by a Reed Spickers, caught my attention. It was a cleverly written comedy about Broadway show biz people; he obviously knew his material. With Miss Hanchett's approval, I sent a postcard to Mr. Reed Spickers, suggesting a meeting to discuss the play.

The next day, the office phone rang. I responded to a strong, vibrant voice: "This is MISSUS Reed Spickers speaking!" She complained of a temporary inability to walk without help, demanded my meeting with her in her apartment in Greenwich Village. "Plan on dinner at promptly six." A bit taken back, I agreed.

I climbed the stairs to her apartment in a once grand Victorian home. "Door's not locked," she called out when I rang the bell. I entered into another world: dark wood, rich drapery, massive furniture, and a genuine Titian portrait on the wall illuminated by a silver candelabra on a table set for three. A plain but pretty girl in her late teens stood behind her aunt, rolling Mrs. Spickers into the dining room in a wheelchair.

"My niece, Laura," she explained. "She stays with me while I'm temporarily incapacitated." She indicated my place at the table. We sat down to a delicious meal of Russian cuisine, "from downstairs," she explained, adding, "the Three Steps Down is a charming restaurant; I'll have to take you there sometime."

Thus, a door opened to yet another of New York's milieu. Mrs. Spickers, I learned, was a widow, her husband having been a very successful doctor to Broadway theater people. Beyond simply being good friends with actors, playwrights, directors, and such, they were showered with tickets to openings and special performances and lavished in the attention given them. After her husband's death, Mrs. Spickers took to playwriting, her first opus the reason for our meeting. It pleased her that I liked the play and had offered a few suggestions that could make a splash on or off Broadway.

While we ate and talked with increasing enthusiasm about the future of the play (which she unabashedly admitted had been compiled through years of association with people of the theater), I couldn't help but take notice of her niece, who in silence sat politely and listened. Suddenly, my hostess turned to the girl. "Laura, we haven't heard a peep out of you. Darling, you must entertain us a bit." Mrs. Spickers turned to me, "You wouldn't know it from her reticence, but my niece is an accomplished pianist. Currently, she is studying under a famous teacher. Laura, play something for us, dear." She indicated an impressive old piano in a dark space in the far side of the room. "Brahms would be nice."

"If you like," the girl replied and went to the piano, sat down, and from memory played an etude—delightfully. It took no encouragement for me to applaud and show my pleasure. Her aunt smiled. "I told you so. She's just too modest for her own good." And then she added, "You must come over again sometime soon; the three of us could take in a show or a concert. There's always something good on."

I don't recall the subway ride nor the walk to Don's apartment, but I slipped in quietly, went to my room in the dark, undressed, and fell into bed, even neglecting my usual glance out my window at the receding rows of clotheslines strung from one side of the buildings to the other. I thought I had dreamt the entire evening.

The Spickers became the foundation of a new life, opening a grand new world, from opening nights in the best seats at the theater (she insisted on seventh row center) to events operatic and from the world of dance. Sadly, I doubt that Reed ever saw her own play produced.

❖❖❖

My association with the Spickers led me to the best of my living situations during my three years in New York. Laura happened to be looking for someone to sublet her apartment on the Upper West Side while she apartment-sat for several months for her piano teacher (off on a European tour for the year). I gladly volunteered, because I sensed that my presence was encroaching on Don's need for privacy and because it offered yet another opportunity to sample more of the exotic Big Apple.

On W. 95th Street, I moved into the second floor of a small, ancient apartment building now squashed between a pair of high-rise apartment residences, surrounded by Jewish and Cuban markets and restaurants, and, immediately below my window, an easily accessible liquor shop (good French wine was often on sale cheap). My landlady was a quixotic delight, as French as the wines in the liquor shop. She took to me immediately, called me "M'sieur KeerKESH" in her amazing mix of French and New Yorkese. Her name? Mrs. Callahan. Her husband? Absent, a mystery to us all.

The room was a walk-up, second floor, first door to the right. It was small but not cramped, sparingly furnished with the best one could buy at Goodwill. There was a kitchenette to the left of the door, and at the right, a long sitting room with a grand fan-shaped Georgian window at the right end that lit up the room from occasional sunlight slipping in from around the surrounding high-rise buildings; from below, a constant fusion of bustling street sounds and odors of bus traffic day and night.

I heard through the grapevine that some fellows from Camp Nebagamon were living, hardly a block away, in one of the newer high-rise apartment buildings. I dropped over to introduce myself and found a trio living there: brothers Jim and Bill Goldman, writers as yet unpublished, but who eventually became famous: Bill for novels and macho films including *Butch Cassidy and the Sundance Kid*, *All the President's Men*, and more, while brother Jim concentrated on historical plots with more seriously developed characters. He was then transforming *A Lion in Winter* into a stage play (later, also to become a successful movie).

Bill met me at the door to the apartment—in his briefs, welcoming me extravagantly with a warm greeting and vigorous handshake. Jim remained seated, observing more than participating in our conversation, as we exchanged anecdotes from our summers at the camp. The third member, John Kander, was away at the time, playing the piano on national tour with British comedienne Beatrice Lillie.

While the ex-Camp Nebagamon trio was destined to become famous in their individual pursuits, not all the guests who from time to time graced their spacious apartment were equally fortunate. Dan J. was one such person.

Dan arrived after graduating from an Ivy League school in upstate New York, where he'd proven himself talented by playing the lead in a Shakespearean production. His performance was noticed by the most successful theatrical agent in New York, who left his card, suggesting an interview at some time in the future. Prompted, Dan arrived in Gotham to follow up. But first he needed his composite. For a modest salary, I was recruited for the job.

Aside from Dan's promising theatrical work at the university was a secret career during WWII, when he had posed as a count in Nazi Germany, actually becoming a spy for the United States. Stories told to me while I traveled around the city with him searching for interesting Manhattan sites as backdrops were like the subjects for a gripping spy tale. His accounts seemed too exotic to have been true, and yet the expensive garments, his demeanor, German weaponry, and other props were impressive enough to reassure the truth in these narratives.

I took more than the usual time with the photographs; it was a fascinating experience to work with someone who, at my suggestion, could switch at ease from one personality to another, changing from a military officer to a casual New Yorker on command. Both of us were more than satisfied with the results.

Then one day he visited me in my little apartment with serious intent. It turned out, he said, he had impressed the talent agent sufficiently to be "shown around" by him—at first, with excitement, then with a hint of suspicion. Ultimately and openly, the suggestion was that he enter into a sexual relationship with the agent in return for following favors. What should he do? He had earlier spoken of a moral bent in his life, now here causing a serious conflict. My frank comment: what he planned to do was prostitute himself … if that seemed worth the results. Tortured by indecision, he exclaimed, "But I know I have talent; if I could just get my foot in the door…."

For weeks, I did not see him, then one day, there he was, walking in the opposite direction on the other side of the street; he pretended not to see me. I called to him, we talked. I noticed he had an impressive tan. Oh, he told me that it was "because the agent liked him that way." He gushed with promise for a future onstage. He took his chance, lost his virtue, and nothing resulted. After that brief encounter, I never saw or heard from him again, but often wondered what became of him.

❖ ❖ ❖

The arrival of out-of-town visitors during those years gave me a chance to share my ever-growing knowledge of the Big Apple. Occasionally, while living in Don's apartment and then at Mrs. Callahan's, I would get a message from parents of boys I'd met at Camp Nebagamon (either on their visits to the camp to see their sons or at end-of-the-season Family Camp). Feeling I was familiar with the great city, they'd make requests to see me there, to show them around during a short stay. I enjoyed the interruptions; it became a chance to help them out and was a pleasant diversion for me.

The most memorable of all these visitors was the father of an older CN camper, Bill Rosenthal, who spent most of his time at camp with me doing photography. Mr. Robert Rosenthal called from an apartment at the Barbizon-Plaza, asking if I knew of any good musical event for the evening. I recommended a new opera, *The Consul* by Gian Carlo Menotti, now growing in popularity. He was excited, asked if I would like to have dinner with him, then attend the opera. Of course. I met him at the hotel, where, he explained, his firm, the Frank Tea and Spice Company, kept a room, nicely overlooking Park Avenue South, for their business visits. We ate at a luxurious restaurant in the hotel, then walked to the theater. The opera proved such a tremendous success, we left in something of a daze and, before we realized it, had walked into Central Park; fortunately, when we realized the potential danger we'd placed ourselves in, we hastened out without incident.

Mr. Rosenthal came to New York often; each time he'd appreciate my suggestions for, as he put it, "something I couldn't do with our less-demanding clients here." Then one day he called, said he was bringing his wife who would like to meet me. Could we have dinner somewhere together? Without thinking, I suggested they come to my (Don's) apartment and enjoy something of my side of New York for the evening. He was delighted.

What to do? Tallie came to the rescue. Gifted, capable of turning a cheap meal into a minor masterpiece, she planned a chicken dinner with fruit for dessert. Don tactfully left to spend the evening with his girlfriend, leaving the apartment to us. The Rosenthals were a bit late, apologized, and explained that Mrs. Rosenthal had a serious internal condition (in fact, it had taken nearly an hour to climb the five flights to the apartment). The evening was a great success, and then a week after their visit, a huge, very heavy box arrived on our doorstep. It was tough carrying it up to Don's apartment, but I opened it with great curiosity: it contained two of every product the Frank Tea and Spice Company offered for sale, which along with the spices, included peanut butter, apple butter, etc. Of course, I shared half with Tallie and we used the results of that generous gift for months.

The Rosenthals shared their novel New York experience with Bill (then a senior in high school). He was so excited, he talked them into bringing him to the city for a weekend "Kirkish adventure." Tickets to hit Broadway shows, orchestra seats only, for the four of us. While his parents busied themselves, Bill and I, at his insistence, took our cameras to photograph interesting sights. I brought him down to Houston Street, then a rather shabby part of lower Manhattan. Bill was enthralled with the Bowery, but as we passed some fellows on a stoop, one of them chided, "Slummin', eh?" and we returned chastened to join the parents. We still managed to get some good black and white pictures.

One time Mr. Rosenthal asked if he might bring Mr. Frank (the company's straitlaced founder) with us. "Let's show him a really interesting time," he said. So, he and the Rosenthals came with me, well uptown, to the second floor of a Greek community center, where the infamous and contentious Living Theatre presented its unique avant-garde productions. I had seen several of their experimental shows in the Village, before they were evicted for political and moral reasons and decamped uptown, and was sure the evening would be provocative. It was!

We entered a room filled with wooden crates for seats, sat down, and waited for the exotic extravaganza to begin. Mr. Frank seemed very uncomfortable. He asked if he could visit the "washroom" and was directed, he told the Rosenthals later, to an open toilet seat in the dressing room with the cast preparing around him. He returned immediately, asked if we could leave at once. We did. The Rosenthals thought it was hilarious. I felt I'd made a bad choice for the night, but after all, they did ask to see something different, and even without staying for the play, they certainly did.

Of all the visitors, one stood out as my favorite surprise: a young librarian from Central Michigan University, introduced by letter to me by the head librarian who felt this small Michigan town girl might enjoy something different during her first weekend in New York. In her letter, the woman enclosed a $5 bill to help cover expenses, not realizing that in the Big Apple it would barely cover a tip. What to do? I called her hotel, left a note asking her to meet me at Carnegie Hall (very near the hotel) at 9:30 a.m. sharp. I told her that she'd be in for a real surprise. You see, once I'd discovered a side door to the concert hall and became accustomed to sneaking in to sit in the relatively empty hall, free, as the concert for that evening went through its dress rehearsal. Would she enjoy it? I hoped so. It turned out to be far more than either of us could have expected.

We slipped unnoticed through the side door, sat in the dark, waiting for the orchestra (the New York Philharmonic) to begin. Not checking in advance for what was to be played that night, I was surprised to find a man with a familiar face and tousled white hair come onstage, toss his coat and hat to the floor, and walk to a waiting podium where he produced a wrinkled sheet of paper, folded it out, and set it on the stand. The young librarian gasped. "That's Carl Sandburg," she whispered. I agreed, not knowing why he was there. The music began slowly, almost mournfully, as Mr. Sandburg read from the paper, the lines to his *Lincoln Portrait*; we sat in awe, realizing we were privy to a rare personal narration from the biographer who had inspired Aaron Copland's music and spoken text. To celebrate afterwards, with the $5, I treated her to lunch at a nearby Automat and even had a few nickels left over.

However, my Aunt Bea (who had taught me about Uncle Wiggily adventures) was less impressed by my bohemian lifestyle. After I moved to the studio apartment at Mrs. Callahan's, she came to the city, apparently to visit our Brooklyn relatives, but actually to see and report on me to my parents. We spent the evening together. She seemed pleased that I was doing so well, but a few days later, I received a worried phone call from my parents wondering if I might need money to find a better place to stay. I assured them I was fine. And I was.

❖ ❖ ❖

At my Upper Westside place, I could do as I pleased, entertain as I pleased, pound away on my Royal portable as regularly as

I pleased. All my decisions were guided by myself and no one else. One night a week, though, I would have an "appointment" with Tallie. I would light candles, toss pillows on the floor, and entertain her with crackers and dry red wine. She would finish with her 9:00 p.m. session at the psychiatrist's office, then walk over to my place, settling down comfortably with me on the floor … I became the epilogue to each professional session. She explained quite matter-of-factly her problem, which focused on her being the youngest in a family of what she called "eight mothers," who forever criticized her for her unusual way of life. She'd left them for Wisconsin, then returned to live on her own, paying for her little apartment with money made from a part-time job and directing an occasional play for one group or another. Her sessions with the psychiatrist were a great help with bouts of depression that would come unexpectedly and go after a session or two. We both gained by those "appointments," looking forward to them. They went on for months.

Still working for Miss Hanchett, I continued investigating her stack of manuscripts. One caught my interest—a 20-page account of a man's disturbing reaction to having been co-pilot on the *Enola Gay* and its destruction of Hiroshima; it was amateurishly written but fascinating in its content. My eventual interview with Bob Lewis (then living in New Jersey and working as a manager at a candy factory) and subsequent meetings of a less formal nature, changed my life—again.

Out went my partially written, uninspired novel. In its place, prompted by each interview from the author (who was more than willing to permit me to take on fleshing out the original submission as long as it was written as a novel, not a documentary), a lengthy tome, *Prologue to Oblivion*, was born. It was about the fictitious crew of the fated plane, followed from the flight group's first meeting at a Midwestern Air Corps base to the dropping of the bomb and its subsequent tragic situations.

I threw my energy into the material. Besides interviewing Bob (who out of guilt for his part in the historic tragedy had blanked out many details), I did research at the New York Public Library. As often as possible, I devoted full days to writing, energized by what was growing into my dream novel. Even before the promised commentary from Charles Lindbergh for an introduction was added to the raw manuscript, we received interest from three noteworthy publishers—with the caveat that I revise carefully and slim it to about two thirds of the material before acceptance by any of them.

I poured every ounce of energy into what seemed to be the start of a new career and would have continued, but two complications arose that made hanging on to the dream apartment nigh impossible. Laura would soon be reclaiming her apartment, and once again, I would have to find new lodging. A call from my parents—actually a summons—before I left for my planned summer stint at Camp Nebagamon, though, was the deciding factor: for health reasons, they were determined to go south to Florida for the winter, and they requested my return to "supervise" my wayward brother, now 21, and to watch over the house. They were worried because he had fallen in with a bad bunch of young card sharks.

For 10 years (since my Army days), I had been able to follow my star and become independent, but now family obligation weighed heavily. I relented, assuming it would only be for a part of a year until they returned. With my academic credentials, perhaps, I might get some kind of teaching job at Michigan Tech.

So, reluctantly, with a reasonable explanation, I bade farewell to Mrs. Callahan and her entertaining dog, and the immeasurable experience of living in the vicinity of Central Park, where you knew it was spring only when its trees and shrubs burgeoned into buds. I knew I would miss the quaint elderly lady who lived a floor above me, someone who occasionally needed help coping with old age and her handicaps (bad eyesight, confusing meds, etc.). She always put on a good show for me, played the grande dame she once might have been, even permitted me to photograph her in her threadbare finery.

And there was Brenda, the cleaning lady, an immigrant with an air of suspicious knowingness—eyes, ears always ready for juicy gossip I might be capable of sharing with her and telling me about the rarely seen occupants on all three floors. There were twin sisters whose *raison d'être* was caring for a French poodle in the high-rise building next door, which they fed chopped filet mignon while they ate ground beef. Or the two fellows who lived on the third floor who were quiet and virtually invisible, only spotted when they were hauling themselves up the stairs, returning heavy-lidded from one of their all-night orgies.

I had grown accustomed to the fluidity of a bohemian life and since serendipity had landed me so many opportunities during my time in the city, I figured that when I eventually returned I would find another place and resume my photographic and literary pursuits. These had been the happiest three years of my life—and I still feel that way about it now.

Before leaving, I took a final casual walk along what was called "the Gay White Way" of midtown Manhattan, soaking up for the last time the noise, the crowds, and the glitter of Broadway that once enveloped and entranced me. When one of the ubiquitous con men did not try his regular hustle on me, I realized that I was no longer a mark, but transformed into a bohemian. Sadly, almost melodramatically, I returned to the apartment from that farewell walk, packed up my car, and headed for the tunnel and the day-long trek westward for who-knows-what waiting for me.

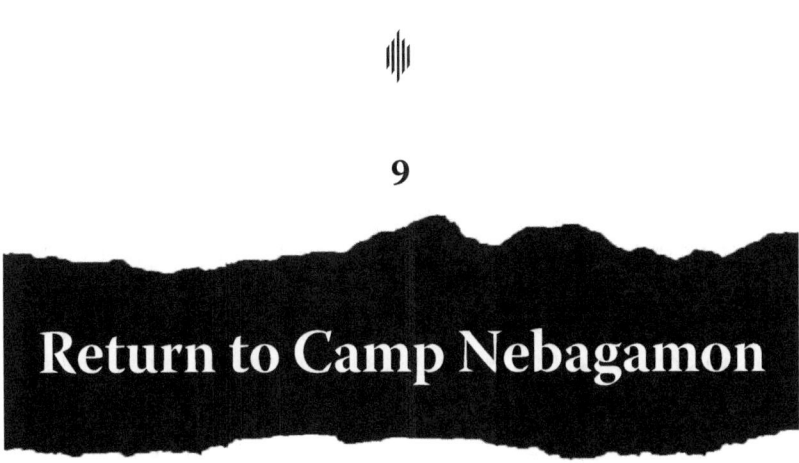

9

Return to Camp Nebagamon

W ith more confidence, I returned to camp, not just once, but for all three summers while I lived in New York (1954–56). Tallie had tried to convince me to work at a camp in the Catskills where I could earn more money, but when I wrote to discuss my employment with Muggs and mentioned the other possibility that I was considering, he simply replied, "I didn't think you were like that." He reminded me that I was getting his highest salary for my job, but suggesting that if I was, indeed, considering working in the Catskills, he'd be happy to give me a good reference. He added, "But I don't think you're going to like it there." Once again, his understated words got to me.

Since I had been moved from being a cabin counselor to the position of "specialist," there was little reason for me to remain in a Lumberjack cabin on the lake. I was given a home on the second floor of the log cabin Craft Shop, a bunk bed among two rows of them arranged mostly for temporary housing when needed. It was nice—a quiet place and warm on chilly nights, with the craft shop specialist keeping us toasty with a fire in the ancient fireplace below.

Each year's return was arranged with plans for new projects. Muggs had given me some leniency; since I was older than the average counselor or specialist, he now trusted my judgment (up to a point) in my offerings. With his permission, I purchased new equipment for the darkroom and broadened its capabilities to draw more older campers along with the steady flow of younger ones. I also proved to him that my own more portable, newer 35mm Kodak camera was preferable, especially in capturing better action pictures and, with its long lens, sneak exciting "caught" portraits.

I continued to ask myself how I could fit in to the accepted mold, since I was more an introverted intellectual than a lover of physical activity, a person who possessed so few of the stereotypical counselor characteristics. In my free time I would wander around the property, eyes everywhere, seeing the place with my own personal vision, and shooting faces—wonderful, gleeful, soulful, petulant, watermelon-eating, shouting, suddenly surprised or thoughtfully pensive. Timing was the trick, capturing on film so many varied faces day and night.

Campers plunging into Lake Nebagamon

Informal shooting was my preferred activity and one that Muggs picked up on and encouraged. He seemed to enjoy the results, would encourage me to do location shots where no one else had ever approached, and also to photograph camp visitors in key places—in front of cabins or the Big House, on the waterfront, on Tuchas Hill. They were well appreciated; I learned years later that my pictures were on walls in homes everywhere, on proud display.

He also suggested I glance through annual albums in the Big House sitting room, added to each summer as historical permanent keepsakes. I did and learned to lean toward his favorite subjects, locations, and activities; I was rewarded with genuine compliments. I grew confident, extended the subject matter, shot plenty of extra photos, and was pleased that the single annual album grew to many more each summer.

❖ ❖ ❖

I'm not alone in believing that the camp belonged to Muggs (and his wife, Janet)—lock, stock, and barrel. There was also general agreement that he seemed to possess mental powers, all-seeing, nothing ever withheld from him.

I almost got away with a major fumble on Cruiser Day. Cabin counselors were given one free day a week, and if the counselor did not have an assistant, he could always count on me to sub for the day. I enjoyed, most of all, the opportunity to spend time with the youngest campers because I knew that there was something about a boy's first year that makes him malleable to camp and all that it stands for.

So, subbing for a Swamper counselor on a Cruiser Day, I guided the eight youngsters, nose-bags (camp jargon for prepackaged lunches) in hand, to the destination of their choice, in this case, near an isolated creek about a mile from camp. Lunch, of course, was the prime focus for any Cruiser Day, so we settled down on the banks of the rivulet to eat. The water looked inviting, and there was a small boat sitting near us, so, shoes off, one of the campers leaped into the boat, and before I could prevent it, boat and Swamper slipped away, headed toward an overhead bridge, and jammed there.

No panic about it. Well, not much. After surveying the situation, we took off shoes and socks, slipped into the water, surrounded the stranded boat (and whimpering camper), and gently rocked it off its mooring, bringing it back to its original place on the bank.

Success! I made a huge issue of it, extending pride to all the helpers in the endeavor, but cautioned them: "You were very brave today, but it must be kept as our secret—just ours—telling anyone else would spoil it."

It worked until Sunday night, at the Council Fire where a ritual of throwing a key log on the fire indicated gratitude for some special act performed for the camper. You guessed it: the little fellow walked to the bonfire, small log in hand, proudly proclaiming, "I put this key log on the fire for my cabin who saved my life on Cruiser Day." Muggs's head shot up. Our eyes connected, an appointment expected ASAP. Again, not a serious result from our meeting but, Kirkish had made another gaffe.

◆ ◆ ◆

The camp tradition of the Follies also allowed me to put my theatrical training and skills to work. The production was an annual show, usually held toward the end of the season, with handpicked "hams" to sing, dance, or act out short CN-oriented skits on a portable stage at one end of the Rec Hall. Many previous campers and staff had stage-struck stars in their eyes and the Follies provided a start. Some eventually made it to fame, like the Goldman brothers and John Kander (whom I would eventually meet).

I heard stories about the original Follies, created and acted by the staff. Black-face comic shows were popular until Muggs felt they were degrading, tried one year with a black-and-white-face show, hardly much better. He finally turned the event over to a volunteer writer/director among the staff, peopled it with campers, without makeup, but with outlandish costumes from the attic of the Big House.

When I heard there was a need for someone to put on the yearly show, I immediately volunteered. With help from Muggs's daughter Sally and Betty, a new, young camp secretary, I brainstormed ideas that ranged from a comic love story to a mystery to a spoof on Cruiser Days ("Who's bag is this?" "No bag-a-mine."), finally reducing them to enough for an hour's playing time. On my weekly days off, I would borrow a rowboat and, with my portable Smith-Corona in hand, would row far enough away from all distractions to script the show. Sally and Betty would edit and embellish the scenes, then we recruited a cast of extroverted actor wannabes, while creating a budget-controlled setting and costumes for the final project.

It was not easy work but it was fun. That is, until Muggs decided we were neglecting the non-talented campers whom he felt should be given their moment of fame. He even drew up a list, filling our cast with shy, untalented, and the least acceptable actors imaginable. He also trimmed our rehearsal times, cut our budget to next to nothing, and seemed to be doing everything possible to create a total failure.

But we obstinately plugged on and presented as fine a production as possible. During the show, Muggs took me aside and whispered, "Joe, you're ruining it with details." For the first time, I shot back that it was entirely his fault, and stalked out of the hall, planning to get into my car and drive away. Behind me, at show's end, I could hear him onstage, working up the traditional camp applause—cries of "How" for a "wonderful show." Cooling down, I returned to my cabin and sulked in silence, knowing that Muggs would evaluate the event, then track me down, put a gentle arm around my shoulder, and apologize as he was wont to do on such occasions. I dodged him for days, until I bumped into him coming around the Big House. Arm around my shoulder, the Al Jolson smile. How could I not accept the apology?

Muggs Lorber

Because I was a few years older than most of the regular staff, Muggs granted me the pleasure of his company on rare free occasions. Ubiquitous pipe in mouth, easing back into one of the easy chairs in the Big House living room, or on pleasantly warm nights, on the porch, any subject was open for conversation. Religion? Though a practicing Jew, he professed an admiration for a simpler, quieter, less ostentatious group like the Quakers, adding that, "Your religion and mine are a bit too much in the opposite direction."

He wanted to know more about my family background. At one time I complimented him on how good he was, not only in fathering boys summer after summer, but in raising his family equally well. His response, "Well, it comes naturally when you love someone very much—the way your father does, right?" I didn't respond, didn't confess that he, Muggs, had already begun to replace my father. Nor was I alone in that adoration. One day, a former camper, up for a short visit with his son at camp, lay on the beach with his wife. As Muggs walked past, he looked up and with admiration in his eyes, said, "There goes the father image of 20,000 kids"—the Pied Piper of so many boys grown into manhood with similar feelings. That was Muggs!

Our little talks shed new light on his personality—not just a famed football player from Indiana University cum director of a boys' camp, not a dilettante, but a very knowledgeable man about people and what makes them tick. He was not always right in his judgments but, when found wrong as with the Follies, could graciously admit it.

When my parents dropped in on their way to Duluth one day, Muggs came out to meet them: hearty handshake, Jolson smile, and some kind references to me. My father was more than uncomfortable; at home he was embarrassed to admit that his son was working at a camp for Jews. He was flustered. I was as well but stuck to my guns. Eventually, after meeting Muggs, his feelings actually changed for the better.

❖ ❖ ❖

As soon as the regular eight weeks were over, I stayed around a day or so to enjoy the sounds of silence, of camp fading; I cleaned up the darkroom, packed up, and headed for a week or two at our cottage on Lake Superior before resuming my life in New York. During that end of summer break, I remember that my dreams somehow involved showdowns with Muggs ... my unconscious letting me flush out my pent-up frustrations and restore once again my admiration for this powerful father figure.

I had heard about Family Camp, and during my second return summer, Muggs was searching for volunteers to help with that special week. Curious, and with no rush to get home, I volunteered and said I'd keep the darkroom open and give adult programs in creative photography. I also planned to become the group photographer for families who would want one. Most of them did.

I'd also met parents who might show up during regular camp for a quick visit with their boys and, more often than not, meet and talk with them from a counselor's point of view (frankly but never too personally). They liked and appreciated it. Often, our conversation would wind up with an invitation to visit them during the winter season or later trigger a surprise call to me in New York of an upcoming trip to the Big Apple, hoping I would be their guide, which was always my pleasure.

But Family Camp, I found, was almost daunting: dozens of families up for a week of relaxation and reminiscences, with use of all supervised facilities. Many of them were "old timers" returning year after year with high expectations. The families usually moved into the now emptied and cleaned-up cabins, with some exceptions. Mothers with very young children, for example, might be favored with a room in the Waldorf Castoria.

From the start, it was exciting to meet the parents, especially of campers familiar to me, and it was a delight to see them change into camp gear and almost immediately don the CN mode—relaxed, polite, gregarious. Unlike regular camp, the darkroom was quite popular and used often. It was open to anyone interested but almost always, it was the wives who would drop in, usually out of curiosity about what their youngsters had enjoyed, but also to just talk *tête-à-tête*. And at times they were astonishingly frank.

During that week, I simply wandered among the groups, asking if they'd like a family photo taken (of course, yes!), getting to know the parents at the predinner "cocktail hour" just outside the Rec Hall—attractive table setting with hors d'oeuvres, drinks in paper cups, and loads of *joie de vivre!* Besides the more formal family portraits (usually in front of their cabins), I'd shoot candid photographs, while mingling informally with them during the hour. I began to feel quite at home with them and even enjoyed eavesdropping on the men discussing business or political issues, and the women, well, more personal issues about home social life or their youngsters.

Being at Family Camp made me feel that I was truly part of the Nebagamon family. Being a loner, I was accustomed to remaining within my own world, usually creating pastimes for myself by doing so, but among the families here, informally, I began to feel a part of them ... perhaps the hypnotizing effect of the CN atmosphere? I also wondered if the family campers did not share the same "all family" experience among themselves.

Two months (or more) at Camp Nebagamon was the perfect complement to my unstructured life in New York. At the end of each summer, I could decompress on the rocks at our family cottage on Lake Superior, while thinking about my upcoming literary projects, like turning the Bob Lewis material into a novel. In my quiet, peaceful milieu, I actually jotted down ideas for elaboration, winding up with the 29-page short story becoming possible material for over 500 pages to be worked, of course, into a more carefully edited expansion in Gotham.

After my parents' call in the spring of 1956 pressuring my return to Houghton, I decided to go there first before heading off to camp, to inquire about teaching positions in the newly formed Humanities Department at Michigan Tech. Since I had yet so little preparation for professional teaching, Professor Burt Fryxell had no intention of hiring me. Then, at the last minute, with two weeks to the fall term, he contacted me to let me know that one of his four new teachers had backed out. Did I want the position: teaching six sections of Freshman English with a one-year contract, salary of $4,000 a year? Did I! Serendipity again, I took the job.

So, at the end of the 1956 season of camp, this time I was not heading back to a week of relaxation, but for several months in the Copper Country—uncertain when I would return to New York, to the place that had given me so much freedom and ever-unfolding creative opportunity. My extended educational odyssey had ended, and now I was returning home to test my knowledge and teaching capabilities as a college educator.

%%%

Joe on a Brooklyn photo shoot

PART 3

Careers in and beyond the Copper Country, 1956–88

10

Becoming a Humanities Teacher

My teaching career did not begin auspiciously. My first day at Michigan Tech lingers in memory as the opening scene of a screenplay.

FADE IN

EXT: DENTON HOUSE (former grand family residence turned into an academic building); early fall on a Monday, 7:30 a.m.

MEDIUM LONG SHOT: Mr. Kirkish, 30-year-old teacher (dressed formally in suit and tie), climbing steps

CUT TO: his face, CLOSE UP. Clean shaven, hair in place, black-rimmed glasses

INT: HIGH-CEILINGED LARGE ROOM

PAN THE ROOM, following his gaze: obviously once a former grand dining room, now converted into a classroom with six very tall windows looking out on campus, then to the plain, tan interior wall with a large clock (ticking loudly) to 36 chairs with armrests loosely scattered around a spacious floor.

CONTINUE PANNING: to desk with a blackboard behind him. He picks up a chalk and writes his name, Mr. Joe Kirkish, in large letters on the board, surveys it for a moment.

MOVE IN FOR MEDIUM CLOSE UP SHOT: He lays out articles from his arms—two pencils, some notebooks, a list of student names, and a thick, brand-new textbook. CLOSE UP on his fingers playing listlessly with the cover of the book.

PAN: up to his face, move in for VERY CLOSE UP and in a series of LAP DISSOLVES for quick flashback sequence of people from the past who shaped his notion of a revered teacher. We see but don't hear him, as a young boy, Lord Krishna, seriously talking to a group of kids around him, then Professor Bloom, hand on shoulder, talking to him as he listens earnestly, then Professor Stein in a similar situation, and finally, paternal Muggs, smiling, apparently lecturing him—DISSOLVING clearly back to his face.

PULL BACK: as we hear a clatter of feet coming up the stairs.

MEDIUM SHOT: as Kirkish hears them, quickly sits down at the desk, as the first student, mature and appearing self-confident, casually dressed in khakis, walks through the door and stares at Kirkish in surprise—as do the other students, also, seeming older than typical freshmen, as they enter and find seats.

PULL BACK, THEN PAN (as room fills up): to expressionless Kirkish, trying very hard to appear authoritative, but not doing well at it. When bell rings outside the room, he stands, hands flayed on the desk, clears his throat.

CUT TO: male students looking expectantly up to him, then back to Kirkish (CLOSE UP)

Kirkish: "Good morning. I am your instructor for HU101, Freshman English. As you can see my name on the blackboard, it's pronounced 'Kir-kish,' like the towel. I hope to be with you for the whole 10 weeks ahead. First things first, let me call the roll."

PAN TO: students raising hands as names start to be read out, then fade out.

CUT TO: TWO SHOT, Kirkish in profile facing listening students.

Kirkish: "I realize this isn't going to be one of your favorite classes. You're here to learn about technology and the sciences, not how to stuff yourselves with classical literature nor when to use a semicolon, but this is a required course that everyone must take. I'd like to prove to you that what you'll learn here is important, how to communicate."

CUT TO: a hand going up, and PULL BACK to reveal a student raising it earnestly, then MEDIUM CLOSE UP

Student 1: "Yeah, how will you be grading us here?"

CUT TO: MEDIUM SHOT, Kirkish

Kirkish: "When I took a course similar to this one, that was my first question, too. I know how important grades are to all of you, so here goes: your textbook, you might have noticed, is divided into two parts, the first half containing samples of some of the finest essays ever written, the second on grammar usage. I will assign one sample each week; you will read it, and after we discuss it in class, you will write a paper on it."

(Big groan heard from the class).

Kirkish: "I will read your papers—and by the way, they will be written on one sheet only. Preferably, they should be typed, single- or double-spaced, on one side or both. It's what you have to say that will interest me, not how you can stretch it out."

CUT TO: CLOSE UP of his face.

Kirkish: "I will grade it this way: one grade for content, another beneath it for grammatical correctness, and a third following to determine the value of both other two grades put together. Make sense?"

CUT TO: a student, nodding but not terribly convinced.

CUT TO: Kirkish picking up textbook and opening it.

Kirkish: "Let's start on page 34, an essay by Winston Churchill. You might find him interesting."

DISSOLVE: from CLOSE UP facing camera to MEDIUM SHOT of Kirkish looking directly to the group, his voice in the middle of lecturing. FADE IN on his voice:

Kirkish: "You'll find as we progress that grammar is simply a tool to 'fix' communications."

CUT TO: Another student raising a hand and pointing to a page in the textbook.

Student 2: "What is the difference between a compound sentence and a complex sentence?"

CUT TO: (CLOSE UP) Kirkish, taken aback by a question he cannot answer and then glancing desperately at the clock, then down at his wristwatch.

Kirkish: "That's a good question. It will take a little explanation, but (glancing up at the clock again) let's save it for our next meeting. For now, class dismissed."

PAN EMPTY ROOM, then CLOSE UP: Kirkish alone at desk, head in hands looking down, then DISSOLVE to Kirkish, squirming, being tied up by Nebagamon campers.

FADE OUT

That was just the first class; I still had five more of these to go through before returning again to the original group. I went to my office, rapidly pored over another grammar handbook, found what I was looking for and memorized it in case someone in one of the other classes might ask a similar question. As I drew close to the second class that afternoon, I could hear—and feel—my heart pounding. Did I make a terrible mistake, dropping into this role barely prepared for it? I managed to fake my way through the second and third sections, without any serious goof-ups, then went home ready for a rough sleep. The first three sections were on Mondays, Wednesdays and Fridays, the other three on Tuesdays and Thursdays. Five days, then a weekend to recoup ... maybe.

I called my cousin, Annie Karam, now a nurse, and told her my plight. I knew if I didn't shape up, I'd swirl down the tube in very short time. Wonderful Annie came to the rescue with a packet of three small pills. "Take one each night; this will get you a good night's rest, and gradually you'll pull yourself up." She was right. Her little white pills and a lot of frantic hours between the grammar texts and along with questions tactfully pressed on my colleagues also helped, and by week's end, I felt a surge of relief. Well, almost, but the tension was eased and my natural sense as a teacher kicked in.

The second week began well. My assignment, one of Winston Churchill's remarkable speeches, seemed to draw their attention, and as we analyzed it, each section had someone to bring fresh interpretations, making the following ones easier to handle. Then the papers came in: written (scrawled) by hand, one sheet, one side only—running a gamut in content from dismal to promising. It was getting easier to red pencil obvious grammatical errors, but I was sure I was skimming over many more subtle ones. (I was, but I discovered a smaller, well-written text: Strunk and White's *Elements of Style*—so perfect for beginners, including me, of course) that I eventually assigned it and found to my relief that the students took to it like a Bible.

Grading, a thorn in the side of teaching, caused terrible problems for me. My grading system worked for the written assignments. Students could understand the mathematical method I used, but when it came time to construct an appropriate final exam to grade, then combine with nine grades on the weekly papers to come up with a final grade for the course (and somehow work in their comments contributed during our discussion periods), I struggled to find something fair to both the student and me. I hoped the plan would improve in time, but it never did. And it didn't help when in discussion about grading with one of our veteran professors, he admitted openly that he never found a perfect system, either. I endeavored to be conscientious toward every paper, every test, every final exam—and still I would tumble worriedly into bed for nights before assigning a final grade, and rarely felt 100 percent comfortable with the decisions for the 150 students each term.

As I learned, many of the students were not recent high school graduates, but upperclassmen—and already married—and were taking the class to complete academic requirements. I found, too, they were not afraid to contest a grade. I already knew I was in trouble when I stood by the entrance to the adjacent classroom when students were pouring out with graded papers in hand, saying, "I got an A!" or "He gave me a D." I had to brace myself for a week after each term's end, knowing at least two or three students would storm in about a grade they felt was too low. A few times, a wife would be sent to plead her husband's cause. That was the worst. I couldn't help but recall my mother storming into a high school teacher's office with my brother's inevitably low-graded paper in hand, ever grilling a distraught teacher until, fair or not, she was satisfied with a change in grade.

In other ways, the days grew less tense, I began to feel a certain comfort, even pleasant anticipation, in walking up those steps to my office or the classroom each day, prepared with new material to present, and to expect some byplay between the students and me. Tech students, according to entry statistics, were of a far higher level than at other universities; we had a reputation to expect more from them and we got it. That kept me on my toes as well as the students, and I liked it. As their teacher, I could discourse with them and still permit plenty of leeway in give and take in our discussions. Most of the time I learned as much as they did; it elevated my spirits.

The teaching process that had touched me from early childhood now grew to increasing satisfaction and even, if I may say so, a sense of intellectual power. As with others in our department, I was permitted to associate with the brighter students, invite them home, feed them, and carry on wonderful discussions on anything that stimulated them—and me.

❖❖❖

Of the other new instructors, George Strang and Dick Mason were like me, fresh to the university, but they had a little more previous experience. Both were married, while the third, Dr. Gerhardt Brandt, was not and he was much older than any of us. (He was hired to teach German, but also one Freshman English class.) All three of them chain-smoked; the halls and their offices often stank unpleasantly of smoke. Strang and Mason would dash at the end of the last class of the week to their favorite bar to unwind before heading home, while neither Brandt, who was a loner, nor I, ever joined them. I could never understand why Brandt, with an enviable background of teaching in Austria, deigned to accept a position among us at Michigan Tech until I learned about his unpleasantly complicated life in teaching and working underground during the war. It left him tainted with memories against the Nazis that all too often sifted into his freshman German classroom lectures. He was a delightful person until he drank copious amounts of beer and then would drift back into his fated past again.

Always fortified by my association with my peers, I would regularly join a small group who would gather during free time in the "coffee room" to relax and get to know one another better. My favorite, my mentor from the beginning, was Professor Price, a bespectacled, tousled-haired fellow in his 30s, specializing in philosophy. His comments on anything from class material to news of the day kept me rapturously entertained; our rapport was remarkably good. My interactions with the other newcomers were less enriching; we all felt overworked, and collectively, we joined the rest of the department's faculty to lobby for adjustment to our teaching loads.

Then there was Dr. Fryxell, who had the capability to balance a growing department while playing cautious politics with his superiors in doing so. There would be occasional gestures of cordiality and support from him, but I could not feel at ease around him, particularly after an episode in our department. For years, the one novel every student had to read in the final term of Freshman

English was Aldous Huxley's *Brave New World*. As a literary critique with a clever blend of science fiction and technology, it was a good choice, but one that often focused on things sexual, sometimes quite graphically. A Catholic student had brought his copy to a local priest, revealed the "naughty bits" to the priest's horror, who in turn carried a complaint to the university.

I was unaware of the situation until Dr. Fryxell invited me to have dinner at his home. It was a nice meal with good wine, then a retreat to the sitting room where both he and his wife shocked me by solidly berating me for being Catholic! "Your church, Kirkish—*your church* is ruining our department ..." and he went on to explain the reason: there were now local people from other faiths voicing disapproval, demanding the novel not be taught to students who might object on religious grounds.

The result was that our department held a tense meeting, determining that the book would still be taught, with the understanding we would have an alternate for those who objected to Huxley's novel. I did not take sides but found a perfect alternative in Arthur Koestler's stark novel *Darkness at Noon*, which included our same aims and was exceptional in the literary world, eventually being made into a stage play and then a very successful film. It worked out well for me and my classes; students were all expected to be present for the discussions of both books but had a choice in picking either one or both to read.

Dr. Fryxell, a staunch Lutheran, reasonably furious about the entire brouhaha, focused his ire on me. Tactfully, I reminded him that I was new to the teaching profession and not being politically wise to situations such as this, did my best to compromise with my plan. He accepted the explanation, but the religious label unfortunately would continue to rear its ugly head, albeit very subtly.

Despite hints of hesitation by Dr. Fryxell toward me and my work, he not only hired me to teach a second year, with the addition of a speech class (thankfully reducing the six sections of Freshman English to three), but also, to my surprise, with a modest raise.

❖ ❖ ❖

Meanwhile, I discovered through departmental meetings

and instructional notes in mailboxes that teaching was just part of our job. There were committees to join, meetings for a variety of updates in a common desire to improve the department, and always the strong suggestion that we blend in with the community in one way or another.

In my "free time," I offered various extracurricular services on and off campus. I made my skills as a photographer available to the Public Relations office and picked up assignments such as shooting faculty portraits. I also parlayed my local knowledge into writing articles and photographing local events for the *Daily Mining Gazette*.

Working in the Denton House, I noticed an unused small radio room and studio on the first floor. Knowing that Houghton's better commercial radio station, WHDF, would often introduce programs above and beyond the traditional news and pop music entrees, I decided to take a leap. I figured out how to use the turntables and the recording devices and then forged ahead, creating half-hour programs. I selected material reflecting my own artistic and dramatic pleasures: poking fun at long-haired operas (while actually piquing interest in them), revealing examples of classical compositions that included creations of thunderstorms, etc. WHDF played them, even encouraging me to continue, so I broadened the subject matter to such things as interviews with popular local figures, from on and off campus. The interviews also aroused audience interest and provided a delightful sideline to teaching.

The college was in a growth mode, evolving from the Michigan College of Mining and Technology (MCMT) into the full-fledged Michigan Technological University. With it had come the expansion of our Humanities Department and, in turn, greater involvement in the extracurricular activities. In spring 1957, I was encouraged by the dean of students to be an advisor to two fraternities. The music fraternity, Tri-Beta (later to become Mu Beta Psi), was being revived, and with my love of classical music, I readily accepted to join as their co-advisor (along with a choral director). The second one was a newly created social fraternity.

I accepted the bid to advise the second group for different reasons—first, the excitement and challenge of starting a new fraternity. With the approval on May 8, 1957, by the Inter-Fraternity

Council to form the college's fourth fraternity, the initial dozen men voted Ed Lyon as chairman of the group and named the organization Mu Kappa Mu (later to become Phi Kappa Tau). The early members were, unlike the typical college entrants, mature adults, some older than I, some married; they impressed me from the start with their aims and ideals. For both the dean of students and me, they represented a unique departure from the fraternal norm, even as they hoped to blend into the college's general cadre. Unfortunately, their presence among the students on campus was not met with open arms; whenever they competed—for grades in classes or in various contests—they were met with derision as new guys on the block who had to earn acceptance.

The group grew rapidly from 12 to 28, and a residence had to be found. The former grand Victorian Ray Hill Hotel (which had undergone a few changes to the present vacant residence) in nearby Hancock, with a prize view of Portage Lake, was for sale; it was ideal except for its location in Hancock, a few miles from the college campus, where nearly all other similar organizations were located. After serious discussion with the dean of students and other official members of the administration, they received approval and moved in.

I spoke to the dean about my complete lack of knowledge regarding how to fit in as a fraternity advisor. He gave me one fine bit of advice: always be one step ahead of them. "For now," he said, "you are fortunate in that they are older and more mature in handling their issues, but eventually, as they graduate out and younger students roll in, your duties as advisor must carry more responsibility; you will become, in a sense, their father surrogate." Though more than a little concerned, I found that I grew into the task of mentor and guide, and that for me, too, it afforded a feeling of family bond I always needed.

In my effort to demonstrate my creative talents in the community, I made one significant faux pas. Each year, the Rotary Club sponsored a theatrical production as a fundraiser, and I readily volunteered my services to direct it. What I didn't realize was that Dr. Fryxell was until then the sole director of dramatic productions, both on campus and within the local community. It was my misfortune to innocently worm my way into them, resulting in a gradual shift from him to me as I proved myself a fresh and inexhaustible spirit among the local aficionados. Gradually, it was Fryxell out, Kirkish in. Naturally he resented it and showed it on every possible occasion.

❖❖❖

I don't recall why, but it never seemed earthshaking to any of the family when I donned my professional look and spent so much time on the other side of town ("over there," as people would say from where they lived and worked on the west side). My daily departure—at first on a bicycle and, later, by car across the mile or so through town to my new occupation—simply elicited from my parents, "There goes Joey, off to work each day and back for dinner each night." I was gone most of the day, and in the evening, I'd be up in my room on the third floor, grading the mound of class papers or studying. With my parents away, Jimmy had his poker-playing friends (who might be there well into the night) in the smoke-filled kitchen or living room. As long as their habits did not stretch beyond that, we simply let live. The following year he married a beautiful catch from Hancock and moved into one of the small homes my father had owned since his marriage (a few blocks up the hill in our old West Houghton neighborhood), so we rarely saw one another ... unless he might come by to beg a few bucks when his betting was off.

The rest of the relatives? The George Kirkishes still lived in their original home a few blocks from us, now with just two of their sons still living in the area. When we occasionally got together, Uncle George would eye me with a glint of pride at my choice of endeavor. In the Lebanese manner, he would say, "It looks good."

Of the Karam children, only Annie was in Houghton and still living with her parents. She had soldiered through a nursing program, training as both an operating room nurse-anesthetist and clinical nurse to serve the community (and all of us) with her absolute dedication. I would visit the Karams' home once in a while for a good Lebanese meal and the comfort of their modest, old-fashioned way of living. That was undoubtedly the strongest bond to our childhood in a neighborhood that never really changed, just remained unobtrusively apart from the rest of town.

As it turned out, my homecoming was not that awkward. My family could see that I had not become a snobbish intellectual now that I was a teacher "over there." Like me, they probably wondered how long I would last teaching at Tech.

I began to miss New York—the freedom, being among friends who enjoyed a bon vivant life, the richness of cultural offerings, the foreign eateries—and Tallie. I decided to return during my first Christmas/New Year break. I drove out and stayed, not with relatives, but with friends I'd made in Manhattan. My relatives were no longer living in Bay Ridge; I chose to forsake the tunnel to New Jersey to try to find them.

Of course, I'd written ahead to Tallie, prepared (with money now) to take her to a good meal, a show, and afterwards, hot dogs at Nathan's on Coney Island. It was good to see her again, and much as we enjoyed the food and performance, it was Nathan's that really perked us up ... like old times.

I also attended a solo dance recital by Don Redlich in Central Park, which was beautiful. I went backstage to say hello and compliment him. Don looked over his coffee cup, made a typical slight wry smile, and said almost diffidently, "Hello, Joe," so I just told him I appreciated the dance and left. Of course, I was a bit disappointed and just accepted this as Don's regular aloofness.

For some reason, it never occurred to me to visit my old neighborhood on 95th Street, nor did I try to see Miss Hanchett, but I did visit a few other friends from the U of W crowd. There seemed to have grown a gap between us, with all except Tallie, and even that seemed different from our struggling days together. While there, and as I drove home before the New Year's rush, I felt something missing. We had gone our separate ways, with them still living out their hopes and bohemian lives, while I, having symbolically adopted tie and jacket, was becoming rooted at a university miles away.

I did go back a few other times for different reasons but could never find that "glow" again. I realized I was now just an out-of-towner, gaining some pleasure from a few Broadway shows and for a last time walking down the brightly lit, gaudy, crowded Times Square area, then with some regrets, would leave for home again.

Despite, or perhaps because of the rigors of academic life, I was eager to spend the summers working at Camp Nebagamon, a place (unlike my return to New York) that always renewed a deep sense of belonging and connection. For two more summers, I served as the photographic specialist—and, always, as a willing substitute for counselors on their days off.

I always looked forward to spending the day with any cabin group in the Swamper Village. At home I enjoyed being with my sisters' children, about the same age (not yet 10 years old) and especially enjoyed putting them to sleep either with Harvey the Rabbit to soothe them into a pleasant sleepy mode or making up a story with me as the main character in the story: searching for monkeys in the jungle, tracking down a jewel thief, or inventing a spaceship that would take me to the moon. The first-person technique always worked, especially at camp, and when the campers asked for a spooky story, I was in my element with ghosts, evil magicians, or man-eating flora—always keeping in mind their grand imaginations—never over the edge. I could tell the success of each story by how it would affect them. No sounds when disinterested, but if the story became too dramatic, flashlights would go on from the bunk beds; and if more mysterious, then padded footsteps would sound followed by a creak from someone on my bed. A truly successful story would have the entire cabin of eight weighing us all down, right to the satisfying conclusion—and then, all back in their bunks with visions of the story following them into slumberland. It was great for us all.

In my free time at camp, I got to indulge my passion for photographing professional performers: the Tamburitzans, a nationally renowned touring troop of Middle European folk dancers, musicians, and singers from Duquesne University (Pittsburgh), in residence for a month of preparation in Lake Nebagamon. For decades, the Tamburitzans would stay at a boarding house next to the auditorium in the village and rehearse in the auditorium, diligently training each new group of students to sing, dance, and play traditional musical instruments. Though tightly controlled and endlessly trained, the group graciously allowed onlookers to sit in the sidelines of the auditorium, watching with amazement as the show developed.

They were true celebrities in Lake Nebagamon. Once I

discovered the auditorium routine, I joined the onlookers, would photograph the Tammies (as they were nicknamed) either singly (in costume or work clothes) or in progression as they developed from neophytes to professionals. As thanks to their welcoming generosity to me, I made little sample photos and handed them out. That did not escape the notice of their director, who approached me and asked what it would cost for me to replace their former professional photographer. Cost? I'd gladly pay *them* for the privilege.

We made an arrangement: I'd be paid the full salary of their pro, accept half and donate the rest to the Tamburitzan Fund. Since I had free time at camp, I could easily split myself between camp duties and the Tammies. It was a win-win situation.

Tamburitzan dancer, Lake Nebagamon

Those years were also the beginning of Muggs's succession plan for the camp. Nardie Stein had been hired in 1955 as the senior counselor in Swamper One (usually considered the most difficult cabin since the kids were all young and new to camp), and he handled them with the proficiency of a pro. We later discovered that his introduction was well planned: he'd been dating Muggs's younger daughter Sally! (They had met off and on at various times, struck up a friendship, and while she was at the University of Michigan, he met her again; they fell in love and planned to marry when he would return from a military stint abroad.) Muggs, ready to retire but without a son to take over the camp, decided to test him for a season. It worked: he married Sally in the fall of 1955, and together they began taking on greater leadership in the running of camp.

I continued to spend some off-duty time with Muggs, but I also wanted to build a relationship with Nardie. In fact, because of the location of the darkroom in the basement of the Big House, I was able to get to know Nardie on a personal basis very easily. Adjacent to the darkroom was a bathroom (a "house jop") where he liked to shave. One day while I was performing my early morning preparations in the darkroom, he came down and into the bathroom and began to shave, door open. We chatted; at the time, I was ignorant of his future plans at camp and enjoyed his casual nature and well appreciated his sense of humor, as I stood there, a bottle of developer in hand, and he, talking as he shaved the foam off his face. When finished, he would leave with "See ya" and disappear up the stairs. This scenario happened frequently and led to a nice rapport, even after he developed into camp director. In fact, some of the campers thought that Nardie was my brother; at the time we did bear some resemblance, so when I told him about it, he grinned. He had a great sense of humor, enough to appreciate the disparity in our lives.

I also discovered that Nardie had a longer fuse than Muggs. One time I was asked to bring an older, often unruly camper to the Duluth airport, returning him home for some reason not explained to me. I tried to settle him down for the obviously undesired trip. At the airport, as the woman at the luggage check-in desk took his suitcase and threw it roughly to the floor behind her, I assuaged his concern by saying with a grin, "I hope you packed your nitro carefully," at which he grinned as well. With an hour's wait, I decided to treat him to an ice cream dessert at the lunch counter. As we were enjoying the treat, a man with the nervous expression of Don Knotts rushed up to us and said, "Stay where you are; the FBI will be here quickly."

FBI? An airport joke of some kind? No. In a few minutes, two black-suited men strode up and asked us to follow them to a small empty room. There, they opted not for a strip search (for what?) but quizzed us about the contents of the camper's suitcase which sat on a table in the room. After thoroughly examining it and with my explanation of the private joke, they relaxed, returned the luggage to the check-out desk, and left us standing there, mute, confused.

By that time, we had missed the plane and rescheduled for the next one in 90 minutes, so I turned to the camper and suggested we find a police station for further instructions. Okay, it was not far from the airport, empty except for two officers casually munching on sandwiches at their desks. I explained our dilemma; one turned to the other and with a chuckle remarked, "Hey, Bill, here's the guys that caused the shutdown at the airport." They dismissed us with a laugh and told us to return to the airport for the next flight out. We did, first stopping at the check-in desk to guarantee the suitcase was properly arranged for the flight. The lady behind the counter said with a sigh, "You know, when you said what you did, I had to press the panic button that led to your inspection." I then explained and she relaxed and guided the suitcase to its destination on the next plane. As the plane took off with my charge on board, I said to her, "Watching that plane fly into the air, I had a terrible thought." "Don't even mention it," she said as we both saw the plane disappear into the welkin.

I returned to camp, explained (sheepishly) my delay in returning, fully expecting a harsh response. Nardie, instead, just grinned and said lightly, "Oh, no harm done, I guess; just another Kirkish stumble. Just watch your tongue next time." Red-faced and humbled, I agreed.

Sally's gregarious personality and intelligence were well known, and with her at his side, Nardie readily gained the respect of both campers and staff. We could see that he was not always in sync with Muggs. I overheard several "debates" between the two in the office or as they walked together around camp, but it seemed that Nardie's growth into assistant director went relatively smoothly. He refused to become a carbon copy of Muggs, perfect as he was; instead, while retaining all of Muggs's love and respect for what the camp represented, he was evolving his own style of leadership and dedication.

We knew, too, that Sally and Nardie's eventual co-directorship (which officially began in 1960) would bring some changes and innovations, like introducing women as specialists. The changes came gradually and apparently worked out well. It was still Camp Nebagamon for Boys, still loved—even cherished—by hundreds more to come and leave with the same nostalgia the place created. And it continued even 30 years later, as Sally and Nardie turned the directorship over to other dedicated owners in the same tradition.

◆ ◆ ◆

Near the end of the summer of '58, my parents drove over to Camp Nebagamon. They came to inform me they had made a giant move: they had sold our now big, burdensome, and underused West Side home, so I should come and pack up my belongings. They would be permanently living in Florida for the winters, and then return to spend summers at their Lake Superior cottage. My father said he would help me find a place to stay if I wished.

At such a late date, finding a place to stay was not easy, with all the best housing in the immediate vicinity of the campus already taken. I didn't know where to start. After a few false hopes, I dropped in at the McGintys, friends of my parents who lived near Tech, told them of my predicament, and solicited their suggestions. They exchanged looks, the wife more encouraged than her husband, said they had a nice apartment on the floor above them with a young schoolteacher about to vacate; would I like to see it? Hobson's choice! Without searching any further, I took it and, in a week, moved in. So just as school was beginning, I was settling into a pleasant three-room apartment (and only a few blocks from campus).

In a way, this unexpected move to simpler quarters was a relief. One less responsibility. For my first year at the college, I had plunged almost blindly into teaching—driven by necessity, willing to throw all my personal resources into the profession. I improvised that year, intent on developing effective instructional techniques and gaining confidence and the respect of the students. My pedagogical approach came almost subliminally, in part drawing on memories of my own undergraduate and graduate experience: Dr. Bloom in his formal deliveries; his wife, Magda, in her ability to spice historical material with subtle appeal to our curiosities; Dr. Throckman with his kindly personal attention to one's handicaps; Germanic Dr. von Hagen in his attempt to work humor into serious historical material.

My second year had been less overwhelming. I enriched the basic syllabus of English 101 with content from previous academic studies, drawing on material gleaned not only from lit classes but also from those I'd taken as alternatives (speech, film, etc.). I had learned, too, from my colleagues how to guide our students, many of them city kids from the Detroit area who generally lacked imagination or native curiosity beyond their technical vocations, but who astounded me with their analytical minds.

I had worked hard, as well, to look authoritative. From that very first day, I prided myself on looking, not officious and certainly not severe as did Dr. von Hagen, but never casual like many of my male colleagues who mirrored the students in jeans and casual shirts. It made me feel <u>good</u> to select the right tie, jacket, even socks, in preparation for each class, and I'm sure it did not go unnoticed by the students, especially among the rare few girls when we were fortunate enough to have one or two in attendance. (Immediately after our first day of classes we would gather to brag: "I've got a girl in class," I've got <u>two</u> in mine," etc.)

Though I had made a solid start, I knew as I prepared for my third year at Tech that I had just a few more years to be elevated from instructor to an assistant professor, or my employment would end. And to achieve full faculty status, Dr. Fryxell and the dean of faculty made it clear that I would eventually need an advanced degree.

11

New Horizons

I was eager to expand my teaching repertoire. First, I had introduced that basic speech class, giving students the opportunity to learn the tricks of various kinds of oral delivery. Dreaded, even hated at first by the students, the course enabled them to gain confidence in speaking (later, the top ones would admit they enjoyed the benefits each time they were forced to put these techniques into practice). Then, a class in argumentation and group discussion proved more challenging in that it required the teaching of logic and fallacies before going into the valuable ability to discuss, not argue, over any issues. It gave me the chance, too, to introduce them to non-Aristotelian logic—a concept foreign to minds so steeped in seeing only black and white solutions.

At the same time, I wanted at least one of what the faculty termed "ecstasy" courses—in my case, those in recent literature—and eventually I was given one in American literature, from the Civil War period on. Again, since I knew little about it, I dove in with usual intensity and managed simultaneously to teach both myself and the students about the few great authors from that "gilded age" (so called by cynical Mark Twain) including Twain himself, Melville, Poe, Thoreau, Whitman, and others. All the classes involved lectures, easy for me. With a mind that endlessly attracted information from all sources and with the God-given ability to compose on the spot, I never needed to write out a single lecture. Keeping the overall aim of a course in mind, I would prepare each lecture simply by lying on the floor, eyes closed for deeper concentration, and think it through with a beginning, middle, and summary, bookending it into a 45-minute segment, allowing time for Q & A at the end.

The ability to compose on the spot often came in handy. One day, about to begin a lecture on Walt Whitman, a student raised his hand and asked about something else, entirely unrelated to my prepared lecture and yet fitting as an aside to the general content. I delivered it, wrapped it up in the allotted time and, since no one had questions (astonished, I supposed, at the fullness of an unplanned lecture), thanked them for their attention and closed out. (One very bright student told me years later that he was "blown away" by that extemporaneous incident; for me, it was nothing more than just being a well-informed teacher.)

Besides the importance of getting a doctorate, Dr. Fryxell had impressed on all of us in the Humanities Department a list of 26 criteria necessary for continued employment, such as service to the community, papers published, designing new courses, etc. So, while I realized I could never fulfill all the criteria, I continued to devote as much time as possible to what I knew best: extracurricular activities in and beyond the campus, always being eager to try new things while continuing to write and photograph for the *Gazette* and even the *Milwaukee Journal* (eventually as a "stringer" covering local and campus activities).

One early creative venture was a brief success. When I was a youngster, on one of our outings, Aunt Bea had brought me to the biennial spring Tech Fair, an exciting, all campus open house for the public, with scientific demonstrations from amazing lighting sources to experiments with mercury, chemical magic, and even a demonstration in the beginnings of television. (In fact, this was the only time I can remember being at Tech during my youth.) It "blew my mind," going from building to building to get such enticing samples of what a technical or scientific training could reveal. So, I decided to introduce a new spring Tech Art Fair (TAF) which would fill in the off years with artistic events.

Through my association with local art and drama enthusiasts, I organized the weeklong event that included locally created art exhibitions, short theatrical productions, musical programs, and anything else to prove that Michigan Tech was a well-balanced institution. Besides coordinating this extravaganza, to add to the event, I wrote a one-act play titled *The Circus*; it was a tongue-in-cheek comedy, a parody of the currently popular Theatre of the Absurd style. Judging from comments in the local newspapers, the play and our week of TAF was a hit. However, it had required such a monumental effort, with little later encouragement from overly busy volunteers, it was presented only once. But, with proof of the university's broad cultural interests and a pleased group of volunteers—as well as local citizens who spoke to me about it for months—it did its job. (A decade later, a newcomer to campus revived TAF as an annual spring event and I willingly served, but just as an advisor.)

On an ongoing basis, I continued advising the two fraternities, one of which (Phi Kappa Tau) was considered by the dean of students as the finest student organization on campus, while the other (Mu Beta Psi) grew to become recognized for its contributions to musical and other entertainment programs. No question that this responsibility did require time, but I relished being a part of these student-run groups, and it gave me very personal insights into the lives (and loves) of the members. What's more: as they grew under my counsel, I grew, too.

Living at the McGintys also opened up new dimensions to my social and cultural life. I first met Professor and Mrs. Roman through Irene Greenleaf, a mutual friend who thought I would enjoy this transplanted Polish couple; like Irene and me, the Romans were members of St. Ignatius Catholic Church. Professor Roman had been hired in the mid-1950s to teach mining engineering (in fact, I had earlier shot his portrait as a school assignment as he worked with students in his huge motor-filled lab), and she worked in the library. Through the photo of Professor Roman, it was easy to see his dedication to teach one-on-one in his professional field. In Mrs. Roman, there was the same dedication, not only to the students in the library, treating them not just as students, but more as young men and women.

The Romans lived in an unpretentious but well-built frame house on College Avenue, fitting comfortably among the other century-old, still fashionable homes, not far from my apartment, just a block farther from the campus. They had turned their living room and other parts of the main floor into a "Polish home," with art, books, and objects that were typical (or so I've been told by other Polish people), guarded over by an impressively framed Black Madonna. All I knew was that their home was modestly furnished, understated, and very, very comfortable.

Now and then they would invite me to attend a concert or a lecture with them at the university, while I would invite them to a poetry reading or some other cultural event. Occasionally I came at their invitation for a rather curious meal—curious because I found it was always the same: a toasted potato, green beans, a slice of pork, plain Jell-O, and tea. Turned out, it was partly because they'd become accustomed to eating frugally, but also because, as I learned later, each of them suffered some sort of internal problem that demanded a rigid diet.

I would visit them at home, but we would also take little trips together, often, at Mrs. Roman's bidding, to drop in on a large Polish family named Vishnevski in nearby Painesdale—obviously a family of limited means who had prompted sympathy from her on a previous meeting or, perhaps, to inhabit a bit of their homeland. The pattern was always the same: met at the door with exuberant pomp, brought to their rather humble living room, where two easy chairs were plumped up for the guests, wine served with special homemade Polish pastries, small talk during which the professor was ever referred to as *"pan profesor"* with his appropriate noblesse oblige response as his wife (who seemed to adapt easily to American familiarities) smiled and spoke to them as equals. Professor Roman accepted the obsequious farewells as his wife would take hands, kiss a cheek, and wave a smiling farewell as we'd drive away.

They were two very different people: she, with her Old Country finery in modest hairdo and dress, and he, always unnecessarily formal in shades of gray, in suit and tie; she, the extrovert, he, an impressively tall man with an Old World noblesse oblige air. They obviously loved one another very much and proved it with their willingness to compromise comfortably at nearly every challenging moment of their New World lives. That, I thought, was the reason they never went anywhere without one another. But I learned differently when, one day, he and I arrived at their home to find her gone, and he went into a sudden mix of concern and anger. When she entered with a bag of groceries, he flew into a barely controlled fury. They spoke in Polish—he admonishing her for going somewhere without his protection and she explaining they were safe now, it was no longer necessary.

And so, little by little, I pieced together the horrors of their recent life as refugees from what must have been an aristocratic life: at the end of WWII, when the Russians were approaching Warsaw, leaving a magnificent mansion, traveling through Europe constantly in danger for their lives, then immigrating to India where he managed a mining operation and trying to adapt to a totally different lifestyle in a strange country for seven years. Mrs. Roman told me she knew immediately when they entered their home in India that it was inhabited by evil spirits. A religious Catholic (as was her husband), she immediately sprinkled holy water room to room before they could live contentedly there.

In the early '50s, when it was safer, they left India for an equally strange county, which became their final residence (first to St. Louis where Mrs. Roman took classes in library operation, then to Houghton with an offer for her to work in the Tech library while her husband became a welcome addition in the Mining Department). For her, America was pleasantly free and democratic, but uncivilized to him. (I heard a confession from the professor many years later, when he acknowledged their different views of American life: she accepted it immediately, while he, upon leaving the plane, muttered, "I don't think I'm going to like it here." I'm not sure it ever changed.)

It must be added that Mrs. Roman had developed a way to dig information from people and then sift it with a superior mind. One day she asked if I had a companion they might like to meet; I had—a girl, Dell, from one of my earlier classes, older than most of the rest and somehow more interesting. We dated casually, seemed to enjoy one another's company, so when Mrs. Roman asked me to bring her over, I delightfully agreed and brought her the following evening. Like two schoolgirls chatting, the two women dominated the evening, and when we were about to leave, saying good night at the door, Mrs. Roman whispered in my ear, "Get rid of her." I was both astounded and puzzled. She never again made another comment regarding Dell; she knew I knew, and that was that. In time her intuition would prove correct.

◆◆◆

As a further demonstration of my willingness to extend my teaching responsibilities, in the summer of '59, I volunteered to teach in the intensive, five-week summer term at Tech. Though it meant no longer being able to spend the entire summer at Camp Nebagamon, instead I could return for several weeks as a welcomed guest.

It was in the late '50s that Muggs's last years as the camp director were imminent, and there were already signs of the next era: Nardie and Sally had hired a very talented young woman to replace me as the photographic specialist. She went, I recall, by the name of Margie, and when I was introduced to her, it was friendship at first sight. To begin with, we had a mutual pleasure, not only in photography, but in teaching it as well. I assisted her in the darkroom, went on photo hikes with her and camper enthusiasts, and, in general, made myself as helpful as possible, even putting on an exhibit of photos I brought from home for such an occasion.

Since beginning my teaching at Tech, I had recommended to Muggs a few students whom I thought would be good additions to the staff. So, knowing of Dell's need of a summer job, and of Muggs's need for kitchen help, I wrote him on her behalf and he hired her. When I arrived for the second month of camp, midway through the season, we would arrange to take our days off together and visit nearby parks, waterfalls, and beaches in Wisconsin and Minnesota.

Muggs, ever observant, noticed, called me in one day. He made a suggestion that, while occasional visits with her were fine, he had rules about emotional liaisons between staff members, and hoped that, as a mature person, I'd know better than to take advantage of having her at camp with me. I assured him our relationship was a casual one; he accepted that, and so I continued dating her.

On a visit to Superior, Wisconsin, Dell became quite interested in the town, drawn to its life as a port city (like nearby Duluth, but smaller). She surprised me when she never returned to the university in the fall. We continued our friendship with postcards and letters through which I learned that she decided to stay on in Superior, had a menial job at a hotel, and would be happy to see me when next I returned to camp. I began to understand Mrs. Roman's caveat but continued to correspond with her and even spent one evening (the following summer) together in her inauspicious room at the hotel.

What drew me back to her? What always draws one person to another? From the first meeting in class, when I pronounced her name and she looked up at me with that unusual half-smile that spoke volumes, and said, "Present," I was licked. It was that da Vinci-esque "La Giaconda" smile, her acceptance of me in the odd relationship of student/teacher, and the way she would alternately open up frankly and then clam shut as to conceal things she did not want me to know. All that, along with a naturally brilliant mind, captivated me.

After that hotel evening, though we kept in touch by mail, her correspondence grew less and less optimistic, and when she began quoting fatalists Nietzsche and Schopenhauer, I felt we were drifting apart. Always in my mind was her comment—knowing that she gave up a brief career in grade school teaching—that it was nigh impossible to train ignorant minds safely and correctly. The pitfalls, she believed, were dangerous and overwhelming. I took a different approach: that careful, dedicated teaching could, not ruin, but improve individual lives. I did meet her briefly once more in Milwaukee (while visiting relatives). It ended, not with a bang....

12

Heartland Studies

W hen it became obvious that I was dragging my feet with studies to complete the PhD, Dr. Fryxell prodded with a not too subtle option: get it quickly or leave Michigan Tech. I opted for the former, applied for acceptance at the University of Iowa … chosen because it was close both to home and Camp Nebagamon.

One further reason: my novel *Prologue to Oblivion* needed cutting and polishing. Since my return to Houghton, I had kept in written contact with Bob Lewis, letting him know I'd tackle the job in free time, but free time never happened. The manuscript remained in a box on a shelf, boring into my conscience each time I'd glance at it and realize that I, too, might disappoint the fellow as had others before me.

I thought if I could be accepted into the university's famed Iowa Writers' Workshop, I could kill two birds with one stone: work on the novel with professional supervision to make it salable and also have it accepted as my PhD dissertation. I built Bob's hopes with my plan and then sent to the workshop a chapter from the novel (with a very sensuous tryst) which elicited interest. I was accepted into both the workshop and the university, so off I went, feeling at the time that dividing my free summertime between summer classes and Camp Nebagamon could work out very well, though it disappointed my Tech critics for not rushing the PhD program to a more immediate conclusion.

A comfortable "rural Iowa" atmosphere seemed to permeate campus life at the university, along with an easygoing town-and-gown relationship. The University of Iowa is divided on two sides of a river, connected by a high arched bridge. I could easily bicycle back and forth from the graduate student dorm on the north side (where the theater and art complexes were also located) to the academic buildings higher up on the south side, just adjacent to Iowa City's business center.

For three summers (1960–62), I had a packed academic schedule between my advanced literature and a few other humanities courses and the Writers' Workshop fiction-writing program. The workshop was created to accommodate promising writers of every ilk and age, though most of the 17 students were male. Two professional writers, both renowned and having published extensively, were the faculty: one was a quiet, laid-back fellow who read and returned our scripts rapidly; the other, although very good with his criticisms, always let us know how brilliant he was and always expected us to revere him openly as such.

The workshop was a mix of group classes and private work with one of the faculty—mine, regrettably, was the ego-driven writer. The sessions with my advisor were hardly productive: the more I praised his work, the kinder he was, bestowing his criticisms subtly in his own magnanimous style. But I did find the group sessions valuable. We had occasional assignments, short pieces, to turn in for group discussion (everything from character studies to a plotted mystery story); it was then that I could assess the varied works of others in my stead, discover new possibilities in style and content, and improve to some degree.

The drumbeat of the successful path to being a published writer was a constant. Early on, I learned from my faculty specialist that he had made most of his publishing money by writing pornographic stories and novels, suggesting with my descriptive talent I could easily do the same. I found some of his novels in the library, thought they were cleverly written but too graphic for my taste. Also, my first summer, among our group was Walter Tevis, a rather unassuming fellow whose novel *The Hustler* had been picked up by a movie studio and was now in production with a star-studded cast. His discouraging account of being flown to Hollywood to be on the set (but only as a bystander) gave the rest of us a sobering picture of the powerlessness of a writer in the film business.

Surprisingly, it was a series of creative photography classes taught by Professor John Schulze (pronounced "Schultsee") that were truly transformative. (I initially had enrolled thinking that all my photographic experience would make this an easy five-credit course!) Though I struggled with a huge load of reading to be absorbed in literature classes, his art photography courses dominated my life. Casually beginning each day, he would walk in with his usual smile, his shock of prematurely white hair bouncing with each step, put a photograph on an easel in front of us, sit down, and wait for responses, which sounded like a variety of grunts: "Uhh," "Mmmm," "Yeh," "Ohhh," as meaningful opinions. That first session, in between grunts, I'd come up with a detailed diatribe about hidden meanings in the photo. Astonished glances in my direction from the art majors. A student sitting next to me, with shocked trepidation, asked, "Are you a lit major?" I had to admit it—and after that learned how to grunt like the rest of them.

In contrast to the Writers' Workshop faculty, Schulze never discussed his own work. He delivered his information sparingly, prodding us with a silence to fill on our own, or questioning subtly to open the dams he suspected to flow from our own talents. Each week we'd produce photographs for his analysis; we'd have to watch his face for reactions—a raised eyebrow, a broadening smile—that spoke volumes, as his finger would weave across each photograph he held. Then, as he grew to know us by our work, he would on occasion require a presentation. For me, one day, it was the surprise command that I prepare a talk on the work of Richard Avedon, famous for his prodigious portraits. As I studied for the presentation, I began to realize what he saw in my portraits and opened my eyes to extending and improving them. He would do the same for other students with their lectures on Robert Frank, Harry Callahan, etc. That was his skill: making us discover ourselves through our cameras, not prodded by him.

In subtle ways, Schulze would guide us to see our pictures as personal expressions; for me, having spent years as a contributor to campus and regional newspapers, it was an entirely new concept. We were assigned to "get acquainted with the territory," i.e., for our weekly camera shoot to go down any of the roads leading from campus to parts east, west, south, north. Every Saturday, I would point my car in any direction and, after a mile or two, would pull over and walk into whatever happened to be there (mainly fields of cows, pigs, plenty of corn and alfalfa, and, as I accidentally discovered, wild marijuana). I met farm families, construction workers, and others who introduced me to their lifestyles, their simple living and their easy acceptance of a stranger with a camera. All of the photos were shot on black and white film which I would process on Sunday afternoons, ready for each Monday deadline.

Rural Iowa proved fascinatingly different from my life in the U.P.—rolling hills, corn cribs by the mile, typical farm odors that penetrated everywhere. But like Michigan, it was populated by deeply religious Protestant groups with more Apostolic churches than I'd ever seen before. And, as part of my exploration of the countryside, I discovered an Amish community in an isolated area and became fascinated by their simple way of life ("if it's not necessary, it's a sin").

I met one family, the Beachys, visited their home, ate simple meals with them, often talked generally about things religious. I could never discuss the geological history of the Iowa terrain ("How do you know God didn't just put it here that way?"). Though photographing them was completely out of the question, one day, as I was studying their farm fields with my camera, Glenn seemed interested, so I let him look through the viewfinder; he then pointed to the natural scene, and said, "I prefer it that way." I even bought a complete set of traditional Amish men's clothes—straw hat, sailor-type denim pants and shirt, handmade suspenders—and often wore them when I went to Camp Nebagamon, just to see how it felt to be Amish.

A different eye-opening experience was when Professor Schulze selected a small group of us to discover figure photography in a new way. We were driven to an isolated forested area and then turned loose on a young woman, unclothed, obviously trained as a model, who would simply move freely around the area as we followed—at first in some confusion, then gradually enjoying the experience of hunt and catch, creatively as possible.

The results netted me an opportunity to photograph one

similar model (for her portfolio, she said). We headed for an abandoned farmhouse, she with her pet cat and I with an old blanket and a head full of ideas. A few hours later, flushed with the experience and time in the darkroom, I was pleased sky high, and when she saw the results, so was she. It turned out to be a win-win afternoon: she graduated, went to San Francisco where her portfolio snagged her a lengthy, choice job as model for a noted painter, and future sessions with other artists after that; for me a breakthrough—the inspiration and the confidence to move beyond commercial photography. (Professor Schulze, in his understated way, decisively singled out the images from these shoots as "keepers" for my portfolio.) The blinders had come off ... portraying women, not as the Virgin Mary (for which one of my classmates once chided me), but as living embodiments of their own special making.

Unlike my days at the U of Wisconsin, there was very limited camaraderie among the students at the Writers' Workshop, but also, I had limited time to socialize. One of the local churches did open up its kitchens to students and invited all to a late Sunday morning brunch created by volunteers. I volunteered often, enjoying the preparation and eating of the meals with so many new people, students, and locals alike. I even experimented with local foods, and once I sneaked into a field of alfalfa and brought back enough of the cow feed to add to a novel salad: it proved difficult to tempt the locals but made something of a sensation in general—one person calling it "moo-rvelous."

❖❖❖

To my surprise, beginning my sixth year of teaching at Tech (1962–63), I gained appointment as an assistant professor in the Humanities Department. Dr. Fryxell had been continuously reminding me of the need to meet all the criteria for advancement; though I had not fulfilled some, I had stepped up a few off-campus activities—most notably, by having a weekly column in the *Daily Mining Gazette*. I called it "In the Catbird's Seat" after a James Thurber short story, which was ironic given my lowly status, but I did use it to provide thoughtful commentary, particularly on local arts events, social and cultural trends, and important personalities.

During my annual interview, Dr. Fryxell (who did occupy the cat-bird seat) coolly told me, "There had been an accumulation of on and off campus services" that was acceptable for the promotion and continued teaching within the department.

I still needed to complete the PhD program, so in the fall of 1963, I enrolled more seriously for a full year of study at the University of Iowa. During the summers, I had lived in the graduate school dorm but this time rented a second-floor apartment in the southern part of town. It was not exactly Skid Row, but close, with families reminiscent of those of Dust Bowl fame which I did manage to photograph on occasion, including half-dressed, dirty-faced kids sitting in front of a small television set, chewing on their fingers in passive expression or planted around their parents, also expressionless.

Three local fellows shared the other half of our floor; doors left open, easy back/forth experiences (they, feeding from greasy pan fries, spending evenings drinking, preferring cars, women, field sports, avoiding anything on or near campus). With casual mien, they accepted me as a foreign curio. Interesting encounters for me, including one frightening evening—nearly getting shot when the most frequent drunkard of the trio wandered into my room, pistol in hand, waving it around and threatening himself and me alternately, then passing out.

I did part-time work on the daily campus paper—writing articles, entertainment reviews, and doubling as campus photographer, which enabled me to use both the paper's darkroom and those in the art building. (On occasion, for pocket money, I sent off photos of regional interest to the *Milwaukee Journal*.)

To my great pleasure, the Art Department presented a modest series of art films, mostly campus-created shorts and some longer films from foreign countries. I mingled with the film aficionados, got to know a few, and even went with them on excursions to see avant-garde film programs on other nearby campuses.

My life was also enriched by attending free concerts organized by the university's renowned Music Department. I got to know a delightful family (the father was a professor in that department) who introduced me to a shy, charming girl living with them who played the cello; she in turn introduced me to Joel Krosnick, an equally charming cellist who went on to become a member of the famed Juilliard String Quartet in 1974! (I would later see him when they performed at Marquette University in the U.P.; he entered the stage with his three associates and, in bowing, almost fell off the stage when he saw me, grinning and applauding in the first row.)

My most haunting and unforgettable experience in Iowa: driving in the rain to class on November 22, 1963, when I heard on the radio that President Kennedy had been shot. In class, I was told that he was dead; we disbanded, with a heavy pall settling over us all. I left the classroom, drove aimlessly, winding up at the campus chapel, which was dark except for a single candle burning on the altar. A man was there, up front, sobbing piteously. When he walked out, I recognized him as a member of the Art Department and saw him in a different light ever after that event. I returned to my apartment, settled into a chair to study, listlessly, while the campus radio station played somber dirges for the remainder of the day.

November 22, 1963, came to symbolize a doubly sorrowful day in my life.

On my way to class that day, I had written a letter to Tallie in New York and was about to drop it into a mailbox when the shocking news came over the car radio. I hastily wrote on the envelope: "My God, Tallie, the President's been shot!" I knew she revered Kennedy and awaited her reaction, but for some unexplained reason, I never ever heard from her again. I wondered if she'd fallen into a depression so deep she found a reply too great and eventually simply put it and me out of mind. I never found out.

❖❖❖

My main reason for choosing Iowa, of course, was to work on *Prologue to Oblivion*. My faculty specialist had taken the time to read my entire unedited manuscript, telling me that it would make a great potboiler. In his strange way, he considered that a compliment. Well, coming from him, that was encouraging; I spent long hours in trying to polish it according to his suggestions, even while realizing that cutting it from 500 to 300 pages was going to take far more effort than I had originally thought.

I left Iowa still facing the prospect of studying for a

comprehensive exam and the daunting task of producing a finished, publishable manuscript. The enthusiasm which had prodded me waned and I worried about how long I could drag out the completion before censure. In truth, what I was most excited about were the possibilities of abstract photography, image overlays and more, that I had discovered taking Professor Schulze's courses. I wanted to explore my personal interests, and did, eventually leading to recognition in both my home territory and the photographic art world.

13

Camp Nebagamon Connections

As I had planned, for several more summers (actually, through 1967), I continued my shortened, but yearly visits to Camp Nebagamon. The changing mix of new and old campers and counselors always made the experience something special and I so enjoyed seeing the maturation of the boys into young men.

Alan Bennett, in particular, was one. Initially he was a pesky little guy who delighted in sneaking up on me and making me jump with a pinch on the upper leg. He followed me around, year after year, always looking up at me with a special, bright-eyed smile. Never said much but appreciated it when I would go down to the waterfront and watch him gain skills in sailing. And, later, he returned as a strong young adult, patiently teaching the art of good sailing to young campers. He would drop into the darkroom, rarely, but always to watch me as I worked on some of my own creations. Gradually, he outgrew counselor duty, yet continued to be drawn back to Family Camp, where his affable personality captivated every-one. Because he took such an interest in me, I was equally interested in him, but also worried that his outgoing cheerfulness was forever concealing something. He admitted to me that he was actually not a happy person, always seeking something more than his aimless life. It took several years, but then in his late 20s—after a life-changing trip to Europe—while at Family Camp, confided his decision to become a rabbi, which brought me great joy to know he had found a calling for his skills as a teacher and his empathic character. And eventually, he also revealed that he was gay, but thankfully, by that time, that did not change our relationship.

There were other CN stalwarts, like me, who came for short visits. One of my favorites was Bud Herzog, an exuberant former camper and counselor, now very content in his Chicago home with wife, Hazel, and two young boys (who eventually spent their summers at camp). Camp Nebagamon was a lodestone in his life, as it was for Alan and me. He would pop into the dining room, sit at the piano, and leap into a nutty, meaningless song of his—over and over he would return, singing away to his own delight and that of the campers and entire staff—an unforgettable, likable fellow who lived on forever with so many hundreds of us.

Oh, and so many others, from the U.S. and abroad—names, faces, and personalities who still make me smile when I look at my camp photographs.

I also deepened my bond with Nardie and Sally Stein, now in charge. While I had liked and admired Muggs immensely, I could only respect him. With Nardie—and later, Sally, and even their three offspring—it was different. Over time, they became one of my unofficial "adopted families" in an on-again, off-again manner as I would return to camp as briefly but as often as possible for years and years.

Joe and Harvey the Rabbit
with Janie and Ted Stein

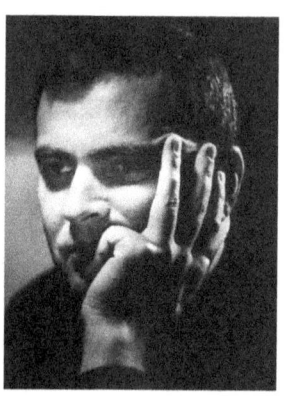

John Kander, 1961

Ever conscious of Camp Nebagamon's local recognition as "that Jewish boys' camp," Nardie set out to make known its true identity as a camp for anyone regardless of faith. Muggs had already established the idea of introducing campers to people besides Americans by hiring counselors from Denmark, France, and even Egypt, most of whom worked out well. As the person who created the sign on the Big House lawn, declaring, "This shall be a place of welcome" to all people regardless of race, creed or belief, Nardie went the next step, not only continuing with foreign counselors, but also adding staff from local areas and inviting people to visit and get to know the place more personally. Once, he invited a group of visiting Catholic nuns, gave them an afternoon's free range; playing four square with the campers was their delight. The campers equally enjoyed these women who referred to one another as "Sister," bringing a roar of laughter from them as a young camper asked where their mother was. To everyone's delight, he also invited the Tammies to drop in for an afternoon; they did, even putting on a miniature concert for the entire camp.

And there were more changes, some surprises, but all very successful with the campers, their parents, and the community at large. While Muggs considered the many albums I turned out regularly as showpieces for camp visitors, Nardie and Sally went a step further, taking sample albums—and later, movies—around to current and prospective camp families on winter recruiting visits.

Under Nardie and Sally's direction, the end-of-season Post Camp grew to a special week for adults and families with projects and outings as an expanded Family Camp. Part of its appeal was the relaxed mingling of talented and influential people working in a variety of fields from all over the country. I had the sense that it was a week where they could comfortably express their true selves whether they had been or were a CN camper, counselor, or parent. Over those 15 years, I came to understand that Camp Nebagamon was truly an alma mater to its alumni and friends.

One summer, for instance, it was my good fortune to share the upstairs lodgings of the Craft Shop with John Kander, who had come alone from New York, partly to relive old memories, but also to visit with his brother and sister-in-law and their camper son. At the time I didn't realize I was "bunking" with the composer/songwriter of future mega-hit Broadway shows (*Cabaret*, *Chicago*, and others) and movie

Family Camp, 1961

successes. We had long chats—he in his bunk on one side of the room and I on the other—like a pair of campers enjoying talking much too long before going to sleep. He confessed that, though he treasured his camp memories from the '30s and '40s, he had vowed not to return until he had made it (which he had done in 1962 with *The Family Affair,* written with brothers Bill and Jim Goldman whom I had met in New York). During his visit, John modestly took over at the camp piano one evening, playing songs he'd written—and I realized that his lyrics drew from some of his own family story.

An informal relationship and correspondence resulted during those few days; he even allowed me to photograph him for a portrait in a simple setup I used for shooting other visitors. He liked the results well enough to use one on the album cover for his next Broadway success (*Flora the Red Menace*). Of course, I was honored.

The darkroom continued to be a magnet at Post Camp. My favorite "customer," from Chicago, was Jean Abeles; her husband was an executive in the undergarment business and they had two boys at camp. She was a charming person—and with a secret she delightfully shared with me: she was wearing the first pair of pantyhose, testing them before husband Jerry's Formfit business put them on the market. She laughed; all her friends could not understand how she'd become so shapely practically overnight. In turn, I shared with her my experience teaching a course at Tech that included the subject of propaganda and lectures on the power of advertising.

Later, Jerry and Jean cornered me with a full-page photo in *Life* magazine of a model leaping in the air, hair flying in abandon, wearing an attractive bra and panties. "This is our latest ad," he said. "I hear you teach a course in propaganda. Ads are propaganda. So, what do you think of this?" That resulted in a business proposition: to work as a consultant to review product descriptions and go around to owners of women's shops in the Upper Midwest to get their reactions to Formfit's sexy advertising campaigns on their customers, and then potentially, to a rather impressive job in their Chicago offices. I felt, though, that my obligations as a full-time teacher at Michigan Tech had to take priority. I stalled with some inadequate investigations, then had to admit failure. In the meantime, Jerry passed away, and I was freed of any further obligations to the organization. (I still have some regrets.)

Post Camp yielded a whole new network of friends with whom I corresponded and, in several cases, visited as I traveled around the country, particularly throughout the Midwest and as far as New Orleans. Unlike the atmosphere of Tech and Houghton where arts and humanities were generally considered nominal, I found immediate kinship among others of the Camp family who shared my passions as a culture vulture. For instance, among families in the Chicago area were Bob and Babs Benton, with Bob as a longtime photo hound when he wasn't writing professionally and, later, Babs revealing herself through their foreign travels as a remarkably talented photographer all on her own. Brief visits with them were a rushed delight, always. Our correspondence by letter continues.

In Detroit, again among many others, there were Bud and Sue Kaine. Art buffs, there was never a dull hour with them, from finding out what was new at Detroit's famed glass art gallery (they owned a bowl of Dale Chihuly's delicate glass shapes which was their pride and joy) or lectures at their huge synagogue (where we could be surprised by meeting other CN alums). I still recall my weekend trips to their home, enjoying Sue's remarkable cuisine, Bud's photo trips around the area, and over the years the pleasure of watching their family grow and multiply.

And so many others. But of all the CN families that I regarded as most special to me were the Geismers from Shaker Heights, Ohio. Our introduction happened through observing Bobbie washing her younger daughter Mollie's red hair as day was descending into night—in the wading area of the lake! You might say, it was love at first sight. Alan and Bobbie spent time with me during their first summer at Post Camp, talking about music and their dedication to the Cleveland Orchestra, their love of art and visits to the art museums, and we quickly bonded. I did my obligatory family photo: Alan, in appropriately informal camping clothes but looking impressive and serious; Bobbie properly smiling and bright eyed; slightly plump Mollie (who always reminded me of a youthful Carol Channing); petite, pretty Meg, only hinting at the charms and active mind she beheld; and freckle-faced camper son Alan Jr. (Lanny) with an early adolescent, reluctant smile and distracted air. One of my most pleasing family portraits among the plethora of similar families from around the country.

The next year (1962), Bobbie sent a formal invitation to attend the family Seder. I couldn't resist the offer (never having participated in one), drove the nearly 700 miles to Cleveland, arriving at magnificent Shaker Boulevard with its rows of stately homes to finally locate theirs, comfortably situated among them. The grandeur and ambiance of the Tudor-style home and rear garden almost "blew me away." For a moment I actually hesitated to ring the bell—it seemed wrong for a country boy to invade so impressive a place. But the anxiety vanished as soon as Bobbie met me at the door wearing her decorative wraparound kitchen smock, hugged me, and ushered me to my room. In their exquisitely decorated home of European and American art and antiques, I was thrilled to see a few of my photographs on display. Apparently, as with others from Family Camp, they were impressed with my "art," as well as with the fact that I was teaching in academia.

That first Seder meal is etched in my memory: meeting Monnie, Alan's grande dame mother, witnessing Bobbie's attentive preparations of food and elegant table setting, participating in the extended ceremonial dinner with its heartwarming conclusion of songs and recitations, and then, the decanting of a last dusty bottle of Château d'Yquem, a special French dessert wine saved from an earlier family event.

My spring visit included other memorable events. The Geismers were longtime patrons of the Cleveland Orchestra, and I was thrilled to accompany them to a concert at magnificent Severance Hall. As was the custom, we dressed rather formally to enjoy the event from their seats in the prestigious Dress Circle. As we were climbing the stairs, Alan (a highly-reserved, erudite lawyer with the finely chiseled appearance of a British statesman) stopped for a moment to introduce me to a dean from Case Institute of Technology. As we continued to our seats, Alan casually mentioned that I had an appointment with him in his office the next day!

Surprised and curious, I went to the interview; he told me that the Geismers felt I was underselling my talents at a small university in Upper Michigan and hoped he could find a position for me there. At the close, he thanked me, said I had more than convinced him that the Geismers were right. But, he added, until I completed my doctorate, I could not be hired. I know they were disappointed when I told them about it, but they—and I—understood. We agreed, it was something to consider in the near future.

A week later, at home, I received a very kind letter from the dean, repeated his approval, reminding me to let him know of my doctorate as soon as I received it. Unfortunately or not, with all the possible benefits of being in proximity with a city so brimming with culture and the "Gs," as I grew in importance at Michigan Tech, and grateful as I was to Alan and Bobbie, I never again pursued the offer.

I did return on numerous occasions over the ensuing decades, always welcomed royally; on one special occasion in the late '60s, I even got to meet Maestro George Szell at a party after a special concert for orchestra patrons. In the formal reception line, I shook his hand, was briefly introduced and ushered on. Afterwards, he came over to me while I was at the sumptuous buffet table and asked, "Und tell me, Professor Keerkeesh, vere is diss Meechigan Tech?" We then conversed for several minutes (under Bobbie's watchful eye). On the way home, she complimented me saying, "You and George had quite a conversation," but I was so stunned by his attention to me the hick, I couldn't remember a word we said! Still, a miraculous encounter I continue to cherish.

14

Students, Colleagues, and Friends

M y successful "audition" for a corporate job and the interest from another university gave me an added sense of the value of my knowledge and talents, but at age 40, I felt I had carved out a niche at Tech and wanted to capitalize on my gains.

I had to accept, though, that being a humanities faculty member at Tech was a nomadic experience; as the department grew, we were continually being uprooted and reassigned quarters. The classrooms were temporarily borrowed in any building, including a full year teaching one time in the boiler room of a mechanical engineering building! (This cyclical disruption gave me a recurring nightmare of not being able to find my classroom on the first day of classes.)

Our offices were also juggled around but not nearly as often. One year, after leaving the Denton House, a group of us were transplanted into a basement room in the old chemistry building, made over to accommodate five of us. When we moved in, we sighed at the cramped, windowless quarters but adjusted to our cubbyholes without much discussion. I was at the far end, the darkest little closet-sized space barely enough for a desk, two chairs, and a small bookshelf to one side. My first glance was to appreciate the fact that the walls were a light tan, helping to brighten it from the single, unshaded light above the desk.

Some of the group were familiar, others newly hired; we got

acquainted easily since all of us were sharing the same make-do setup. By a singular coincidence, four of my colleagues were Jewish, so we christened our new quarters "The Ghetto," with me, the oddball, cordially included as their companion. It became a learning experience as a *goy* to recognize and appreciate differences within their religious heritage (far from stereotypical, ranging from highly observant to one who professed totally atheistic beliefs), but all with one thing in common: their love of academic teaching.

My colleagues and I in The Ghetto used the place as little as possible. After two weeks with my freshman English class, though, by departmental order, I had to meet with my students individually, to assess them from the start (how they wrote, how they reacted in class, etc.). I had 24 freshmen in the class, with time enough for each of them in morning and afternoon sessions for about 15 minutes each. No problem, I thought; after going through two assignments and six class sessions, I felt I'd established a good rapport.

Not true. During the morning, they entered nervously, one by one, oblivious to my smile and indication to sit nearer the desk, either arms folded and tight-lipped or silently passive, contributing little to our discussion. Just as we had stopped for lunch, the lights went out; clumsily, we found our way to the stairs (also dark) and went our ways—they to the dorms, I to my apartment at the McGintys, hardly a five-minute walk away.

I found a few large candles around my rooms, bagged them and set them up on the office desk. They lit up nicely, almost cozily. I waited for the first student with some discomfort about repeats of the morning's disappointments, but something happened that I still find hard to understand.

I confronted the first student, who wrote well but never responded during class discussions. Why not? She looked at me through the soft flickering light and explained with a shyness I had never seen in her before, then went into a kind of confession about a recent romantic adventure with a sad ending (or, more honestly, no ending, just nothing). In or out of class it was forever on her mind. Honestly, sincerely, I listened and probed until our time was up and she seemed openly relieved; I became the sympathetic ear she never had from her roommates nor counselor in the dormitory. She thanked me, asked if she might visit me in my office again sometime. I said, "Anytime," and she left with a slight sigh and smile. That 15 minutes astounded me and lifted my spirits as well.

The next student was a youthful, 17-year-old fellow who approached the desk quite fearfully. When I referred to his paper written unabashedly about the difficulty of leaving his family for the first time and now crying himself to sleep, I reached for my phone and had him call home. From his "Hello, Mom" to the end of a touching four or five minutes, I witnessed his emotional release, for which he then thanked me heartily for helping him. I reminded him what a sage counselor once told me: for many people, entering upon a different life might take as much as a month to adjust. He nodded eagerly over and over, then left, a totally different person.

That's all it took to find the key to a successful rapport? No, it was also the intimacy of the visit—not just being with someone who cared, but within the atmosphere of an intimacy in that diminutive space ill-lit with candlelight. Only then, with the final student gone as the lights came on again, did I realize the obvious: as with a girl in my speech class, who gave the appearance of a brash extrovert but who fell apart when she faced her classmates (and me in the back of the room, pen in hand, recording extensively and grimly as the superior instructor I thought I should be), I discovered two things that lifted me a step closer in any teacher/student relationship: the need for full, sincere attention, showing I really cared.

And it took the few moments in the right environment to cinch it.

Some years later, for a final course evaluation, a student wrote, "Yes, he fulfills all the requirements for teaching the class, but he does it as though he really cared about me individually, and I actually think he did that for all of us." I was touched, of course, and while her gratitude was repeated by most of the students after that, it took a long time before I realized it was a two-way street I'd paved. I needed their appreciation as much as they did mine. That candle-lit session would carry me to the day when I finally retired, two decades later.

Camaraderie with my Jewish colleagues led to a new dimension of my ecumenical life and to a new group of local friends. Harley Sachs from The Ghetto (along with new neighbors Marshall and Joanne Keltz) encouraged me to visit Temple Jacob, the proud little edifice on the other side of the Portage Bridge that would glow in brilliant colors through huge stained-glass windows when services were held. Always willing to expand my knowledge of anything, I solicited elderly friends Ted and Louise Reiss to take me with them to allay my concern about "butting in." They invited me to accompany them for a Friday night Sabbath service, and as soon as I saw Joanne with a shawl draped over her head lighting the candles on the altar and hovering ethereally over them in opening prayer, I was hooked—line and sinker—into the beauty and sincerity of the event.

Under the Reisses' guidance, I felt comfortable and welcomed. Their warmth and that of others drew me back again and again for weekly and holiday services. I learned the ritual procedures and even prided myself in partaking in reciting and singing and sharing in the frequent potluck meals sure to follow most of the services. That was also where I met sophisticated Chicagoan Susan Burack who landed in Houghton when she remarried (eventually, to become president of the congregation). Her shared passion for the arts made her a fellow culture vulture, and she became a close friend.

My photography was the source of another unexpected and long-term friendship. It began with a fierce knocking at my door—a highly unusual event in my second-floor apartment at the McGintys—during an early winter blizzard. I had forsaken my office on campus that weekend to correct papers in the warmth of my apartment.

"Come in," I called. The door opened to reveal a pair of adults covered with snow. They came in, unwrapped layers of heavy clothing to reveal a bearded Mr. Keith Walters and his smiling wife, Patricia. They explained: they were new to the area from a Detroit suburb (and previously, Canada), now living in Copper Harbor with their grown children and intending to open a new gift shop. They'd heard about my photography, and after glancing through some prints scattered about the room, they were assured of their salable quality. Would I like to give them samples as a starter for the summer tourist season?

We chatted while I brewed tea for them and listened with interest about their plan for the business, reassured by the straight-forward tenor of the conversation. Frankly, I told them, I'd not yet attempted selling photographs but if they liked, I'd bring some next time I drove the 40-some miles to the Harbor on a frequent photo jaunt.

"Good!" said Mr. Walters, looking much like famed film and television actor Monty Wolley complete with trimmed beard, stern expression, and elegant voice. I agreed to gather samples for them to take away. His wife was effusive: "Bring us as many as you like, the sooner the better." She laughed, glancing at the storm raging outside the window, adding, "seems that spring is a long time off, but we're anxious to get started before the season sneaks up on us."

As they dressed for winter again, she turned at the door and suggested, "Keith, why don't we invite Joe to my birthday party next week?" and to me, "The family's giving me a surprise party—all Mexican food and drinks, if you think you'd enjoy it."

Would I? I was enamored by their blend of formal and familiar mien, attracted immediately and wanting to know them better. They left down the stairs to their heavily snow-laden car, and as I watched them vanish into the blizzard down College Avenue, I could only wonder about this strange interruption, which, I thought—cor-rectly—would open a whole new world to me.

Then, a week later, I received a phone call from the Walters' daughter Alta, reminding me of the upcoming "surprise" 40th birth-day party for her mother. "Please come, Joe," she said, adding, "and don't bother about a gift; just bring a good appetite." The lilt of her voice, the mellifluous pronouncement of my name, was all I needed, not only to enter into the spirit of the party, the box of photographs in my arms, but the intrigue of hearing Alta's voice again—both sin-cere and openly friendly—was enough to assure me that, providing good driving weather, I'd be enjoying myself there.

December 2 proved uncommonly mild; I reached their bun-galow home easily, but with some trepidation at the cacophony of voices, laughter, and an occasional shout. When Alta immediately thrust me into a whirlwind of individual family activities, I felt as if

I was an old friend with no cause for introductions. I learned that was typical of the family in any situation.

A greeting was shouted to me by Patricia, in apron and wearing a silly paper hat, inviting me in. "Make yourself at home," she commanded and in no time, I did. Four girls were busy in preparation for the meal: Vaughn the oldest, then Alta, Kelly, Gabrielle and a few husbands I knew I'd never remember.

Alta said to me, "I hope you like hot stuff. No ordinary meal for my mother; we all agreed on the least birthday meal we could come up with; isn't that great?" And, of course, I agreed; even the standard birthday cake with candles had been replaced by French sweets—amazing and somehow absolutely appropriate—which they'd created together.

I drove home in the dark, still wondering if I'd actually experienced one of the most captivating birthday parties I'd ever attended.

When spring rolled around, Keith's simple one-room gift shop opened. Again, to my astonishment, not the typical touristy things in copper, but paintings, statuary, and unique *objets d'art* to attract the sophisticated buyer. Hand-blown glassware from a Canadian artist were the featured wares, but also included were a variety of glazed pots from Patricia's kiln, baskets woven by Kelly's husband from scratch, and later a variety of other handcrafted works from among the clan. I felt honored to have my photos represented as well.

Soon, I made it my habit, each time I drove to the cottage, to include at least one visit with that remarkable family—such joy in getting to know them in their endless surprises and ever astonished at how easily they accepted me. One summer day, while visiting them and allowing them to pore over a box of new photographs to sell on consignment, Alta pulled a few from the lot. "Joe," she said in her expressive voice, "I really like your work, and I'd like to buy some but just can't afford it. Here's an idea: I did some modeling for art students while in Ann Arbor; would you care to trade time for photographs?" Keith, busy reading a newspaper, looked up in surprise but without a touch of negativity. Before he could butt in, I readily agreed, and a new relationship began. As often as we were both free, we'd wander the countryside, find an abandoned home or a secluded open bit of scenery, and, without more than a quizzical expression, she permitted me to photograph her in all her natural beauty. I cherished those private moments, and afterwards, she gathered anything she liked in exchange. Eventually, she allowed her parents to have several from our photo shoots. Many of them still hang on the already filled walls of their home—reminding me of some of the finest shots I've ever taken.

My friendly rapport with the Walters slipped into a delightful kind of relationship, feeling as part of the growing clan, but also singly or collectively with each of them in a natural progression. I thrived on their curiosity, knowledge, and cordiality, and time spent at their Copper Harbor home always left me energized (and well-fed)—an experience that has lasted decades.

Upon my return to Houghton from the University of Iowa, I was eager to renew my friendship with the Romans. Besides our in-town socializing, occasionally I took them up to our family cottage at Copper Harbor. They politely enjoyed the visit; ever class-conscious, their equal dedication to the Catholic church (and St. Ignatius) provided a common ground with my parents. It was perceptive Mrs. Roman who once surprised me by asking, "Joe, have you ever photographed your parents?" Never thought about it until then. "No," I replied. "I guess it's very difficult for me to aim my camera at people so close to me." Followed by another of those "I know" looks from her.

I also began to realize that Mrs. Roman was having health problems. As we went for an evening drive, she wrapped her shawl around her and said, with resignation, "This will be my final plea-sure." I did not understand at the time, but as she showed definite signs of illness and was taken to the hospital, it became obvious that cancer had reduced her to a slow but eventual end.

Before her final decline, a teenaged niece came for what I thought was an extended visit, but in reality their hopes were that she would stay and care for them in their aging days. Zofia, obviously a caring niece of Professor Roman, attended to them constantly; all four of us would go for a drive or just visit like old friends. I noticed that she had in common with them (particularly her uncle) an air of birthright superiority; gradually, putting pieces together, I suspected the privileged life they'd lived "in the old days." She left abruptly, disappointing them with her announcement that she intended to become a nun. She did join a teaching order, writing to me, saying, "I cannot say that I am happy with my choice, but I am content—and that makes all the difference." Exit Zofia.

Mrs. Roman's death, as expected, devastated the professor; he went into a cave of his own making, visiting her grave punctually at noon and 5:00 p.m. daily, praying at the hospital door where he'd spent day and night (with a provided cot) for years before it was deemed difficult for the hospital staff. He wore only black after her death. He turned to me as their closest American friend, with a kind of mutual surrogate father/son relationship.

15

Zigzagging Toward My Doctorate

After my return from the year in Iowa, to expand the departmental course offerings (and to pursue my constant interest in things dramatic), I submitted a plan for a class titled "History and Technology of Movies, 1900–Present." The proposed course would take students from circa 1900 to the present as we learned how the same subject (comedy, war, generation gap, romance) would change according to the times, both socially and technically with the original simplest machine to make people move on film, then with the addition of sound, color, etc., as they advanced through the century. I also proposed teaching a new course introducing photography as art. Unfortunately, I could not convince the dean of the scholastic merits of either, though, and had to mothball them.

So, what else could I do? With my first ventures into creating radio programs, I decided to enlarge my horizons and develop a small FM radio station. The inspiration grew from my experience working at night in the Camp Nebagamon darkroom when I discovered WHA-FM (the U of Wisconsin radio station, broadcast across the entire state). The programming covered an astounding range, including classical music and jazz, a host of lectures by their faculty and guest specialists on subjects ranging from foreign history and literature to current topics: political, social, serious, humorous, etc. Standards were the highest I'd ever heard—and no commercials! I listened for hours late each night, often leaving the darkroom, reluctantly, well past midnight. Each time when summer camp was over and I returned to teaching at Michigan Tech, I felt I'd lost a friend. All those people in the Upper Peninsula without an FM signal and nothing but commercial radio—they, like me, needed far more.

In early September 1967, I approached a group of students with a variety of technical and electronic skills. That brainstorming session advanced into a group of three of the most proficient, most eager students to develop a plan for a 10-watt station. Where? In the top two floors of an abandoned water tower mid-campus (with the first three floors of Sperr Hall, the Mining Department, beneath us).

Next step: get the approval of the administration. After an unenthusiastic reception from my dean, I decided to discuss the plan with President Ray Smith. Through photo assignments (including one where I accompanied him on an inspection of a copper mine), we had developed a rapport, plus he and his wife were neighbors, and I would often drop in to their home for a personal visit. President Smith, who had spent his earlier life tinkering on mechanical projects, listened to our proposal to design and build the station at a third of the usual commercial cost; he said if we could actually put it together as planned, he would even roll up his sleeves and help complete it. Besides his financial support of the project ($10,000), his backing and interest turned out to be essential to winning over others to the project.

President Smith (in white) inspecting a copper mine

We built the station, bit by bit, with the studio on the top floor of the cramped tower and the tech equipment (the heavy stuff) on the floor below. On the tightest of budgets, our engineers scrounged everything they could use from the little radio room I had used for my original Denton House programs and with any surplus equipment from every other possible source. With the president's help, we were able to enroll the head of the Electrical Engineering Department—who had initially been less than helpful—in constructing the transmission tower.

Meanwhile, as word was out that a new FM radio station was soon to broadcast in our area, the sudden demand for appropriate radios was brought up. Once again, as luck would have it, a relative of mine worked at a radio manufacturing firm near Grand Rapids; they were willing to sell $90 excellent quality AM/FM table radios for $29 each in quantity! The president told me we could sell them ourselves as long as we were not to make a profit on them. So, with my own money, we purchased 30 radios, gave word of their availability, and within hours, faculty and staff bought me out. I ordered 50 more. By that time word was out in the community; we sold them as well in less than a week. (Yes, I got my money back. It was worth the expenditure.) We were now guaranteed a small waiting audience for the promised FM station.

Receiving FCC clearance for the FM tower was the final hurdle. Typical delays from the Washington, DC-based department held us up for days, then weeks, then months. With a planned spring 1968 launch on the horizon, I won the approval of our department to work half-time as the station manager of the new WGGL-FM station.

WGGL-FM (91.1 MHz) went on the air on March 30, 1968, as a 10-watt station, reaching a listening audience at a distance of approximately 10 miles. A few weeks before, while in Washington, DC, for an educational conference, I had wormed my way into the labyrinth of FCC offices, met a "little/big man" in charge of discharging requests; flattery, a pair of tickets to a concert, and future promises worked—within a week the release arrived at Tech! The call letters were our third choice; jokingly, we referred to it as "wiggle" and, jokingly, "the wiggle in the miggle of your dial." It caught on!

Talented, eager students came on to help with free time to act both as announcers and tech crew. I felt confident in overseeing the programming. I knew what I liked about WHA and wanted our station to be (as our motto) offering "a change and not a repetition" with as much of the WHA format as possible (even to lectures and discussions by the best-suited faculty willing to join us), all of us learning as we progressed, as we were stuffed into that closet-sized space, sometimes with as many as three or four people in attendance.

Joe with Tech students in the first WGGL studio (in Sperr Hall)

A huge problem to overcome, though, was in training the announcers, who, accustomed to commercial stations, had to learn a new technique: how to be heard as dedicated, learned men and women (yes, we hired women, too, more interested in talent than gender) who sounded intelligent yet with that tinge of humility that made them informative and believable. Some adapted quickly, but then the classical music programs provided another challenge.

I was working in my basement darkroom in one of the academic buildings, listening to the station as it played Beethoven's Fifth Symphony. As it went into the coda in that magnificent series of climactic closings, the piece faded down and the student announcer, in his best commercial tone, said, "Well, guys and dolls, it's time to close out this program ..."

I dropped everything, shot out of the darkroom, found a phone, and the wires were scorched with my disapproval. That sort of thing never happened again.

At first we were on the air with an entirely volunteer crew five hours a day (4:00 p.m. to 9:00 p.m.), six days a week—later adding Sunday afternoons as well—and, also, we had to shut down over the summer and during other holiday breaks when students were away. Besides the faculty interviews and lectures, we broadcast tape recordings from free national and international radio services, even one from Radio Moscow (prompting a slew of outraged listener responses). Saturday afternoon opera brought in our first, most favorable reactions; our record album stockpiles grew appropriately, and eventually we were able to satisfy most of the popular requests.

I must confess, aside from my initial impetus from the Wisconsin radio network, I have to credit the U of Wisconsin's Idea Theatre director, Bob Gard, for giving me the opportunity to work across the state in areas including theater and radio. He was a visionary, who influenced me and scores of others: were it not for his creative ideas about the role of academic institutions in the improvement of community information systems and in local arts development (and connections with influential people who believed in him), I know the cultural landscape across the country today would be quite different.

❖ ❖ ❖

I had hoped the success of this new venture and other extracurricular activities (advising the fraternities, writing and photographing for the *Gazette* on a weekly basis) would distract my superiors from my incomplete doctoral work. What's more, my photographic work by that time was gaining recognition: besides occasional small, local exhibits of my work, in February 1968, *Popular Photography* published two full-page abstract color photographs—one of metal pieces with the light glinting off the edges and the other a double exposure of a Ferris wheel against a water scene—and then in March, a black-and-white overlay portrait close-up.

My "sleight of hand" ploy worked for a while—and I even gained promotion to associate professor. After I was turned down for a sabbatical in 1967 to work on the dissertation, I finally had to admit to the dean the impossibility of finishing at the University of Iowa ... but I did propose a Plan B to zigzag my way forward. Since speech rather than English was now my focus, why not pivot and pursue a PhD in speech/communications? The plan was accepted, but there was no longer any chance for delays, side steps, or disappointments, so a final decision had to be made: where to get that damnable degree as quickly as possible?

With any number of universities available, I wanted to keep to my tradition of remaining in the Midwest. Why not right here in Michigan, where tuition would be lower and the distance would be negligible? In my typical into-the-fray attitude as if to purchase a new anything, I drove, first to East Lansing, to Michigan State, to "check out the lay of the land." I found it not to my liking so then went off to nearby Ann Arbor and the U of Michigan, which seemed to have everything I'd appreciate in a campus—expansive, but well laid out around a broad diagonal and, as at the U of Iowa, a kind of friendly blending into the city that surrounded it. A casual discussion with the head of the Speech Department and I was sold.

U of M accepted my application and I got credit for previous courses at the University of Iowa. In the early summer of 1968, I packed my car with enough supplies for a small army and an address (and a key sent in advance) for a summer rental. What had I to worry about? I'd been teaching long enough to feel comfortable in any grove of academe, buoyed by enough past campus experiences at large state universities to feel ready for anything Ann Arbor had to offer. However, this time, I had to pay my way (with no subsidy).

Within the first 24 hours, I made my first blunder. I found the small apartment building (just across from the city library) and parked in the broad garage behind it. Then I unloaded the car, making several trips up a flight of well-worn groaning stairs to the Number 3 door, and filled the empty two rooms in less than half an hour. Tired from the nearly 500-mile drive, I fell onto the partially made bed and slept ... to be awakened early the next morning by a pounding on my door. It was the landlord—a fellow with a heavy Mideastern accent. Shouting with a fusion of rather exceptional vulgarities, he gave me to understand that I had taken up the space of two other cars with angry phone calls dragging him out of bed, across town, to rectify the problem. In his anger he even threatened to throw me out of the apartment.

I was naturally alarmed. I picked up on his accent and calling him *Uhmmu* (friend or brother in Arabic), explained and asked him to forgive the error. He did. Guiding me under his glaring frown, hands on hips, I pulled the car into its proper place and apologized in ineptly phrased Arabic. He softened, told me I could stay, and drove away in his sleek black Cadillac.

Mark one for Joe Kirkish, goofballing his way into what actually became an edgy friendship with him and his Syrian family, including a wife who made tasty meals and even invited me to share a few Sunday meals with them, and two shiny black, curly-haired little girls who took forever to win over from behind their father's protective legs.

My apartment was adequate for an old, made-over wooden building, and surprisingly quiet. That, I was told by the fellow across the hall, was because walls were filled with what he called "pigeon shit" to baffle outside noises, perfectly. It was just four blocks from Madison Hall, a building on the north side of the campus and the locus of the Speech/Communications Department with three floors crowded with lecture rooms, practical studios for radio and TV operation, and faculty offices.

I quickly oriented myself to the U of M campus and, in the first few days, met my summer term classmates in Speech/ Communications—no one under the age of 30 (mostly graduate students, teachers on leave, and robed and plain-clothed nuns). Like me, they were working toward that "gold star" degree, and we fell easily into company with one another. Competition was less intense than at Iowa, more varied than at Wisconsin, but all with a common interest in getting on with our individual goals.

I had been warned earlier by a graduate of the university that getting a bachelor's degree was something of a snap; for a master's, a bit more difficult; and for the highest degree, pure hell. The course-work that first summer offered a chance to ease into that challenge, with a combination of lectures and hands-on classes in subjects new and old: TV and film production, library studies, and commercial advertising.

The basic class in TV production turned out to be demanding but lively. None of us had ever experienced working in a TV studio before, though we were familiar with its general use. Our room was spacious, high-ceilinged to hold batteries of bright lights, and padded to deter unwanted sounds. We entered through its only door, glanced around at the scattered assortment of furniture, bulky cameras, and at the farthest end a broad, glassed-in room, which we learned would be used for visual examination of our work on the floor.

Through various assignments and shifting roles from in front of and behind the cameras, we learned the technical intricacies of shooting a show. Our instructor, Professor McConnell, was not an academically trained professor, but an experienced dropout from the commercial demands at ABC-TV; he and Professor Marshfield taught in tandem, both efficient, experienced, and capable of putting us at ease in the most trying experiments as we shifted roles from in front of and behind the cameras.

Included among our disparate group of teachers from around the country was Doris Hall, a housewife from Detroit who openly came "around for the ride," wanting to see what it was like on the other side of the camera. From struggling with new equipment and performing for one another under lights, she pulled us together with her Erma Bombeck ease. Guided by our "outsider" Doris, I tried to make light of each experiment, for example, as when I had to create a five-minute how-to-do-it demonstration with our comedienne housewife. We began with the camera on me, close-up, but with an upside-down face on the screen and my comment, "Don't touch your dial; it is I that is upside down." As the camera pulled back it revealed me in an upside-down handstand; I dropped down to introduce Doris as she would demonstrate the art of frosting a cake. She faked a cooking show attitude, with a cake and a huge tub of gooey frosting before her; wielding a large spatula, she talked us through inches of frosting to cover the cake, then with a phony smile of conquest, looked up and said, "You see how easy it is," as her hands sank slowly into the gooey mess, trying hard to keep from breaking up.

Quite unlike the lively fun of this class was a project for the introductory film production course. I was paired with a Sister Mary Camille and only lukewarm to the idea (as a schoolboy having been under the influence of nuns good and bad, likable and disagreeable). But one look into that hardy, smiling face, a modern version of Ingrid Bergman in *The Bells of St. Mary's,* and my attitude changed, instantly and correctly. We clicked with our very first brief assignment ... and it was she who saved the day when our plans went awry.

Memories of that near-disastrous experience—as vivid as my first day of teaching at Tech—are best captured as a film scene.

FADE IN

EXT: The SWAN, a deli near U of Michigan campus—weekday, early afternoon in mid-June

Joe Kirkish, serious, dark-eyed, bearded, middle-aged man with Middle Eastern features. An experienced college teacher, trying to be a super-achieving graduate student

Sister Mary Camille, upbeat, "take charge" nun (30s), also a college teacher, wearing civilian clothes, a silver crucifix around her neck, but no veil

LONG SHOT of deli window, students passing by, then MEDIUM SHOT past the swan image on the window to a MEDIUM TWO-SHOT of Joe and Sister Mary Camille having tea, obviously engaged in serious discussion.

INT: Deli interior

CUT TO: MEDIUM SHOT of the window, looking out at the street, then move in, MEDIUM TWO SHOT of the pair, still talking as they enjoy their tea.

Joe: "Well, what do you think of a scene along the Diag, students walking across, maybe a couple with books, talking as they walk, or something like that?"

Sister Mary Camille: "Oh, that's too ordinary; I'm sure every first-year student in Making Films class must have done it dozens of times." CLOSE UP of her face. "I was thinking about a little hillock not far from here, near where I live. It has a bicycle path running down from the grade school toward the family homes below. We could do our short film about the kids riding their bikes."

CLOSE UP of Joe (looking interested): "Yeah, that might work—long shots of kids on bikes going downhill, close up shots of bike wheels, handlebars, faces …"

CLOSE UP of Sister Mary Camille (getting excited, too): "Yes, that's it. Not very complicated but filling the requirement of people in action."

MEDIUM TWO SHOT, as they work up enthusiasm

Sister Mary Camille: "We could easily fill several minutes with a few kids, won't need more than that."

She puts her cup down. He picks up his books, looks at his watch.

Joe: "It's just about time for grade school to let out. We've got our camera, don't have to use sound. Let's go!"

EXT: Grassy hillock with elementary school at the top.

DISSOLVE TO LONG SHOT. We see them from behind, looking over at the hill.

Sister Mary Camille, pointing: "See, there's the school up there."

PAN to school above, then back to MEDIUM TWO SHOT:

Joe: "Ah, and the kids are pouring out. Perfect timing. There's a girl coming down; I'll catch her."

PULL BACK as we see the girl on the bike. Joe rushes into her path, shouting and waving hands. FOLLOW THEM as girl sees him, looks frightened and peddles faster.

MEDIUM CLOSE UP of Joe (waving his arms): "Hey, stop!"

CUT TO: girl, as she moves still more rapidly away down the hill.

PAN BACK to Joe, disappointed, still shouting after her.

CUT TO: MEDIUM TWO SHOT, Sister Mary Camille and Joe (from behind)

Sister Mary Camille: "Well, that didn't work out too well; let's see if we can't catch someone else … Oh, look there's a boy coming down; maybe we can catch him."

LONG SHOT, boy descending on bike, then PAN TO LEFT, LONG SHOT where the girl had vanished, a trio running quickly toward them: in front, woman brandishing a baseball bat and a police officer with little girl pushing her bike behind.

Police officer (shouting): "Stay where you are, you."

MEDIUM CLOSE UP of Joe and Sister Mary Camille, standing several feet apart, looking at each other in surprise.

Joe: "You mean us?"

PAN TO rapidly approaching police officer, the other two puffing behind.

CLOSE UP of girl (pointing): "That's the man; he tried to grab me!"

CLOSE UP of Joe (astonished): "Me?"

PAN TO police officer rushing toward him. "Yeah, you. Who do you think you are, scaring this little girl here? What's your name?"

MEDIUM TWO SHOT as he approaches, menacingly.

Joe: "I don't know ..."

Mother rushes up and stops behind the police officer. Mother: "You've got a lot of nerve. What're you trying to do to my little girl?"

CUT TO Joe, CLOSE UP: "Me? We? We're just ..."

CUT TO Sister Mary Camille, coming up behind Joe. "What is it, officer? All we wanted to do is complete a film assignment—just filming someone riding down the hill to home."

CUT TO MEDIUM GROUP SHOT. The trio notice Sister Mary Camille's dangling cross and then look in consternation at Joe.

CLOSE UP of Joe: "Yeah, that's all, just wanted to get her to stop so we could explain and then have her ride again down from the top."

CUT TO GROUP SHOT. The three looking embarrassed; Mother starts to explain: "Oh, I'm sorry, I thought ..."

Officer (also calming down): "Sorry about that. See, the kid's been warned about strangers. We've had rumors about some guy trying to lure little girls ..."

CUT TO MEDIUM SHOT of mother, with arms around daughter: "I'm so sorry. We just thought—well, Joanne here, she ..."

CUT TO GROUP SHOT. Sister Mary Camille: "Oh, I understand. Neither of us were aware."

CUT TO Joe, CLOSE UP: "Yeah, I'm really sorry; it was my fault. I shouldn't have rushed at her like that."

CUT TO mother and daughter, MEDIUM SHOT. Mother: "Whew, I'm so relieved. I'm sorry, we were so frightened."

As the trio moves away, CUT TO: MEDIUM SHOT Joe looking wide-eyed at Sister Mary Camille. Joe: "You saved me, thank you! I'm not sure who was more terrified ... the little girl or me. I've done thousands of candid photos of kids at play, but I guess filming them is a different matter! Guess we better quick come up with another idea ..."

CLOSE UP of Sister Mary Camille, with sly smile.

FADE OUT

We ended up shooting a less adventurous short film with students crossing "the Diag," trying for a variety of angles, and occasionally playing with speed for humor. That seemed to work. With some careful editing, we managed to turn in a final piece for which we received a grade of A-. Working with Sister turned out to be a pleasure; I looked forward to being paired off with her again sometime in the future.

While the two lab courses comprised most of my class time that first summer at U of M, I also did two graduate seminars, one in "Materials for TV Advertising" and another in "Values in Film Production." Both required additional reading, some of which I was able to accomplish at the public library across from my apartment, with its huge supply of film and radio television magazines. (Unexpectedly, I discovered a feature article about the now successful John Kander and his partner Fred Ebb, which prompted a brief round of correspondence—but then dwindled since I was now far removed from his glamorous theatrical world.)

Between my readings and the lectures, I had plenty to write about in the required essays and was able to impress the instructors. When I returned to Tech for the fall term (now teaching just a few speech courses while also being the part-time station manager at WGGL), I drew on this additional information—particularly what I had learned about viewer manipulation from a renegade CBS executive—to make my lectures fuller and more interesting to students.

My studies at U of M also fueled my determination to introduce new media courses in our department but knew that I would have to bide my time.

❖❖❖

For my second summer, I had arranged to share an apartment in a new building (very near our classrooms) with Ralph, a student I'd met from my film class the previous year. I thought the comparatively low cost in rental was odd but accepted it readily (found out later why the low rent for a ground level existed ...).

Leaving the relatively sedate life on the campus of Michigan Tech was actually something I looked forward to. I couldn't wait to experience the contrast between the two campuses, while at the same time looking forward to being immersed in the areas of interest—radio, television and film—that also beckoned. I had resigned myself to putting in the extra hours necessary to prepare for the comprehensive exam. The summer of 1969 also proved to be filled with all kinds of historic events: the antiwar and social protest movements that permeated campus activities; the arrival of guru Steve Gaskin and his cross-country caravan of pot-smoking, ecology-loving, communal-living group of acolytes mid-session; the July landing of our spaceship on the Moon.

Aside from having to endure a useless (and required) course in library science, labs in TV/radio production occupied most of my hours with almost as much enjoyment as being instructive, always with lots of teamwork. Professor Overby, a professional once in commercial radio, concerned himself with the value of learning, not just broadcasting, but experiencing the entire process from news gathering, writing copy, to fitting in as newscasters on the material—all within specific time allowed—as would be found in everyday news broadcasts. First, he paired us off with professional newsmen, observing how they did their daily reporting; I accompanied a popular Detroit radio newscaster following up a street shooting.

We had weekly team assignments, which culminated in a recorded 30-minute televised broadcast for criticism and analysis. Toward the end of the summer, we began to feel quite confident in our practices. A CBS professional, who monitored our overall presentation, told us candidly that we had achieved news-casts worthy of actual airing.

When it was my turn to be the on-air announcer, I arrived at our studio early to gather and prepare material for the broadcast. It was a particularly hot summer day; the studio had no air-conditioning, so I decided to dress formally from the waist up and then, as I'd heard professionals often did, wear only summer shorts, out of sight of the cameras. As the students came in, took their positions at their television stations, I went into my "Walter Cronkite delivery," apparently (from Professor Overby's expression of approval) doing a satisfactory job—no flubs, on cue, looking very professional to the end. As we shut down, I stood up, revealing what had been hidden underneath the table, and the cries of surprise and laughter from everyone including the professor cinched the day and the class for me, and warranted a solid A for the course.

Meanwhile, I spent spare time looking for interesting events to record on tape to send back to WGGL for a weekly 15-minute program. Not hard to find on a campus so rich with exciting and novel occurrences almost by the minute. When I read that Tom Hayden (then Jane Fonda's co-conspirator in probing contemporary political doings) was on campus, I tracked him down. I interviewed him in my car and spent half an hour getting it into a strong recording that covered everything from his political beliefs to his relationship with Miss Fonda, which nicely reproduced for my WGGL program, but also became fodder for a subsequent course in radio production.

Reading about the coming arrival of California guru Stephen Gaskin (then on a national tour with his growing caravan of followers being sponsored by the American Academy of Religion), I planned with some anticipation to attend his evening lecture and record as much as possible of it. Gaskin had a fascinating background: after serving in the Marines, then teaching at a West Coast college, he was now spreading his highly unorthodox philosophy as a free thinker and proponent of marriages of fours, as well as a believer in the sacramental use of pot. How could I miss this?

Armed with my tape recorder, I did attend the lecture, held in a small music auditorium almost bursting with both the caravan attendants and curious onlookers like me. It was an experience I'd never forget: the audience sitting in rapt attention while the group (both onstage and off) left their children of all ages rambling everywhere, unattended. Adding to the atmosphere of the program was the sweet blue smoke permeating the space. Whenever I could during the very long session, I talked with some of the Gaskin group, all smiling and seemingly without concerns, about their lives, including the fact that they followed their leader's commitment to marriage in fours, his love of peace and harmony with nature, and a desire to live eventually as a community with him and his two wives and their offspring.

It was like a fantasy, in that smoke-filled auditorium, with Gaskin's voice commanding attention despite all the chaos surrounding him. When the program finally ended, I cornered him long enough to gain about 15 minutes of enthused, sincere comments and returned to the apartment, eager to see what I would do with the recorded material. I dropped the recorder machine into my clothes closet with two hours of tape waiting to be examined the next day, after classes were over.

Disaster! When I returned at the end of the day, I encountered my roommate with the news that our apartment had been broken into (from a ground-floor window) and the recorder, his new leather jacket, and other precious items were gone. The police were called; they told us that other main-floor apartments had been equally ransacked, suggesting we conceal anything of value in case the culprit(s) returned.

What to do? Nothing about the stolen items, but as for our typewriters and other vital equipment … well, the wisest hiding place was no longer in closets, but inside the kitchen oven. It worked.

The big event that summer was cramming for and taking my comprehensive exam. After a tremendous amount of time in the library and reviewing of the pertinent class materials (along with knowledge gained through my teaching at Tech), I hoped I was prepared for the exam. On a Saturday afternoon, I was given a room in our now empty building, carting my portable Corona typewriter, a sheaf of paper, and nothing else, was told I'd have from noon to 5:00 p.m. to write. I took the sheet of information, sat down and read two statements upon which to write as completely as possible: one, on the history of BBC radio, and two, on the history of the film industry from 1895 to the present.

I was in luck, having focused on both issues in my studies, typed away, thinking it would take only a few hours. But the more I typed, the more details I filled in. Then a surprising knock on my door startled me: it was a fellow grad student who was being given his last opportunity to pass the comprehensive. We'd discussed the material a week earlier; he was exceptionally well versed, smiled wryly, but pure terror had always made him clutch.

And here he was now, illegally at my door, white-faced and with a sickly expression, asking for help to calm him down. What to do? Luckily, "just in case," I'd brought a pill for that event. I gave it to him, he thanked me and left. A few minutes later, he returned looking even worse, telling me he'd just vomited, pill and all. I picked up a phone on the desk, called the professor in charge, asking for help. He sympathized but said only, "Have him order out a light lunch; that should do some good." I relayed the suggestion, he looked piteously at me, and left. I never heard from him again and have no idea whether or not he'd won or lost.

At 5:00 p.m., the professor came in, took the thick sheaf of typed pages, and let me out of the building without a comment. It seemed I'd done a fairly good job but was on pins and needles until two days later a letter came from the department: no comment except to say I'd passed the exam. That's all I needed. Now, onward and upward, the weight of the next great step hovering: producing a dissertation.

That fall, I suggested to the dean of faculty at Michigan Tech that I do my dissertation on the National Film Board of Canada (NFB), whose films I had shown frequently in my weekend foreign film series. From its beginning as a producer of wartime propaganda films, the NFB had expanded to become an innovative producer of documentaries and gained enormous recognition for attracting highly talented animators. The dean felt the subject of Canadian film was satisfactory and encouraged documenting the lives of its originators. I readily agreed, said I'd look into it immediately. And then, in a gesture of frustration, I asked him why I should be forced to spend a great deal of time and effort on a dissertation, when after

14 years on the faculty, I'd already proved my value to the teaching profession. He pursed his lips, smiled, and replied, "To prove you can do it." End of discussion.

My first step was to contact the film distributor from whom I'd rented the films screened at Tech to get their advice about doing the research on the NFB, and they immediately directed me to John Grierson. I was familiar with his extraordinary documentary films (in fact, he was considered to be the father of British and Canadian documentary films), but I was not aware that he was the visionary founding director of the NFB. Switching from a budding career in Britain in the making of short explanatory films (like *Night Mail*, about the speed in which the British system operated so successfully), he expanded to three- or four-hour documentary extravaganzas which were presented over the Canadian Broadcasting Corporation system. He had also encouraged experimental films that drew actors like Hollywood's Fredric March to play in his internationally recognized productions.

I corresponded with Grierson, who was enthusiastic about the project. Now, I actually looked forward to working on the new dissertation, but just had to figure out how to set aside time to pursue it.

To show proof of trying to finish my PhD work, I had previously applied for a full year's absence from teaching at Tech, which both times had been denied. Reason: there was no one to replace me during 12 months of absence. Two summers at the U of M, plus having passed the comprehensive exam, and, just as important, the arrival of Bill Powers, a new department chair, helped my cause. Bill offered a solution: from among the department's cadre of instructors, find one for each course I'd be missing. Voila! It was accomplished; I would head for Ann Arbor the fall of 1970 for a nine-month (unpaid) leave of absence to complete the roster of lab courses and deal with the "Sword of Damocles" hanging over my head … the dissertation.

My residence this time was a room in a private home on the southeast edge of Ann Arbor, a real find thanks to the owner's brother who lived in Eagle Harbor (near Houghton) and who pointed me to the curious rock-studded home owned by Elizabeth Haven, widow of a retired colonel in the U.S. Army. She was a pioneering sort of strong-willed woman, greying hair pulled severely into a bun on the back of her head, not a sign of makeup on her regularly rigid face (except for a dusting of powder for "dress-up" occasions), plainly dressed in work clothes (attending her forest of blue spruce which daily brought in a steady income).

She lived a very regimented life, including managing her daily housework, cooking, working the fields around the house—and still taking the time to call me with a clanging school bell (a remnant of her grade school teaching days) to three massive meals a day. Given the continuing turbulence at the U of M campus, being in her midst was an interesting time warp and, as it turned out, except for those endless mounds of food, a respite. (After gaining weight after the first few months, I learned that telling her I would be spending the day and evening on campus gave me an "out.") I enjoyed, too, bicycling back and forth to campus, which allowed me time to decompress. Compared to the personalities at U of M, she appeared ageless, tireless, and dogmatically ever in control. She took kindly to me, and I photographed her a few times; the most successful image I shot was while she was tending her grape arbor, which looked like something out of a 1930s WPA photograph.

Upon arrival at the university, I was assigned to Professor Edgar Willis, chair of the Department of Speech, as my dissertation advisor. Canadian born, he had British-style delivery and speech patterns. He was the opposite of my U of Iowa advisor—a taskmaster and stickler for precise language and academic convention. We discussed my proposal for the NFB/Grierson dissertation, including my planned approach to doing research and getting the proposal for the NFB history approved as quickly as possible. I mentioned the fact that from exploratory correspondence, Grierson, along with his wife, planned to visit me for a short stay at our cottage on Lake Superior while the two of us detailed information for the project; Willis was obviously surprised and interested in what he called an "extrordin'ry" arrangement.

With little effort, I was able to get approval for my dissertation proposal. Professor Willis wanted me to work on the introduction while I was still doing background research. I drafted text, but time after time, it was met with disdain. In desperation I went to the basement stacks of our building to check on other completed theses; to my sad surprise, I found that all were written in one formal style, as if all from the same source. Okay, if that's what he wanted, I'd give it to him, planning to rewrite it for myself once he'd accepted his version.

Still, he continued needling me. I would sit up half each night redrafting, then wait for his response by phone followed by a session with him in person as he would berate me over tiny details. Example: he crossed out "the meeting began with … ," changing it to "commencing with." I changed it and in our next session found he'd tossed out "commencing with" and writing above it "beginning;" when I exposed the error—wow—I'd made an enemy for the rest of my time at the university.

Meanwhile, I enrolled in the required classes for completion of the degree and readily signed up for advanced filmmaking. It was my good fortune to find Sister Mary Camille in the same class, eager to work with me again, this time on a project she had planned for a long time: a documentary on teenaged, unwed mothers-to-be, in a Catholic home, safe from prying eyes at a time when such occurrences were much less common than today and far less accepted in public. Immediately, my mind raced to unrealistic, dramatic scenes; Sister calmed me down to reality, and after the initial instructional classes had been completed, we were off on our own.

For our initial work on the half-hour planned documentary, Sister and I drove to the facility, which was about halfway between Ann Arbor and Detroit. It was situated on a pleasant field with a pond, the building looking more like a family home than an institution. Mother Superior greeted us, brought us into her office, and we explained our plan—Sister's plan, actually—to show the place as a comfortable hideout, away from the city's prying eyes, where the girls could live dorm-like, get to know one another, and learn to face facts (gently tempered with the kindness of the nuns assisting there). We agreed on the plan for our weekend visits: I would initially shoot generally around the grounds, then more specifically as the "story" worked its way out, while Sister would use her tape recorder to get bios from the girls willing to relate them (their backgrounds in the suburbs, how the pregnancy occurred, the plans to enter the institution, and how they felt about it).

On our second visit, camera and recorder in hand, we walked around the outside of the building with Sister recording the sound of birds, etc. for atmospheric purposes, and me watching girls pasting Halloween pumpkins and ghouls on the windows—always keeping in mind what Mother Superior had reminded us: no faces shown.

As the filming progressed, I had fun designing shots that were explicit: ubiquitous hands with cigarettes or folded comfortably over growing bellies, silhouettes against the sunlight, etc. Some of the girls' anecdotes were touching; most seemed to have been pushovers in their relationships, with promises that the "father of the child" would make financial and social reparation afterwards; to a person, it ended in unkept promises with the father making a slow exit. Sadder still was the waiting for their calls, which came less and less, finally dribbling to silence.

Sister, through her perceptive interviewing, began to realize the most serious issues were not what to do about the unwanted babies nor how they would return to fit into their earlier lifestyles, but the need for the girls to regain their faith in men. Cleverly, she would encourage me to sit and converse with one or another of them—sympathetic teacher style—which she felt I was good at; truthfully, I did enjoy the discussions, camera aside, on short but frequent sessions. And I grew to appreciate their plight more and it was gratifying to see them light up with each of our return visits.

I can say frankly that working with Sister was the most fruitful part of my time at U of M and proudly that the resulting film, *Choices*, was screened at the 9th Annual Ann Arbor Film Festival in March 1971!

❖ ❖ ❖

Early on, I landed a job at the university's public radio station, WUOM-FM. During registration week, I found a notice that trained radio announcers were needed. Why not me? I had training as a broadcaster at WGGL, knew I would have some spare time, and needed some income. During the interview, I was given a stack of musical broadcasts to announce, each one scattered with names from different countries. A snap, except for one in Hungarian; I slipped it inside the other sheets. The director lifted it out and with a knowing grin asked me to try it, too. Apparently, I did well; he noticed, also, when handed a sheaf of news items to organize them for broadcast, that was also a snap.

I was hired, first, weekdays for a five-minute news summary, later with a 15-minute conclusion before the evening classical music hour, this time (gratefully) with a regular staff partner. Fine, until the station needed people for Saturday mornings (a full hour and alone) to give the day's upcoming news. Of course, I had to accept my once-a-month session, but was rarely satisfied with the results too rushed in preparation, and my poor knowledge of sports became evident each time I had to digest them.

It didn't take long to pick up the sophisticated tone of the regulars, but I always felt I failed by not having a "voice of God" quality that the rest of the staff did. I was adequate, not much more in that respect. One fly in the ointment: the supervisor of the news programs was a stickler for perfect productions. One day when I failed to recognize the board man's signal to speak, I was left with radio stigmata—a full half second of dead air! Immediately after my time was up, the phone rang with the supervisor berating me for that horrible dead air. The director of the station heard about it and calmed me down while chastising the supervisor for his overdone criticism, but I remained tightly on my toes after that.

A nice thing about the Friday 5:45 p.m. news—if I planned to drive to my sister's home in nearby Battle Creek, I'd close out with weather around the area; when I'd include Battle Creek, it was a subtle signal of my imminent arrival. Cis's children would listen and spread the news; I'd arrive there in half an hour with a welcoming meal awaiting me. It became a frequent break from campus and its drudgeries.

Further testing me, the director sent me out on an assignment to interview a visiting celebrity and then produce a seven-minute piece, no more, no less. Another snap from my experiences at WGGL. One interview followed another, and I was delighted to be paid to visit and record so many interesting people I'd never otherwise have had the opportunity to meet. He even sent me to Detroit to record the opening of Arthur Miller's new play, *The Price*, and interview him afterwards.

I also interviewed the ultramodern "Music by Chance" composer John Cage, and demonstrated my ease discussing his controversial work. I followed my fascinating brief interview by attending his evening performance in the School of Music main auditorium, which was the strangest, most disjointed 20-minute musical event I'd ever witnessed: a group of mimes removing and changing everyday garments in an arena while four musicians, outside the ring, busied themselves by piercing music sheets from the blank sides and turning them over; when signaled by Cage, they played whatever notes were created by the pinholes on the regular sides—dissonant, obviously haphazard, played repetitiously off and on as the spectator/composer, arms folded, smiled devilishly in approval. I enjoyed the experience, especially after having heard Cage's earlier comments, but the totally confused audience was not amused.

That experience moved me to consider creating a short experimental movie. I envisioned a young man walking into a very small house, then with a series of clever edits, have him walk from one room and floor to another, gradually aging into maturity, to a final wrinkled old man, motionless on a mattress in the attic—all to the sound of the controversial musician's contentious music.

I never made the movie. Simply creating it in my mind was sufficient, and, instead, indulged my passion for film through going to evening screenings of independent films around Ann Arbor (many to choose from with a host of local film societies).

My other favorite intellectual pursuit was finding interesting classes which I could audit as a graduate student. My presence (always taking copious notes, but never participating) drew the attention of Professor Abraham Kaplan in his five-hour class in which he examined ethical and philosophical issues in different religions; he would seemingly speak directly to me at times. Eventually, we walked together from the classroom to his office—his arm carelessly over my shoulder like a parent to a child, making inquiries as to why I audited the class, assiduously scribbling notes without making comments. I explained my interest in him as a world-renowned philosopher, wanted to know more, but could never afford the time to fulfill his overwhelming class requirements. That seemed to satisfy him.

He invited me to be a part of regular, small, weekend gatherings

Abraham Kaplan

at his lovely home, always filled with flower arrangements done by his wife. Once again, I was being granted special access to a great scholar and teacher. Like Lord Krishna, he would sit among us, enjoying us as his ardent followers, engage in fascinating conversation on any topic, from the ongoing battles in Israel to the emancipation of women. He appeared to be a rare master of all topics as we, obviously his chosen intellectual few, revered those evenings. A few times, I visited him on my own, and I caught his Lord Krishna quality in a photograph that I shot of him "attended" by his wife and daughter in their backyard, which pleased him very much.

And then I discovered an unusual connection. I would type up my notes (for future reference) and send a copy to Professor Roman. One day, after having sent him many typed pages from a brilliant lecture, I received a surprise response. Professor Roman had left behind in Warsaw a good friend and philosopher on similar subjects regarding religion and had been forwarding my notes to him. When I told Professor Kaplan, he smiled and said, "Ah, yes, how many times I'd spent in Poland with my good friend, sitting in a bistro and sipping vodka as we discussed so many things!"

When I left Ann Arbor, I hoped somehow in the future to bring him to Tech to lecture and meet Professor Roman ... and almost succeeded. The following year, through my involvement in a university board that selected guest lecturers, I received approval to book him, but the day I called to invite him, his response was, "Oh, Joe, I am talking with you in a barren house with nothing but this phone and a cot to sleep on. Tomorrow I fly to Israel where I will begin teaching at the University of Haifa! You must come and visit us there sometime."

It was an impossible invitation to accept, of course, but a generous one from a remarkable, unforgettable person. Though our acquaintance only lasted several weeks, Professor Kaplan made a deep impression on me: he was both brilliant and a brilliant teacher—too often a rare commodity in academia. Later, when asked to define his identity by an interviewer, he responded: "I am by training a positivist, by inclination a pragmatist, in temperament a mystic, in practice a democrat; my faith Jewish, educated by Catholics, a habitual Protestant; born in Europe, raised in the American Midwest, hardened in the East, softened in California, and living in Israel." He became my model of a living, breathing humanist and truth-seeker.

One other unexpected souvenir of being at U of M was the result of volunteering to be a guinea pig for psychology grad students designing personality tests. Often the experience yielded unexpected enlightenment: the most astute researchers helped reinforce my own personality and approach to both photography and teaching. Most impressive to me was learning that my sense of composition was the equivalent of having "perfect pitch." And I made money doing it!

After nine months being a deferential graduate student, I was more than ready to regain my faculty status at Tech. While I had not gotten as far along with my dissertation during my leave as hoped, I had gained new material (and inspiration) for teaching, and become a more well-rounded broadcaster, ready to begin the next era of WGGL as an NPR station.

16

WGGL and NPR

The popularity of WGGL supported its growth in just a few years from a 10-watt to a 550-watt station; then in October 1970, the Corporation for Public Broadcasting (CPB) invited our young station to be part of National Public Radio (NPR), a new network under formation. In May 1971, NPR became the first nationwide, noncommercial public radio network in the United States, with 90 member stations, which were required to be on the air at least 18 hours a day (6:00 a.m. to midnight), seven days a week, 52 weeks a year. The results of a discussion between President Smith and the CPB that spring were that our listening area needed to be broader and with programming other than the usual "sandbox" type. So, with a hefty grant, the operating power of WGGL grew to 100,000 watts stereo, along with stereo production facilities which enabled it to reach nearly 100 miles' coverage with nearly 300,000 potential listeners.

Soon after my return in the spring of 1971, the station, with its expanded, state-of-the-art technical capacity, relocated to more spacious quarters in the basement of the old administration building. I went from being part-time to full-time station manager, overseeing a full-time secretary and part-time staff of students plus faculty and community volunteers. In almost no time, we were broadcasting to most of the Upper Peninsula and large parts of Wisconsin, Minnesota, and even across the lake to Canada!

One of the programming additions was a noontime talk show

on which I interviewed people from campus as well as visiting celebrities—entertainers, writers, public figures, scientists—which quickly gained a following. Certainly, the most memorable of these (and in truth, during my whole career as a radio producer) was my interview with Edward Teller, the Hungarian-born physicist dubbed the "father of the hydrogen bomb." It proved a tense experience with, fortunately, a happy ending.

Edward Teller

On request from President Smith, I accompanied high-ranking Tech professors to pick up the physicist at the local airport. He stepped off, his grizzled Slavic features looking still more ominous than ever, glanced down at us, then approached me as his guide. "I haff never had such a horrible trip," he confided; "the air was blowing on my ear and now I haff an earache." As we walked from the tarmac to the awaiting car, he continued commiserating in preparation for the interview. Looking down at me, he asked, "How vould you like to be called the father of such a terrible thing?" adding more jovially, "Vy don't you ask me if I beat my vife in the mornings?"

I took it all in, sympathetically, said nothing until we were crammed into our tiny conversation booth at the station. No air-conditioning. It became stifling with our radio technician, two professors, two bodyguards, Teller, and me. I tactfully allowed the professors to carry on the Q & A. Teller became increasingly uneasy, giving uncomplimentary responses. Something had to be done. Impulsively, I turned to the physicist and, innocently, asked, "Tell me, Mr. Teller, do you beat your wife in the mornings?"

The tension nearly blew the room apart. The professors were aghast. The bodyguards' hands went to their shoulder holsters, and the technician froze. Teller broke into a bellowing laugh. The air was instantly uncharged; I took over the rest of the hour to record one of the most informative programs I ever made. Whatever happened to that memorable piece I'll never know; after playing it in segments on the air, it was stashed with other similar recordings on a shelf— then, one day, simply vanished.

❖ ❖ ❖

We were importing *All Things Considered (ATC)*, the groundbreaking 90-minute weekday afternoon national news program being produced by NPR staff in Washington, DC, to get the news behind the news. Interviewing the "people in the streets" was the focus then and still is today (though the reports gradually spread beyond our country to people the world over for their interpretation of newsworthy events). For that reason, the use of those original 90 local stations became vital in complete news coverage. It led to us at WGGL in our isolated Upper Michigan area becoming a perfect source for plainspoken perspectives, and from time to time, I got to work as a stringer on a story. I would take my trusty tape recorder onto Houghton's main thoroughfare and speak to people (most of whom recognized me and were willing to talk)—and then deliver a ten-minute segment that met their reporting (and technical) standards.

At our first national network meeting in Washington, DC, after being on the air for a year, I felt confident in expressing my personal ideas for growth. To my surprise, I was listened to, not only by the station managers, but staff of the newly formed Washington-based organization. Hearing nothing but individual disappointments from the station managers about the flagship *ATC* program (which I knew from my long-distance interactions with the pioneering NPR staff was being developed with care and sincerity), I could hold back no longer. I raised my hand and with passion explained that our disappointments originated not from what we heard, but from what each of us wanted to hear for our own specific stations. I pleaded for a change of attitude, of joining together as a unit that could add our own tidbits to make it a unified picture of, not single stations, but of all of us combined. Wow! Did I say all that? Yes, and more, as I noticed changes of expression from station managers around me, listening to something none of them had until then thought about. And, later, I was invited to visit with some of the top NPR personnel to continue with the discussion.

That visit to the NPR offices also gave me a behind-the-scenes glimpse of how *ATC* was produced and the maverick, improvisational style of Director of Programming Bill Siemering. On May 15, word came in that Alabama Governor George Wallace, who was then running for president, had been shot while at a campaign stop in nearby Laurel, Maryland. In a flash, Siemering's team of reporters bolted into his office, each picking up a lightweight tape recorder and rushing out, telling him where they were headed (a multitude of locations around the area to search out anyone with information about the shooting, including specific personal comments regarding it). A few hours later, the team returned, went into a frenzy of editing, while Siemering sat behind his desk, hands clasped behind his head, approving of the action but never butting in. By 5:00 p.m., *ATC* gave the country a blow-by-blow description of the event, filling the 90 minutes admirably. Amazing!

I was always pleased to get a call from Susan Stamberg—becoming known playfully as the "Big Bird" of the *ATC* program for her rich, warm delivery—requesting opinions from the street. One day in 1972, Susan called and told me about a new segment for *ATC* that was in the works—"The Village Well"—featuring a singular figure from a particular area discussing a very personal issue. Immediately, I thought of my Professor Roman, who still mourned his wife's passing after several years by visiting her grave twice a day—at noon and 5:00 p.m. on the dot. He accepted my proposal to accompany him one day just to show me what he did there.

With the sound of us crunching on the gravel surrounding the grave (fully fronted with flowers) and crickets announcing the close of the day, he fussed around, seemingly oblivious of me, freshening the flowers, kneeling down, hands bent in prayer, and spoke to her, in that gentle voice of his, asking her to know how much he'd loved her, how much he missed her, and how he hoped that if ever he had done or said something to disappoint her, that it was never done on purpose. He concluded with another silent prayer, then stood up and still staring at the gravestone, turned and walked back to the car.

We returned to his home in silence—he in his reverie, I in my eagerness to turn his delicate words into a ten-minute tribute. It succeeded; not only was Susan pleased, but at the end of the series, she called to let me know that in a unanimous vote, that recording was considered the finest of all. (She even included the incident in her book *Every Night at Five* regarding her years at NPR.) I was relieved to find that my good friend never heard the broadcast, but he was most pleased to hear, later, that "Miss Stamberg" had liked it.

Being a part of this exciting new media enterprise—both running WGGL and being involved in the evolution of the network— proved fortuitous. Though most of my time was consumed with WGGL, I did continue my preliminary research on the National Film Board for my dissertation. I corresponded with John Grierson, then teaching at McGill University in Montreal, with the intention of meeting him in person to do an in-depth oral history. We agreed on a plan that he and his wife would come to the cottage at Copper Harbor the summer of 1972 but, then sadly, he died suddenly in February of that year. Up in smoke went my dissertation! Where next? Into my backyard, with a new idea quickly taking root: a history of the early days of National Public Radio. I submitted a proposal to my committee at the U of M, which they immediately accepted.

My plan was to chronicle the network's development as well as its early period of operation. When I began, I had not yet decided the span of years I would cover and instead would let the research determine the time frame. My first round of research took place in early summer of 1973, when I spent a month "in residence" at the NPR offices (which had moved from its original, cramped space on Eye Street into larger quarters on M Street), doing preliminary interviews, reviewing documents, and observing the general management of the fast-growing organization.

Details of the backstory of NPR were only vaguely known to us faraway stations on college and university campuses. Upon my arrival in Washington, DC, Kathy, a friend whom I had met while at the U of M, volunteered to give me an orientation tour; our conversation yielded information about the important role several people from Michigan had played in authorizing legislation in 1967. Now a staffer for Senator Robert Griffin, she explained that President Johnson had been eager to improve the poor quality of television through support of a noncommercial system, and I learned that the original Public Television Bill was broadened to include radio, thanks to the intervention of a small group of men. Jerrold Sandler, an educational radio lobbyist and former production manager at WUOM at the U of M, realized that public television producers and managers did not want radio, which they considered inferior, as a news medium; he enrolled the last-minute aid of Dean Coston, also a former WUOM engineer and currently serving as the undersecretary at Health, Education, and Welfare (the federal agency submitting the bill), to slyly insert "and radio" into the draft language before the vote by the Congressional committee. Senator Griffin successfully advocated that the term "broadcaster" encompassed both television and radio, and retitled it the Public Broadcasting Act—thus, unifying at least 500 small stations (most of them just 10 watts in strength) into a new system.

My first day at NPR, I was checked at the door by a uniformed attendant, then walked to the second floor, where I felt I had parachuted into another world: the floor was shaped like a huge square donut with doors leading to staff offices, recording rooms, and a small "overflow" room for miscellaneous uses. But it was what I saw coming in and out of those rooms and down the halls that told me "I wasn't in Kansas any longer": a parade of people, some in turbans, saris, casual clothing—skin coloring from white to deep ebony— all going quite nonchalantly about their business, ignoring me as though I were not visible. What's more, there were so many more women than was usual in the mostly male domain of local radio.

I engaged a woman floating by in a billowing colorful sari, inquiring about President Quayle's office. Without stopping, but with a slight flowing gesture, she pointed me to a door. Though it was ajar, I knocked. A voice called out for me to "come in," and there

I was, facing a portly man in dark blue suit and striped tie, behind a desk piled high with multitudes of papers carefully stacked in front of him. At my introduction, he reached across the stacks of papers, shook my hand in a steely grip, and indicated a plain wooden chair in front of the desk for me. I'd already explained in a letter about my intentions; Quayle was pleased, feeling it was time someone recognized the already new radio kid on the block (noting casually that NPR was ensconced directly across from the CBS offices).

My immediate impression of this impeccably polished member of the Church of Latter Day Saints (as he casually slipped in) was reflected in his VP Lee Frischknecht's equally officious and precise manner, who led me from Quayle's office with the intention of introducing me to various members of the still new offices, starting with a charming Elizabeth "Liz" Young who offered to take over. In charge of station relations, Liz had been the sole female member of the planning group of local radio executives. She was especially friendly, and before the tour, she invited me to share a quick lunch with her in a room reserved for staff, complete with a refrigerator and table settings. We munched on homemade peanut butter sandwiches, drank milk from a quart container, and finally finished off with doughnuts from a specialty shop just down the street; she also shared tips on local restaurants, especially a Greek one a few blocks away which was affordable, a rarity in DC.

As we dropped into her colleagues' offices, I quickly got the feeling that all were eager to see a history of NPR put into print, as well as their 100 percent dedication to the organization above any individual difference in management. I made an instant connection with Jack Mitchell, whose brother I knew as a student at Michigan Tech. Mitchell was now the director of programming, and his office became my unofficially shared space. Since he was in on the creation of NPR almost from the start, he became my best "tap" whenever I needed questions answered about the organization's modest beginnings four years earlier.

By the end of the day, I'd been introduced to at least half a dozen people, all very informally, and my head was spinning. Before leaving, I poked my head into Quayle's office, thanked him, and said I looked forward to a more in-depth discussion. The walk back to where I was staying allowed me to decompress, although I had to keep my wits about me since I had to walk along several dangerous blocks carrying my tape recorder. (I was soon instructed by NPR personnel to always carry a $20 bill in my shoe for this daily routine. Robberies, especially at night, were frequent; the bill would save me from physical harm.)

Frischknecht's guiding continued the second day, even to stock rooms, recording quarters, and the more officious offices filled with files which, he said, were open to me, anytime I felt need of information from them. That surprised me, even more so when we stopped at one file that I opened out of curiosity, to discover it contained information regarding salaries. I looked up at Frischknecht and said, "I don't think I should be seeing this." He looked seriously at the files and replied, "No, I don't think you should." We agreed at that point that I should use my own good judgment as to what to examine and what to leave untouched. Amazed at his confidence in me—and more so at his entrusting a key to the second floor, which he thought I'd need for work over the weekends when the offices would be unlocked but void of traffic. "You'll feel freer to come when the place is inactive," he said, adding that even Quayle's office would be available to me.

At first, I resisted the permission to roam freely from office to office, nosing into desks and files at will, but gradually, I came to enjoy the freedom and spent as many Saturdays and Sundays there as possible. Among the material I took note of were several antagonistic memos between Quayle and Bill Siemering about the vision for the *ATC* flagship program; Quayle was demanding specifics with Siemering responding, "We'll all hold hands and run this race together." It was evident that Quayle worried that detailed, long-term planning was being ignored and feared that *ATC*, demanding nightly feeding (not oracular utterances), would fail.

Unfortunately, my own incompetency chilled Quayle's original cordiality with me. After granting me an hour during which I recorded his personal feelings about the development of this new kind of broadcasting (free from commercials, looking to the people for local information, etc.), I returned to my hotel room to find that somehow I'd botched the tape; when I returned the next day and requested a repeat conversation with Quayle, he icily declined.

However, he did permit me to observe a tense meeting with

a small group of Native Americans demanding representation on the NPR staff and more coverage of their community. Quayle had done his utmost to broaden his own concepts of NPR and, with his ability to observe, then act, seemed always to be on track with the organization's goals. Invited to sit in on what he called an "interesting situation" in progress, I followed him into the small private room to find the visiting group and most of his original staff. The tribal chief called the NPR team "you stupid idiots" and used more bluntly accusing language, for totally ignoring them until now. They munched on the catered lunch, hurling one insult after another, as the staff sat in mute silence until Quayle spoke up. He stated that NPR was dedicated to a totally inclusive program but doing it slowly with great deliberation to add to the total mix and would certainly include this minority group in the future. Afterwards, Quayle and his team appeared both relieved and somehow diminished by the accusations, but there was little immediate follow-up.

I knew that Quayle's biggest concern was the financial future for the blossoming NPR network. He never discussed it with us personally, but it was widely known within our network that President Nixon, angry at sharply critical attacks on him on public television, had retaliated by seeking to cut CPB funding. Quayle, in a powerful presentation to Congress, made it clear that the television sector was entirely separate from radio, and while it was indeed politically critical, radio had evaded such controversial positions. Sadly, he was ignored; both broadcasting networks' budgets were slashed, and the battle for money began. At the station managers' meeting that May, a representative of Nixon's blithely mentioned that local fundraising was going to have to be part of the picture—but put a spin on it by saying that it could go hand in hand with the growth in listenership.

On weekends, I also found time to visit a little movie house two blocks down on 21st Street, which seated less than a hundred people and showed double features of golden oldies and foreign films. That proved to be a weekly delight. For a dollar, I'd enter between the black velvet curtains and sink myself into a pair of Alec Guinness comedies or a couple of films made in China (with English subtitles if I was lucky). But there was one problem: hot summer air gave way beyond the curtains into the coldest air-conditioning I'd ever experienced. So, I brought a raincoat with me, carried over my arm into that frigid space, put it on (to everyone's suspicious stares), and enjoyed the films that way. One day I discovered the temperature control alongside the curtain and would surreptitiously raise it considerably and never needed the raincoat again.

The month went by quickly. Besides the top NPR managers, I had gotten to observe the rising on-air stars in action—Susan Stamberg, Barbara Newman, Gwen Hudley, Linda Wertheimer, Robert Conley, Jeff Kamen, Mike Waters, and others. A very unexpected encounter gave me entrée to a key, but aloof, member of the team. Out of curiosity, one day, I went down to the first floor, where some interviews were held in formal studio settings, and where in cubby-holed rooms NPR audio producers and engineers turned daily tapes into perfectly timed segments for broadcast. I happened to walk into one such studio and, to my surprise, heard my voice! I said in amazement, "That's me!" The editor looked up and asked, "You sent this to us?" "Yes," I said, and explained that along with other submissions (most of which were used after a bit of editing), was this nearly hour-long interview with a good friend, Father John, in charge of the religious life of the Chippewa community not far from Houghton.

Though tribal members were generally suspicious of the White community surrounding them, they had reluctantly permitted me to visit them with an idea: creating a 15-minute weekly program, taped right there on the reservation, as a sort of documentary. (I had childhood memories of visiting the reservation with my father and envying their lifestyle.) Reluctantly, they had agreed, allowing me to get out the recorder and just talk with them in general about their lives. When the first program was aired, my introduction—"This is a weekly program about the people on whose land we live"—and my sincerity won over the community, including Fr. John. He eventually granted me an extended interview about being only one of five Catholic Indian priests left in the country, and how he managed to be a priest and an Indian. It was a remarkable taping, despite the fact that he spoke hesitantly, with long, silent gaps which I edited out to improve the final documentary. (I would later learn that when the program was aired on NPR, it attracted huge listenership across Indian country.)

Through the editor, I met the revered and feared manager

of operations, George Geesey, who casually remarked to me that he must have been hired in that important position when Quayle heard of his life in both radio and television (his driving passion since he was sixteen). He lorded over every sound that was to be broadcast—a stickler about timing, consistency in levels, and anything else that, as he said, "No one else would be aware of anything less than perfection, but I will." As an example, he told me of an important interview made on location, during a heavy rainstorm; he ordered it cancelled, said the rain spoiled the final effect, and that was that. George had the customary laconic attitude of people who work behind the scenes, yet excited to talk about his one love: broadcasting.

By the end of the month, I had sampled the Washington scene and my initial research had grounded me in the personalities and internal and external political currents shaping the fledgling network's birth and evolution. I left the NPR offices with the feeling that I was being made privy to something amazing, something that revealed why the organization was achieving such success (albeit only among a small percentage of radio listeners).

Later that summer, after my return to the Copper Country, however, a surprise visit from former Director of Programming Bill Siemering afforded me a missing perspective on NPR's growing pains. He appeared—unannounced—at our radio station, eager to talk to me. Gone was his relaxed smile that I remembered from the previous interaction: he was "reconstituting" after his divorce and his sudden departure from NPR. Bill Kling had recently hired him to be the first station manager at KCCM in Moorhead, Minnesota, a part of a rising empire of stations Kling was assembling along the Mississippi in Minnesota and Wisconsin.

Siemering's story was a remarkable one, a continuation of what I'd first learned about him and his on-again, off-again relationship with then President Quayle. Growing up in rural Wisconsin in the 1930s and '40s, he had developed a passion for radio, early on producing his own amateur programs, then at the U of W, honing his engineering and programming skills at WHA. It was later at WFBO in Buffalo that he was able to realize his humanist vision of the power of radio as the station manager. His success there in the 1960s elevated him to national status, and he had been one of the original members of the NPR Planning Board. In fact, it was Siemering who drafted its mission statement (Liz Young had called him the "Thomas Jefferson" of the group):

> National Public Radio will serve the individual. It
> will promote personal growth. It will regard the
> individual differences among men with respect and
> joy rather than derision and hate. It will celebrate
> the human experience as infinitely varied other
> than vacuous and banal. It will encourage a sense
> of active constructive participation, rather than
> apathetic helplessness ...

After the NPR Board appointed Quayle as president, he had immediately hired Siemering as director of programming, who accepted the position with the provision that he could continue with his unorthodox management style, with his team "all holding hands and running together." In the months after the launch of *ATC*, the difference between Quayle's button-down demands and Siemering's vision of "organic radio" continued to widen the gap between them. Siemering complained, "I thought he hired me because he liked what I was doing back in Buffalo, but here I could never understand what he wanted."

And one day (in late fall of 1972), without warning, he was out of a job—and his wife had recently left him. He tried other work unsuccessfully until word from Kling called him to Minnesota a few months later. "Being fired hurt," Siemering confessed, "but it was good for me. Yes, I was angry, but much of the anger was internalized. I failed to see it coming. But it did me good; my hubris was gone, and with my new job with Kling, I can begin again, and improve."

Our conversation lasted a few hours. I asked few questions, just let him talk, partly because I was unprepared and partly because he had anticipated my interests. I was grateful for the opportunity to have an impromptu session with this great humanist and creative broadcaster who was driven to push the envelope of public radio as well as to get his interpretation of NPR politics. Little did I know that my fate at WGGL would parallel his demise.

◆ ◆ ◆

I returned to Washington, DC, for two months in the summer of 1974. Luckily, the previous year I had had those conversations with Siemering and Quayle, the two towering figures of the network's earliest days—both no longer worked there.

For this round of research, now more attuned to "palace politics," I needed to delve further into the stories of the original leaders involved in the planning. The first six were selected under CPB auspices as an advisory working board. They were largely from bigger, more established stations: Bill Kling (Collegeville, Minnesota), Karl Schmidt (Madison, Wisconsin), David Platts (Tallahassee, Florida), Joe Gwathmey (Austin, Texas), Bill Siemering (Buffalo, New York), and Jon Witherspoon (San Diego, California). They then elected three more representatives: Dick Estell (East Lansing, Michigan), Marin Segelman (Pacifica/North Hollywood, California), and Bernard Mayes (San Francisco, California). With their initial meeting in December 1969, the not-yet-incorporated NPR began to wean itself from its parental CPB and set out to expand on its own, though still guided by CPB's Al Hulsen and secretary Liz Young (who recorded all subsequent meetings).

Besides Liz, Dick Estell was my key source about the founders (he had helped guide me at WGGL and was willing to share his perspectives through conversations and correspondence as the research progressed). I learned that they were a loose-knit group eager to launch an alternative system of broadcasting but with disparate views about membership, content, format, and audience.

From December 1969 to March 1970, the group met monthly around the country to design the system. During their ad hoc meetings, they drafted bylaws and embraced Bill Siemering's vision statement, but their differences surfaced in the appointment of veteran public radio and television executive Don Quayle as the first president. Dick called the decision "a division between the old guard and the young Turks." A few of the group resigned, including the entrepreneurial Bill Kling (the youngest member who would soon create his own rival system). Those who remained, with additions, became the governing board of directors.

When I arrived at the NPR offices in June 1974, I could tell that staff morale had slipped and the clash of cultures was palpable. After three years at the helm, Quayle left NPR in July 1973 (soon after my first visit) to return to the CPB to focus on public television. During his tenure, Quayle had dismissed or shuffled key staff: besides Siemering, Robert Conley, the first on-air *ATC* host, had been let go, and Jack Mitchell, originally an *ATC* news announcer, had first moved into the role of *ATC* producer to give it a more predictable structure, then replaced Siemering as director of programming.

Lee Frischknecht, who lacked Quayle's geniality and public ease, had taken over as president, and the informal flow of staff in and out of each other's offices was less apparent. Consequently, I spent more time among the original cadre—Liz Young and Jack Mitchell—and among some of the new on-air specialists and rarely spoke with Frischknecht, who seemed more concerned with formalizing the functioning and structure of the organization.

New as I was to the investigative business, flying by "the seat of my pants," I enjoyed the private visits in staff offices and the relaxed conversations while they ate lunch or practiced tap dancing in their spare time and sitting in on informal group brainstorming and discussion sessions. It was an experiment in "free flow" investigation; I looked, listened attentively, and rarely introduced much of my own self—an unobtrusive but inquisitive eye, ear, and not much more to offer in trade for this exceptional introduction to an organization that was to hit the ground running during those early 1970s, to become a vital ear to world news as no standard commercial radio station ever could provide.

Though those on the programming side were carrying on Siemering's vision and *ATC* was gaining followers, there was a more orderly, corporate atmosphere and it was apparent that factions were forming. Feeling more restrained about reading files and never invited to attend departmental meetings, I still found enough inside information from staff members like Liz and Jack (and some of the newer members) to recognize the hints of approaching crises. When invited by Lloyd Anderson for dinner at his home in the Washington suburbs, he floated the possibility of my joining his team in the publicity area. I was flattered, but aghast at the idea of a daily two-hour commute and realized his overture was an effort to bring in someone to share his side of the pending troubles.

It seemed that Frischknecht's leadership had changed many things, beginning with his introduction of a manual dealing with internal policies and procedures. That, among financial problems, encouraged a group of the Programming Department to threaten to join a national union. Three key members of Quayle's original staff (Cleve Matthews, Liz Young, and Al Hulsen) resigned in July 1974, apparently due to the contrast of Quayle's relatively informal style—casual dress, first name addressing, open door meetings—and his successor's more rigid policies.

According to Liz, "I had been there for four years, solving the same problems until it became repetitive, no longer challenging ... no growth. Then there were so many things observed at NPR that needed solutions but weren't being attended to. Impasses create frustrations; it hurt to see them continue. And, finally, I wanted more aggressive leadership under which to work."

It was evident that the founders' era was over and the time frame for my dissertation should only cover the launch of the network through 1974. Those two summers witnessing the burgeoning of this innovative experiment in noncommercial broadcasting gave me a privileged view of the work of a dedicated group of pioneers and their admirable principles and commitment to the highest standards. Now, as the network marks its 50th anniversary, I appreciate their work more than ever (I still listen to NPR but am disappointed that it has been compromised into a quasi-commercial format and not lived up to the technical excellence of its origins).

Of course, the summer of 1974 was when the two-year-old Watergate scandal came to a head with President Nixon's resignation in early August. It occurred just a few days before I was due to head back to small town reality, putting a dramatic conclusion to my departure. News of this landmark event spread rapidly and the offices at NPR came alive with it.

Continuing Siemering's technique of pursuing the story not immediately as a unit but individually, the reporters spread out and then brought back building blocks for each day's broadcasts about the unfolding drama. I watched again in amazement as one new member of the news team remained behind, compiling past material on the president's life for background information, preparing a sort of farewell biography to be used once the ordeal had been concluded. Some of the others, tape recorders in hand, were rushing off to gather opinions from people in the street while another team was off to the Capitol for any breaking political news. It was gratifying to realize that the spirit of their original teacher had successfully imprinted the current cadre.

I felt like an outsider looking in, but time was moving me to my scheduled flight and it was with reluctance that I packed my luggage (including a duffel filled with reams of sheets and tapes of gathered information). My friend Kathy picked me up and filled me in from her political vantage point as she drove me to Dulles Airport and left me sitting in the waiting room, listening intently to the latest news on my portable radio which I'd set on the floor in front of me. It drew listeners who magnetically gathered around my seat with absorbing interest.

Without the use of the radio on the plane, I had plenty of time to lose myself, not in the current news, but with the realization that I had spent weeks in that unique city, soaking up more than sufficient material to create a story of my own. Settling into a comfortable state of mind, the drone of the plane lulled me into a retrospective of my own immersive experience in the politics of NPR. I felt enriched by the casualness of Susan, George, and Jack and all the rest who treated me with such friendliness in our meetings, who freely discussed a variety of historical and personal facets. I also felt endowed with responsibility—suddenly aware of the onus almost accidentally placed on me to be the first chronicler of this upstart communications enterprise.

Thoughts and images of my research adventure filled the hours in the air and interrupted my daily life for years following: experiencing the seedy side of Washington (having my car broken into the first summer and, later, narrowly escaping being mugged on my way back to my apartment); observing the eerie smog that colored the sky so oddly and made breathing so unpleasant; discovering the cultural pleasures hidden around the area, including the musical *Godspell* in Ford's Theatre (with a huge flag draped across the tragic booth as a reminder of where Lincoln was shot), a delightful stage version of *One Flew over the Cuckoo's Nest* on the Mall, an afternoon Brahms concert being played in honor of the Daughters of the Revolution (their white hair concealed by gentle shaking of their flowering hats); spending an afternoon at the huge zoo up from DuPont Circle to see the famed pandas; driving on Sundays to attend services at the Kennedy-funded cathedral (so wonderfully air-conditioned during the hot summer days)—none of these experiences, though, recorded by my camera (too dangerous!).

The first thing I did on arriving at home was to cart all the valuable research material (interview tapes, transcripts, meeting notes, copies of internal files plus recordings of the first two *ATC* programs) to our cottage on Lake Superior. I laid it all out in a row of boxes on our long table and settled down at one end, my faithful Smith Corona readied to start and stop, write and rewrite in an effort to fill pages with those experiences that began in 1971 as a manager of one of the NPR charter radio stations. It was not an easy task—where to start, how to fill in with pertinent details, what to include and what to omit—a job that I would tackle over the next several years in "spare" time.

Belonging to the NPR network was a feather in Tech's hat, with dozens of volunteer students working with us and with positive phone calls and letters filling our files. No serious problems occurred until the administration interfered, a result of the station being under the wing of a central, nonacademic office and our finances being managed by them.

In the spring of 1976, I had been told we had to include more women among the staff. In the works on the fifth-floor administration offices, a plan was in the offing: the opportunity to bring in a choice football coach with the understanding that his wife get work on campus ... well, why not send her to the station? I was told she had no background in broadcasting, but she was eager to try.

In fact, we were told we had to take on, not just one, but two women to satisfy the goals of the affirmative action program—and at least one needed to be a minority hire. So I went into zigzagging mode: after a call to Professor Stasheff, my favorite person in the U of M's Speech Department, I was guaranteed two graduates if they were willing. The two young women came up to inspect the area and the studio; they liked the latter but felt too isolated in "nowhere." In desperation, I brought them to our cottage for an overnight goodwill treatment, a fine restaurant meal, and pleasant talk about the richness of prospects for them. They bought it and started in fall 1976.

However, in the process, we sacrificed our most capable student, who was the part-time traffic coordinator. Gene Purdum was an exceptional physics student who also voluntarily hosted a popular classical music program, which he stretched from midnight to 6:00 a.m. When the position was changed to full time, he was passed over, with the excuse that he had no professional interest in radio and would use the degree to pursue a career in physics (or something like that). He quit, filed a complaint with the Michigan Civil Rights Commission, which ultimately ruled in his favor ... and after graduation, went on to work as a classical music radio announcer/ programmer at the Michigan State station in East Lansing, where he lasted for 40 years!

Unfortunately, my zigzagging scheme had mixed results. One of the women was an immediate hit on and off the air, while the other—a young African-American woman with minimal broadcasting experience—struggled as Gene's full-time successor in the "baggage room." In charge of our steadily growing materials from all over the world, she let packages pile up. Even more serious was her inability to fulfill the other critical part of the job: filling the recording shelf for each day's use. Imagine the announcer receiving an hour-long tape to fit into its normal half-hour slot!

What to do? I was already putting in over 90 hours a week including weekends to amend the growing problems; drastic measures were needed. I arranged a meeting of our immediate staff including the tech engineers, asked them what would happen if we simply went off the air for a day and night without explanation, during which time we'd all dive in and straighten out the mess. No problem, the tech crew assured me, though the entire group feared repercussions from the fifth-floor administration. I decided we had to take a chance. No other way out.

I immediately paid the consequences ... and discovered the behind-the-scenes machinations that had occurred during my absences at U of M and in Washington, DC: the acting station manager had been angling for my job and courting a fifth-floor administrator. I had been so focused on the programming, I had not cultivated allies at all levels to protect me.

It was a complete surprise when the next morning, I came into my office to find my immediate superior sitting primly—gloves, umbrella, and hat in lap—waiting for me. Tipped off by my contender, the administrator demanded to know why I was willing to destroy everything going for us so far. No sense in discussing it with him; he was infamous for being more interested in the packaging than the product, and now he wanted me out, putting me on paid leave of absence immediately and indefinitely.

I left the studio in a fury and, at home, through dreary late fall days, listened to the quality of programming slipping disastrously downhill. After three weeks (which seemed like three months), I couldn't take it any longer; I phoned President Smith and asked for a brief discussion. When I met him in his office, he was cold to me, felt I'd let him and the entire university down for trying to destroy the station. After I explained, he fired three questions at me and when I responded favorably, he leaned back and said, "Joe, now I understand where the blame belongs. Administratively, I cannot reprimand your superior; the only decision I have is to either fire you or place you somewhere else. What do you say?"

I told him though I felt the station was too fresh to leave without my oversight, I'd always wanted to return to the Humanities Department and teach again someday. It was final. The WGGL staffer's appointment as new station manager became official, and I was re-enrolled as a humanities faculty member, my ego shattered to next to zero.

17

Thriving in Academia

With the understanding of now Dean of Arts and Sciences Bill Powers (with whom I had shared admiration for writer William Faulkner) and Art Young, his successor as chair of the Humanities Department, it wasn't long before I bounced back. They were determined to build up the department and fully integrate it into the university's academic framework. And, they were very open to new types of courses. Using the syllabus for "History and Technology of Movies, 1900–Present" that had been previously rejected, Art gave me the approval to teach the class.

As an experiment, in spring 1977, it was initially offered as an evening class; the theme was comedy in film. To my surprise, Dean Powers dropped in, sat quietly in a rear seat, said nothing after my introduction, explanation of the course, and summary at the movie's conclusion. He just smiled his enigmatic smile and slipped away. I got the message; he was pleased.

For students, the idea of getting credit to watch movies was too much to ignore. We had to limit the class to 100 juniors and seniors only. Of course, when they found out they'd have to write a paper on each weekly film, several students opted to drop it. But it was deemed a success, and I got approval to continue teaching it in the fall.

Following the successful spring debut of my introductory film course, for the fall 1977 semester I used "generation issues" as the subject of the films being presented. For me, even more than for the students, the highlight of that class one day was a session with a special guest—famed screenwriter and playwright Dale Wasserman who was visiting Tech—when I showed John Ford's *The Grapes of Wrath*. We did an impromptu joint critique, and afterwards, I took him out to dinner. My theater and film knowledge impressed him (I had seen the original pre-Broadway production in New York of his *Man of La Mancha*, recently made into a film) and that conversation spawned a lively correspondence and a long-term friendship.

I then got the green light to teach a second, advanced course in which we studied the films of major directors (Fellini, Bergman, Kurosawa, and even Woody Allen). In addition to teaching film, my new project was organizing a Film Co-op of seven groups that sponsored screenings on campus—with me serving as coordinator and advisor. Plus, I took over the responsibility for running two weekend movie programs (Friday night, films for families and Sunday night, new foreign films, both features and documentaries). There was an immediate growth of audiences, with people traveling from as far away as Marquette. I finagled a plan, too, to do a second screening of the film being featured in my introductory class to allow anyone who could pay 50 cents to attend the Thursday matinee, which became popular. (That helped to cover growing rental costs.)

Success followed success, so in 1978, I dared propose a course in photography with the same mix of technical and creative aspects that had worked so well with the film courses. It took little to persuade Art and Dean Powers and their faith in me was borne out: the class immediately filled to its 30-student capacity, a real change for me from teaching over 100 students in the film courses!

From my earliest forays into photography as a young teen—whether biking to the lake with friends or posing them and relatives in the basement photo studio I had set up—I'd not just shoot, but felt obliged to teach, always explaining what and why I was doing so. At Camp Nebagamon, I'd honed my skills in teaching very young photographers (about the age I had started) the basics of shooting and developing black and white photos.

At the University of Iowa, I had learned so much from John Schulze about ways of developing photographic vision and talents. Through his tenure there, he had discovered how to teach, not so much by lecturing, but by encouraging his students with simple statements like, "A good photograph cannot be created out of ignorance or in a vacuum" or "Good art comes from creating something special out of the mundane," then allowing us to mull over his brief idea and go off to produce the week's work. He applied what he called the "Seven Steps of Photography," starting with the simple idea of capturing anything at a 50th of a second to seeing with a camera deeply, psychologically, into the making of a many-layered statement.

The question was: how to teach creative photography to students at Michigan Tech who, unlike the art students at the U of Iowa, were left-brained thinkers? Much as I wanted to utilize Schulze's subtle methods, I realized his approach had to be adapted for students who had such limited visual training and sensibility. Focusing first on the technical, then introducing the artistic aspect and constantly offering visual analysis became my strategies.

On the first day we played a game. I asked the students to raise one hand and imagine they planned to photograph it. How? Some murmurs, some wiggling of fingers, some manipulating the entire hand to resemble a fist, an "OK" sign, etc. They enjoyed it, so then I did the same with a folding chair on the desk: they found ways to shoot at a variety of angles, chair in various positions from folded closed to wide open and standing in different parts of the room. It was fun, but they were learning to really look at objects with a camera in mind.

To guide similar games as we progressed, I would fill in with introductory short lectures, each followed by a slideshow focusing on professional photos (and some of mine) to open their creative taps. Some adapted readily, others tried less successfully to forget technique to create something personal, from within; with a little coaxing, I could gradually work on students not normally permitted to ignore rules. In a few weeks' time, I was undoing years of training—a new, freeing experience.

Beginning with what makes a simple box camera work and moving on to understanding the complexities of 35mm cameras, I intermixed advanced experiments. For one session, I invited the university's photographer to come in and do hands-on experiments in portraiture. Another time a physics professor demonstrated the exciting potential of film manipulation during the developing process.

In turn, the students had weekly assignments as follow-up to the class presentations and lectures. Following Schulze's model, on weekends they were expected to shoot and develop their film in one of the many darkrooms on campus and bring their results to class on Mondays for "show and tell" (and, later, see me in personal consultation on their progress or lack of it). Time-consuming for me, yes, but worth it as I saw even the least adaptive student show improvement. Most of them enjoyed the freedom to grow with personal tastes, some improved more than others, and once in a while, a remarkable talent even appeared. (One of my favorite students eventually headed a team of photographers shooting for NASA!)

Once again, the only fly in the ointment was grading; assessing the creative results in photography was, to put it mildly, touchy. I decided to ask for a portfolio of at least five photos for a final assignment, which was still difficult, but less so after discussing it with the student in final consultation. Hard as I tried to solve the grading problem, I still noted the automatic "I got an A" or "He gave me a D" routine. Many sleepless nights became common before and after turning in the grades.

Approaching each new class in film or in photography was, despite the time spent on them, absolutely energizing. I even brought the more promising students on photo shoots around the Copper Country. And curiously, as they grew from my personal suggestions, so did I. For example, I asked the students one day to get closer to their subjects: examine, then photograph inanimate objects (such as barn wood, wet pebbles, blades of grass, scrap metal) and thus find a new world to shoot, up close. The results proved interesting, so I took the idea a step further and started shooting body parts up close—hands into fists, toes dug into wet sand, even ear lobes. When I entered a group of these experimental images into a local art exhibition, I was surprised to hear such comments as, "Why do you think a woman's private parts are decent subjects to photograph?" I looked at the picture being castigated and said with a chuckle, "Ma'am, that happens to be a man's armpit." Another reminder of the challenge for an artist to get the viewer to see anew....

◈◈◈

**Kirkish family cottage
at Copper Harbor**

**Reidar Hahn and Keith Meisel
"show and tell" photo session**

I often used our family cottage as a base for extracurricular excursions—a 24-hour excuse for photographing nature in its most vivid aspects: sunrises, sunsets, various approaches to the rocky beach, the huge craggy rocks rising out of the water, the changes in weather, the great lake as seen from endless angles, the physical environment along the shore shaped by wind and waves. In essence, an adventure in recording the wildness, beauty, and harshness that drew me back again and again.

After graduating from Tech, a few of my students, alone or with their families, would stop by at the cottage on summer vacations for a visit. During one such visit, Reidar Hahn and Keith Meisel, two favorite students from an advanced class in creative photography, arrived with their wives and, at my invitation, stayed for a meal and then overnight. They were delighted, returned each summer for years after, mutually enjoying photographic experiences along Lake Superior's endless natural beauty. Once, I asked them to bring some of their recent photos. Reidar arrived with beautiful, carefully studied images taken around the lake's environs, while Keith brought samples of exotic scenes from his travels around the world. I showed a group of black and white portraits and abstractions taken in Iowa under John Schulze's tutelage. It was a special "show-and-tell" enjoyed by all and one of my cherished cottage memories.

My attachment to the cottage had deepened since I began teaching at Tech. Soon after my parents' move to Florida, they contemplated selling it, but I negotiated a plan to pay them a monthly fee from my salary, with the idea that I would eventually own it. From the 1960s onwards, they spent most of the summer in residence at the cottage, with children and grandchildren from near and far coming and going. When relatives came during the summers, they pitched in with everything while enjoying sunbathing, playing on the beach, and exploring the wooded area.

My parents became accustomed to my bringing Tech students and colleagues, friends from Camp Nebagamon visiting the area, and others out for weekends, always welcoming them warmly. From the earliest days, when my father used the place each fall as a "hunting lodge," bringing friends to settle in for a few days of hunting or fishing, it became my mother's task to oblige them as guests, feeding and bedding them accordingly. No matter who the visitors were, their Lebanese hospitality was on perennial display.

My most unexpected guests were the Beachys, the Amish family I had met while I was at the U of Iowa. They hired a man to drive them up to Copper Country early one fall so they could see Lake Superior, which I had earlier described to them. I received a pencil-written note that they'd drop in the following Thursday. However, they arrived a day before, while I was working in a school darkroom. A fellow called me with the news: "There's a strange bunch of people in your apartment waiting for you!" I shot from the darkroom, ran the few blocks to my place, saw a stripped-down Cadillac in the back (permitted for long trips), rushed up to my second-floor apartment, smelled food cooking from inside (I had told them to make themselves comfortable if I was not there, so Mother Martha Beachy had busied herself making a large pot of stew for our evening meal). No special greetings, we just piled into my car, pot and all, and I gave them a narrated tour en route to the cottage.

They settled in and immediately went down to the lakeshore to walk on the beach while the two children threw pebbles into the water. As we gathered for dinner to eat the stew and other dishes Mother Beachy had also prepared in our cottage kitchen, noticing it was getting dark, I rose to turn on the lights. Father Glenn Beachy smiled and pointed to an oil lamp on the fireplace mantle, saying, "That would be nicer." Of course, by their religious belief, life was basic and anything exceptional would be a sin. So, I lit the lamp, we joined hands as Glenn offered a five-minute prayer meant for all of us, and we enjoyed a hearty, delicious but simple meal.

While they did marvel at the sight of the rocks and waves, the two youngsters were as excited by the prospect of taking a shower. In fact, they each took 15-minute showers that night. The next morning, on being reminded that God loves those who are clean, Glenn allowed the two to use the shower again, this time for half an hour each. After a hearty farm-style breakfast, back we went to Houghton, and then they departed.

There's a coda to this experience: in the late '70s, I took a carload of my most promising photo students to a national photography convention in Iowa City. They were excited to participate in the events and lectures, and it gave me the opportunity to see John Schulze again, plus make a short surprise visit to the Beachys. The students were also eager to accompany me, but I imposed one condition: No Cameras! When I stopped to ask a young Amish woman walking on the road for directions to their farm, one of the students tried to sneak a photo of her from the window. Frightened, she whirled around, concealing her face in her black bonnet. I shouted, "Jim, stop it!" He backed sheepishly into the car while I calmed the woman down with an apology, and we continued on to our destination.

I found their farmhouse and saw buggies lined up outside. I made the students stay outside and entered, calling out, "Anybody home?" A moment of silence. Then, an amazed woman's voice from another room: "*That's Joe Kirkish!*" A lump rose in my throat, after nearly a decade without contact....

Mother Beachy rushed into the room, leaving a group of women staring out in amazement. Impulsively, I threw my arms around my old friend; she froze, I pulled back instantly, and cried a huge hello. She relaxed, explained that her son, now 19, was soon to be married, so the men were all down the other side of the hill, digging a basement for Little Joe's future home.

As the group came back up for their meal, yet another pictorial—and unphotographable—tableau formed: the bearded men eating at the long, rustic table, listening curiously while Little Joe elaborately described their excursion to the Upper Peninsula, and, behind us the students, staring in quiet awe at the scene unfolding before them.

Our afternoon excursion was an Uncle Wiggily adventure we'd all carry in our memories for years later, but first capped in the car as we drove back to Houghton, giving me the perfect opportunity to offer an educational lecture on documentary ethics.

18

A Home and a Hostel on College Avenue

B oth when my parents were there and when I hosted visitors, spending time at the cottage was a chance for me to share my "place of the heart" and to let people see another side of me. The cramped quarters at the McGintys did not allow me to entertain, so the cottage allowed that opportunity. Indeed, Professor Roman—who came on occasion to visit me at the McGintys—would often comment that I needed a more spacious place in town befitting a professor.

After his wife's death, Professor Roman and I became closer friends. We had pleasant times together, driving around the beautiful Copper Country, enjoying the changes in seasons; he would sit in the car while I'd get out to photograph. I returned to the car one time, caught him with head bent, fingers linked beneath his chin, in abject thought. He was forever in mourning, never wearing anything but gray or black. (Before I realized why, I innocently bought a nice red scarf as a gift; he politely thanked me, put it in his closet and never wore it.)

He did take a class in watercolor painting and spent most of his time painting scenes of oak and maple trees that dotted the cemetery, always carefully, precisely drawn. When his teacher planned a show of the class's work, she reminded him to invite his friends to see them. His response: "I'm sorry, I have only one friend now." When she told me this, I felt an immediate touch of reality, a hint of what he was silently going through and an onus for me.

We rarely went anywhere for public entertainment (now and then, a concert or lecture), but we continued to attend Sunday Mass together at St. Ignatius, after which we would have brunch at our favorite restaurant (which he preferred for its sumptuous buffet). However, I could see he was slowly aging, ill with something internal, and ever the gentleman, never discussing it.

One time, he admitted his birthday was coming, his 84th, as I recall. Would I like to celebrate with him? We went to a special restaurant, had a nice meal with a bottle of fine red wine. We lifted our glasses and he said, "*na zdrowie!*" as we linked arms and drank. I took a chance. I asked, "Now, Professor Roman, we are true friends. Would you call me by my first name instead of '*pan profesor*' and allow me to call you Jerzy?" He looked up at me and, without a smile, said gently but firmly, "I think not." That settled it. He was forever a superior Pole, of high descent, and I, just a common American.

Throughout our friendship, he found every opportunity to remind me of my commitment to get my PhD. The reason, I believe, was partly to compensate for his never having completed his work on his own doctoral degree, yet another sad result of interruptions in his life during the war. I would compensate for it. Finally, one day

Professor Roman

when I found him in bed with the flu, I promised him that if he took better care of himself and grew well again, I'd seriously start work on the dissertation. He improved readily, and I kept my promise.

When I finally attacked the dissertation with earnest resolve, I ran into the next roadblock: an ongoing intellectual battle with Professor Willis, my U of M faculty advisor. From 1975–79, he endlessly made clear what was substandard—namely, my interest in documenting the human story/narrative of the drama of the founding and early years of NPR—and demanded a dry, institutional history. I wanted my dissertation to be more than the pedantic studies that had been produced under his direction, and I had gotten positive feedback from Bill Siemering and others from NPR, with whom I had shared some early chapters. We clashed about style from the title ("A Descriptive History of the first American Public Radio Network: National Public Radio, 1970–74") to the choice of words in the text and footnotes. (Recently, I discovered a box with three different drafts of it.) In the end, I decided to surrender and just labored to get the project finally completed on his terms.

During those years, I still tried to steal away some time for a short visit to Camp Nebagamon each August at the end of the season. It was so important for me to stay connected with Nardie and Sally, and the visits with parents at Family Camp drew me magnetically back. Regretfully, though, when CN organized its 50th anniversary celebration in 1979, in large part because of a "command performance" in Ann Arbor with Professor Willis, I had to forego participating.

To my great regret, Professor Roman did not live to see completion of my dissertation. In April 1979, he had a massive stroke. On Palm Sunday, I had a call from a lady living across the street from him, telling me something was wrong; he'd gone out to the car in the garage, opened the door, but remained half in, half out. She called an ambulance to take him to the hospital. I followed, sensing uncomfortably a repeat of the previous event when his wife died.

There he was, eyes open but not seeing, mouth open but not speaking, hands trying to grasp at something but not succeeding. When a nurse came to tend to him, he came to attention for a moment and weakly, gesturing to her, mumbled, "My angel," then fell back again. The doctor explained that the stroke could take him at any moment. Did I want him on appropriate machines to remain alive as long as possible in his current condition? I said, "No, he wants to be with his wife. Let him go naturally."

And he did. I spent each night after classes with him, cooling his brow with wet cloths, dabbing his lips with flavored water. One night, just before Easter, I drove home on a crisp spring night, was about to fall asleep, when the phone rang. It was a hospital attendant telling me the end had been reached. I started to say, automatically, "Oh, I'm sorry," and then stopped myself. "Thank you," I said, "He's happy now."

As I mourned the death of my dear friend, I was obliged to suffer through the burial process ... with his niece Zofia at my side. (She had arrived just over 24 hours after my call to her at the Italian convent where she served as a driver for the nuns.) As usual, the casket was open for a last visit. Zofia whispered to me that the ring on his hand, tightly held by the flesh of his finger, was an heirloom to be passed on to her brother. I told the person in charge about it; he understood. Just moments after the casket had been closed and moved to another room, he returned with the ring. I turned it over to Zofia, trying to evade how it was removed so readily.

Zofia stayed for several days at the Roman residence. I spent time with her and two local nuns who busily cleaned the house from attic to basement. Besides locating heirlooms that she intended to return to the family in Poland, she pored over a great stack of letters written in Polish, to and from the family over the years. She broke into silent tears as she read about herself being mentioned at length, from early childhood to her entry into a convent. She then picked up the stack, brought them to the basement, and burned them in a small stove connected to the chimney.

She also found a container with a full set of handcrafted silverware, another family treasure. "That must be returned," she declared calmly, closed it, and carried it with her to the airport (so heavy it caused her to lean to one side as she lugged it aboard).

A week after her departure, I heard from the professor's lawyer. "I have the will; come to my office at 7:00 p.m. tonight and we'll go over it together." He sounded brusque, business-like. I met him, uncomfortably, wondering what final business was yet at hand. He read the will to me—the first 12 articles largely being the personal things Zofia had already taken with her. Then he came to number 13, looked up at me intently and read: I was to receive the ownership of the house and property intact, including everything left in it.

As if hit by a blow, I fell back, speechless. Something arose in my throat. Tears came to my eyes. I tried to hold back. The lawyer politely went to the door, saying he would bring some coffee, but I had the feeling he was listening from outside the door as I put my forehead on the table and audibly cried. I don't know for how long, but the lawyer re-entered, obviously having heard me, sat down with a gentle look and said, "I wondered who this fellow was and what he did to get such a gift. Now I know." And he sent me home with a copy of the will in hand (which remains still in a drawer of his desk in what used to be Professor Roman's upstairs office). I don't recall much after that; I returned to my apartment and found sleep difficult.

I needed to wait awhile before being able to set foot in my future home on College Avenue. The gift still seemed an overwhelming thing to accept. Zofia wrote to let me know that I was chosen at the advice of family members, who knew Professor Roman and his wife would rest better, knowing who was living there. Then one day a former student came to town, dropped by, and wondered if I could put him up for the night. That was my signal. Key in hand, we walked the block to what I still thought of as Professor Roman's home, settled the fellow into what obviously had been their bedroom, and I slept in the guest room opposite. It was a strange, rather unsettling new experience, but slowly, over the following weeks, I moved in. I began bringing my belongings over from the apartment and arranging them as best I could, blending the previous furnishings with mine.

I had only been upstairs in the home once, when Professor Roman was ill, so I took time to examine the place from attic to basement—amazed as objects began to enlarge my view of the lives of these two aristocratic people adjusting to living in a country (which Mrs. Roman embraced for its sense of new freedom, while her husband, always the self-declared snob, found extremely difficult). In the attic, in old-fashioned travel chests, there were white starched suits from India, along with other summer clothing and artifacts. There I discovered a few matted black and white photos of their wedding, taken in a room with a huge tapestry filling the wall. The men were in formal dress of the late '30s, the women in full-length black satin gowns with great puffed sleeves; on the oriental rug in front of them were dozens of vases filled with what appeared to be hundreds of roses. A royal wedding!

On the second floor was a small room at the top of the stairs which had been the "sick room" where Professor Roman lay whenever he was too ill to use his own bedroom, phone next to it. Beyond it, to the right, a door opening onto a small porch, while straight ahead, the bathroom and beyond it, a large office with a grand carved desk, surrounded by shelves of books and writing materials. (Later, on closer examination, I found a row of metal containers filled with newly minted quarters and half dollars, and a British cigarette box that contained various sized rubies in the rough, a souvenir from their stay in India.)

Next, down the hall, their bedroom: twin beds, his side neat and clean; hers untouched since her death, dusty, with women's things on the dresser, including a hairbrush embedded with her gray hair. A chill ran through me as I thought of his adoration, to never touch that side of the room where they'd slept side by side over the years. Across the hall was another large bedroom (that I decided to appropriate) with a walk-in closet filled with Mrs. Roman's wardrobe, including formal clothes, dresses, jackets, sweaters, and rows of slippers. There was also a dresser filled with the professor's clothing accessories.

I saved a few items—ties, handkerchiefs to remind me of them—and piled everything else into the car and took them to the Vishnevski family in nearby Painesdale, who were grateful for the unexpected largesse. I also removed coats and hats for them from the downstairs hall closet. Imagine my surprise when I found the red wool scarf that my good friend had accepted politely, then laid to rest on a shelf above all the other black or gray things. Tucked back in the rear was his carved wooden walking stick (which I occasionally now use when my legs need the support).

The basement was spacious, with the usual washer, tubs,

furnace, line after metal line for hanging clothes in the winter (a complement to the attic where other lines hung for summer drying, along with a maid's room, complete with dresser, sink, toilet, and bed). One day a strange thing happened when I was down there rearranging things: I heard, above me, heavy footsteps leading from the front door across the hallway to the kitchen. "I'm down here," I called. Silence. I went upstairs to find no one. Was I imagining things? The same sound was repeated a few more times, always when I was alone in the basement. Then one day, when a student and I were making space for some of his things to be left over the summer, I went to Jim's Foodmart down the street, saying I'd be right back with sandwich meats. When I returned, he asked if I had a very large dog upstairs. "No," I replied. "Why?" "Well," he said, "while you were gone, I thought I heard some heavy critter walking from the front door to the kitchen. I called and no one answered."

Aha! I hadn't been imagining it after all! Professor Roman, I decided, was simply reluctant to leave yet. I was a bit regretful when the footsteps eventually ceased, but what I thought was talk between "Boretchku" and "Yagenka" did haunt the upstairs now and then—very softly and very gently. It was comforting to have them still around, however faintly.

What a shift for me from a modest apartment to the exposure of so many memories and this opulence! What would I do with it all? Well, a teacher can always use shelves, drawers, and cupboards for academic collectibles, but what else? With all the extra space, why not rent out the third-floor bedroom to a student, to help with home expenses and to have some company at the same time. I set about to do it.

❖❖❖

The spring of 1980 was the target to "get the monkey off my back." My dissertation defense was scheduled for late in May, after the end of the spring semester at Tech. I arranged to lodge for a few weeks with Mrs. Haven while I prepared. On the appointed day in late May, I met the faculty committee from the Communications Department late in the afternoon in an empty office building. Obviously disinterested and ready to finish me off as quickly and formally as possible, they rifled through the pages of my dissertation, stopping here and there to make some prodigious comment or ask some prodigious question, which I answered with equally prodigious replies. They made an occasional mention of some minor typo, then piled the manuscripts for me to take back to the grad school office and stood to leave.

As the committee members shook hands with me and offered half-hearted congratulations for achieving the doctorate, they left me in the room with Willis, whose parting words were, "Please shut the lights when you leave" before heading home, I presumed, for his delayed dinner.

"Is that all?" were the words uttered afterwards by Donald Dixon (a former Tech student who lived in the Ann Arbor area) who had requested to sit in on the final defense. I left the building for the last time, accompanied Donald to his car, expressed my appreciation for his coming to witness the supposed pinnacle of academic achievements which, I had to admit, as I headed back to Mrs. Haven's, was a pyrrhic victory—a mechanically rewritten thesis, and severely trimmed to suit my professor's stringent instructions. I consoled myself, riding my bicycle with its sidesaddles filled with the remains to be turned over to the proper office in the morning, that I had fulfilled the former Michigan Tech dean's demands that I needed to prove that I could do it. Despite the "not with a bang but a whimper" conclusion, I was nevertheless suddenly uplifted and relieved that it was over, and I could return to the university and go full steam without that arduous caboose following me.

The next day, as I began the slow packing, Mrs. Haven walked with me to the car door. In her arms was a pail with a beautifully shaped blue spruce from her yard, hardly a foot in height; it was her farewell gift for what she called "a job well done" along with her good wishes for the future. Back inside, she gave me a second surprise. Since I still had a few more days to settle final details, Mrs. Haven went to her closet underneath the stairs, drew the drapes to expose three sumptuous fur coats which she rarely wore in public, drew out the leopard skin full length beauty and, putting it on with a wicked grin, said, "No home cooked meal, Joe; we're going to celebrate tonight."

Aha! That accounted for her powdered face, carefully braided hair, and dress underneath the apron she took off. As she held out my coat for me, she slyly slipped a large bill into its pocket, saying, "And that's all. I don't want any change left over, either."

She chose to drive in her heavy-peddled jerky manner (never over 40 mph on the highway to an exceptionally fine restaurant in nearby Canton) and we had a grand farewell meal. Mrs. Haven actually beamed with pride and even picked up her speed by five mph on our drive back.

After one last sleep in that odd, rock-covered little building, I took off early with the tree firmly packed along with my bicycle, a stuffed duffel, and sundry other things, waving farewell to a grinning, aproned landlady. I arrived in Houghton nine hours later, not needing to stop for food along the way, thanks to a full basket with three meals at my side.

It was only during the drive that my mind wandered through time and space, until something suddenly appeared: a vision of my wonderful Professor Roman, now dead and joined with his beloved wife, who would never be in his College Avenue home again, waiting to toast me with his customary "*na zdrowie!*" in celebration of the conclusion of his fondest dream, that I get the degree and title he felt I deserved. It would have been the acme celebration, I thought, ruefully, and yet it was possible that he WAS celebrating somewhere, somehow. That thought opened the floodgates of a tearful memory.

On my return, I planted Mrs. Haven's blue spruce on the side of my home, where I could see it from my windows, making sure to space it comfortably far enough from the house to avoid roots and branches from encroaching the house. That was a long time ago; the tree grew to a magnificent height of 30 feet and continued until a friend from the Forestry Department called my attention to signs of old age and suggested strongly that I cut it down. He performed the operation in my absence (I couldn't handle it) and had it cut into a beautiful pile of firewood. I gave it to him and he accepted it joyfully. Now all that remains of that kind gift is a permanent shadow along the side of the house. I'll never paint over it.

◈ ◈ ◈

Through the months of settling into the house on College Avenue, I had become accustomed to having a student in residence on the third floor, but then decided that rather than rent out a room, I would turn the Romans' second-floor bedroom into a respite space. This turned out to be one of the finest decisions I ever made.

As a longtime advisor to the Phi Kappa Tau fraternity, located three miles from campus, I knew that it was difficult, especially during winter nights, for late returning students to get back to their house. (Not everyone had a car in those days.) I rearranged the bedroom into a comfortable space with a single twin bed for overnight stays and hung a sign above the door welcoming users. I let students know that the "Phi Tau Room" was available anytime they needed it—in bad weather or just for a private night of study before a test. It was to be a B&B overnight with a breakfast of their desire, small or sumptuous. Rule: only one person a night (though on occasion the sick room was also used if two arrived) and with the understanding that they would be guaranteed full privacy unless for some reason they wished to break into my evenings of correcting papers downstairs in the sitting room for a late-night snack and talk.

The room saw frequent use after I contacted both Mu Beta Psi, the other co-ed fraternity I was advising, and the dean of students about its availability, and reasons for its use went beyond just a quiet place to study, to a secure place to unload personal issues to a welcome ear. Those nights back in New York sitting on the floor listening to Tallie and providing counsel would prove useful.

Example: the dean sent a young freshman who had experienced a horrible tragedy during the Christmas break. Walking along a street with a friend, his companion had been struck by a car, killed instantly in front of him. He'd returned to school but was suffering emotionally, as one might expect. He came to the door, small suitcase in hand, and timidly thanked me for getting him away from the dorm. I did the usual: brought him upstairs, showed him the bathroom with a special rack of towels, took him to his room, showed him a dresser filled with clothes and underclothes of all sizes (thanks to St. Vincent's) which he could use after showering, told him he was invited for an evening drink and snack around 10:00 p.m. with me, and would have breakfast ready for him in time to leave for class.

He took up my offer of extra hospitality. While I pored over papers that first night, I heard him padding down the stairs; he came in and stood expectantly in front of me, in floppy slippers and woolly pajamas with little creatures printed all over them and asked if he could talk to me. Of course. I pushed out the hassock, he sat on it, and for an hour, out poured all the bile of memory from that tragic day—everything he'd withheld from his parents—until he was spent, then returned to his room. The next morning, he asked if he could return again that night. Of course, I permitted up to four nights, my usual extension. So he returned the next three nights, and by the time he left with his little suitcase in hand, we were friends; I saw him frequently after that.

An even more intimate example of my "open door policy" happened when I had a tearful phone call late one evening from a student who lived a few blocks away. As usual, without turning on lights (the light coming in from two windows brought plenty of soft light from the avenue), I pulled out the "analyst's" red-painted, three-legged chair near the bed, and waited. He came upstairs, a dejected mess. His girlfriend had announced she was leaving him and then took off on a motorcycle with her new boyfriend. He was desperate. He moved to my bed, sat near me, alternately blubbering and describing his feelings. I said nothing. Finally, reduced to a quiet mourning, he took off his clothes and slipped into bed with me, folding in like a baby into my arms and silently falling into a child's exhausted sleep. Next day, after a hearty pancake breakfast, he was off to class; to him, I remained a sheltering, parental presence. Two years after he'd graduated I received a letter telling me of his marriage and a photo of him—with that perpetually morose expression—and a baby couched in his arms. Happy ending.

One final example: I was sound asleep, having politely refused to attend a party with the co-ed music fraternity, knowing that they usually resulted in heavy drinking and dancing, and sometimes drug use. Suddenly, about one in the morning, I awoke with someone tweaking my big toe! And a little giggle! It was one of the young women from the party. She sobered quickly and tearfully told me that her husband had created a row when she danced with others at the party, neglecting him. In a huff, she left, drove to my place, and asked if the Phi Tau Room was available. Of course, but I suggested she call her husband first, tell him she was there, and ask him to come for breakfast so the three of us could discuss the situation. She did. He did. We had a good meal together, and they left as happy as newlyweds.

Eventually, some of the Phi Tau alumni might arrange to stay. It was always a pleasure for me, a chance to get to know them better. One such student, Marty Schendel (from the Detroit area), had been an occasional guest during his Tech years and then, after graduation, returned frequently. I liked Marty and was impressed by his group interaction: he would sit silently during meetings and speak only when he could offer some intelligent comment or suggestion. He had a younger brother (not a fraternity member) who also would appear, on occasion, ready to have a night away from dorm life. Separately, I got to know them, observing typical sibling differences: Marty, the somber Senecan and David, the happy-go-lucky teddy bear. Their mother and father occasionally stayed with me, too; I felt I had a family again.

Even after Marty became CEO of his own metallurgy business, he arranged time to visit me (and the fraternity) for any special event. Always the same routine: drive overnight, park at about 3:00 a.m., come quietly in, shower, and fall into bed. In the morning, I'd make breakfast and we'd catch up on his reason for returning, then not see him again until breakfast his last day, when we'd chat before he headed back to Detroit.

Marty Schendel

But there were wonderful moments when Marty had enough time for an overnight at the cottage, which also followed a pattern: stopping at special places for grand views of Lake Superior, always reaching the cottage for a round of sunset photos, a quick meal with wine, and off to sleep until time to shoot the sunrise the next morning, and then back. It became a ritual we both enjoyed tremendously, giving us time to explore our friendship—I a father surrogate and he the kid brother I never really knew—and has continued through his two marriages and a few grandchildren to this day.

As Professor Roman had envisioned with the bequest of their house, the ample dining room allowed me at last to entertain and host occasional faculty gatherings—and unexpectedly, opened a whole new world of community volunteer activity for me. While on a shopping run for a nice big ham (from a specialty butcher in Hancock) for a small Thanksgiving party with colleagues in 1983, I was listening to a local station on the car radio. On came a plaintive voice, pleading listeners to give whatever we could to Little Brothers-Friends of the Elderly. Impulsively, I switched lanes and drove a few blocks to the address given, found a little house just off the highway, opened the door and ran in—ham tucked under one arm, the other straight out like a football player, and shouted to the startled lady at a desk, "Quick! Take it before I change my mind!" And back out again to find no more hams available. I bought a large chicken, brought it home and served it cooked with enough side dishes to create a tasty substitute.

They called to thank me; I asked questions about Little Brothers and was so impressed that I offered my services. What a history! The original organization was founded in 1948 in France by a compassionate Armand Marquiset, a nobleman who wanted to serve isolated and lonely elderly people who had lost their families in the war. He wished to reach out to the elderly with informal dinners, home visits, and a large supply of compassion.

"The greatest poverty," he said, "is the poverty of love," which became reflected in the motto he attached to his organization: "Flowers before Bread." His example attracted many followers in

France and ultimately across eight countries, finally to seven U.S. cities, of which our locale became one.

Ours began by Mike Aten and his wife, Cathy, a warm-hearted couple inspired by Marquiset's generosity and aware that our community had many elderly people, some living alone in their original homesteads, who needed the same love and aid as those in France. They turned the main floor of their modest home into office space, made the second floor their living quarters, and in 1982 officially joined "Les Petits Frères des Pauvres."

First simply giving a ham, then money, then volunteering at the holiday meals (and driving people there) and, later, volunteering to take them to the doctors, the hospital, or anywhere else when necessary, I became a Little Brothers stalwart. I began visiting these senior citizens in their homes, which ranged from old farmhouses to what easily could be called hovels where I was always repaid with gratitude (and sometimes with an invitation to enjoy an hour in a homemade sauna). And for the community holiday meals at Thanksgiving, Christmas, and Easter—often serving hundreds of local and rural elderly with high rates of poverty and lack of family support—there was always a rose set before each place.

Who would have imagined that the donation of a holiday ham could bestow on me so much joy and satisfaction for years to come? Maybe my father....

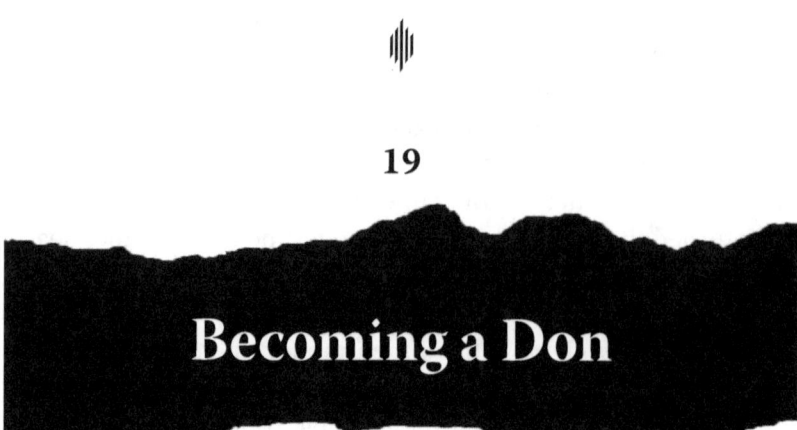

19

Becoming a Don

From my earliest years at Tech, when the Humanities Department was tucked into the Denton House on the far west side of the campus, it was evident that our small but burgeoning department was far from favored either by those who enlisted at MCMT (Michigan College of Mining and Technology) or from the institutional leaders in the administration building. With its transformation into Michigan Technological University, the department grew but remained a secondary academic department, so we were continually being assigned to temporary quarters in buildings around the campus. I must admit, despite the often improvised teaching facilities, that each relocation offered interesting excursions into components of the university I'd never otherwise experience—huge spaces with still more huge machinery in the mining building, silent neighbors in the buildings for teaching classes in mathematics, etc.

Our itinerant situation continued into the '80s, when the scuttlebutt told us that the massive old Sherman Gym, with a swimming pool in the basement and three spacious levels above, was already being gutted and redesigned to house both the Humanities and the Visual and Performing Arts Departments. A real milestone, and the fruition of the vision of Dean of Arts and Sciences Bill Powers for a dedicated facility! I was, of course, delighted when Humanities Department Chair Art Young asked me to design the spaces for my classes in creative photography, which included a "light" room and a "dark" room (though not large, certainly a great improvement over the previous practice of students scrambling around the campus to process film).

Once construction was complete in 1985 for the Walker Arts and Humanities Center, I moved into a fine office on the main floor with windows looking out across the campus, spaciously filled with a new desk, some chairs, a hat rack, and enough shelves for a ton of reading materials. And it was located just down the hall from the darkroom.

My teaching success and my seniority, plus, attaining my PhD at last, had earned me special status. Art, along with Dean Powers, seemed to favor me, allowing me to use my effusive energy and to advance into any area that might somehow garner credit to the department or enhance my own artistic or academic work. For the first time, I was asked if I would like to add classes in Radio Production and Announcing, which of course I was more than ready to take on. Approval also came readily, whether for conference travel or purchase of additional equipment for the photography and film courses (which continued to gain in popularity).

Only much later did I discover the underlying reason for my good fortune: both Powers and Young were actively building the national profile of the department (and became recognized for an innovative program called "Writing Across the Curriculum"). They favored me in so many ways that I actually believed that I had become a respected don. As the senior member of the department, I found myself a well to tap among younger faculty (now teaching and tutoring students in various types of writing and communication classes). Bright students came to me frequently in my accessible office for guidance, both academic and personal.

❖ ❖ ❖

With the PhD done, I could devote more time to my sideline photographic career. Ever since John Schulze had opened my eyes to the creative side of photography, I had experimented with the possibilities of visual manipulation, using techniques like double exposure, overlaying negatives to produce surreal or otherworldly effects, and printing on acetate. Most of this work was done with portraits, but my wandering eye often drew me to inanimate objects, large and small, be it a Ferris wheel or a doorknob. And after having those two photos—part of a glistening red snowplow edge and an overlay of people on a Ferris wheel against a roaring wave—published back in the late '60s in *Popular Photography*, I knew that abstractions were where I should keep exploring and pushing the possibilities of the medium.

I could leap from one idea to another, play with it until my interest waned, then turn to another. And sometimes, I would revisit an earlier subject with new insight; my mind always operates on multiple planes with piles and piles of visual memories just waiting to be tapped when needed. One of my most successful "aha" ideas occurred one day in the early '80s on a drive to Escanaba, Michigan, for a photo lecture (something I did with pleasure, often). On the way, at a crossroad, I noticed a field filled with snowplows waiting for winter to be useful again—colorful, sharp-edged wings that changed by walking around them and moving in closely or farther out. My heart actually pounded as I moved from one plow to another; just too much to take in, until the roll of color slide film reached 36, and I was done.

When the film returned, processed into slides, the results were almost too beautiful to be mine. I then started playing around with superimposing the images and getting test prints developed at a photo lab out in Washington—an experiment that also produced exciting results. So, I scouted out an array of weathered snowplows in a nearby field in Hancock, plus used my road trips to and from Camp Nebagamon (200 miles into Wisconsin) to scan the countryside for abstract sculptural forms and accidental juxtapositions. Cast-off furniture leaning in backyards, ornate doors, carved slats— all awakened my interest. Even at the camp, while concentrating on people as my primary focus, I began to notice aged barn wood, obsolete tools and implements and shot them for my personal pleasure.

I debuted the new series at my first major solo show in April 1983, in faraway Boston. As so often had happened before, an unsolicited opportunity thrust me into the limelight, and once again I benefitted from the special interest of someone who knew my work. Steve Bearden (a former member of the Phi Tau fraternity and now a successful entrepreneur living and working in Boston) organized and sponsored a large show at the Arlington Street Gallery on the University of Massachusetts campus. Besides the suite of large prints (20" × 30") from the snowplow series were another unexhibited recent series of black and white photos of the Larry Richardson Dance Company plus a mix of older overlaid portraits and other subjects—99 photographs, which Steve himself matted, framed, and hung. I found out later that he had also painted all four walls of the gallery!

Larry Richardson—"Dancer Posing As If Touched by Sunlight"

Opening night was a first for me in many ways. The gallery was positioned directly across from a well-known, fashionable nightclub; watching well-dressed patrons entering and leaving provided a fascinating sideshow. One of them came over to the gallery, stood first in the doorway, hands on elegant hips, and surveyed the line of abstractions. She walked over to one of the snowplow photographs and, without checking the price, went directly to the desk and wrote out a check, saying, "Send it to me at this address," and left, a smile of success on her face. The first purchase of the evening had happened in less than a minute.

Meeting and greeting people who had come expressly to see my show was even more exciting (Steve had designed a very striking invitation using one of the snowplow images). A surprise visit from Debbie Dorman, a good friend and artist from Houghton, who appeared without previous mention, helped me relax, as did the equally unexpected appearance of members of the Geismer family—Alan Jr and his wife, Susie (who lived in Boston), plus Bobbie visiting from Shaker Heights and Meg from Vermont. Then, at a special grand dinner event afterwards that Steve hosted, the accolades continued.

One disappointment marred the excitement of having my work recognized: Steve had arranged for the art critic of the *Christian Science Monitor* to get a private tour of the show the next day, but an error on the part of the gallery staff blocked his visit and thus, no chance to learn how a professional critic would assess my work. Still, at the close of the show, we glowed in the fact that, as the director of the gallery announced, she sold more of my work than any previous photographic exhibition. The leftover prints were agreeably divided between Steve (first choice, of course) and me; I still have some stacked in my photo workroom, visions of a happy, wonderful, but brief, time in the spotlight.

Another very different kind of event in Minneapolis in 1985 gave me an even deeper sense of pride for my accomplishments in the world of fine art photography: an invitation to be a part of a weekend farewell celebration of the now famous John Schulze with many of his protégés. Me included? I was surprised he'd even remember me. But he did, greeting me heartily when I found him at the hotel where the celebration was to take place—charm radiating as ever, but he seemed older, a bit tired. (We never knew his age, just that he always had white hair with only slight indications of age showing in his features.)

The day began in the dark ballroom, with the 200 invited photographers in attendance, each having been asked to bring two slides to show. One by one they were displayed on the huge screen, revealing an amazing variety of work. Silence throughout, until my two photos came up: a distorted shroud and an abstract. Murmurs of admiration rippled through the group, then fell to silence again as the remainder of the photos were shown. I was both surprised and elated by the experience, which extended into the next day when John gathered about 30 of us for a special lunch together. Again, I was amazed by the group, all now famous in one way or another.

I sat next to a young Chinese woman who was making a name for herself in Asian-themed abstractions. She lit up when she realized it was I who'd created the murmurs at the group showing and spent some time asking questions! As we became acquainted with the others, we understood that this was John's most prized group of disciples—collectively, we were his legacy.

I'd brought a framed shroud photo for him as a farewell gift; he took it, ran his fingers over it and chuckled, just as he had done all those years ago at the U of Iowa to acknowledge artistic success. That was the last time I ever saw or heard from him again, except for a brief note of thanks in his familiar scrawl.

John had never showed us any of his work, so I bought a paperback copy of a retrospective collection of his photographs. He had trained as a painter, then switched to photography, but to my shock, the images lacked originality. I found it hard to accept as coming from this remarkable man, touted as the greatest photography teacher in the nation. And yet, there it was, the artist who could teach others to do what he never felt able to do; he was by extension all of us combined. He lives in every one of us—the 200 and more—who could never have done what we did without him, there, behind his desk, listening, watching, and sometimes chuckling.

As I began to see the sunset of my own teaching career at Tech, there was still one more achievement to which I aspired: full professorship. I fulfilled all the university's requests, which included submitting samples of my personal accomplishments. For that, I included copious information on past photographic exhibits, awards in photo contests, publication of my prints in journals, books, and magazines, and a portfolio of my fine art photography. Except for the portfolio, I received endorsement. The presiding dean thought my photographs were dull and not truly "art." That might have ended my bid, until (or so I heard) his wife, an art enthusiast, contradicted him openly; consequently, he accepted her sophisticated appraisal and, in 1986, the full professorship was mine.

Being a full professor raised my salary, but at the same time, it was evident that my star had started to fade with the arrival of a new crop of younger faculty hired to teach an expanded roster of basic and advanced photography courses. Particularly telling was that an incoming instructor "inherited" responsibility for running the darkroom. I felt some were better teachers than photographers, others better at photography than teaching. I lived for the opportunity to face students who never aged as I did and who were ever challenging, but, after the WGGL debacle, this time I wanted to engineer my exit. It came as no surprise when my favorite departmental secretary commented one day: "Joe, the university has created an excellent new program for retirement; I'm seriously thinking about taking advantage of it. How about you? With the bonus of professor emeritus, too, why not?" The more I thought about it, the more I liked the idea.

I made the request for retirement at the end of the 1987–88 academic year; it was granted. A happy conclusion to an academic career that came about quite accidentally and had allowed me to fulfill both my intellectual and creative sides—and through which I had learned the art of teaching and mastered the art of zigzagging.

Just as my first shaky moments as a college teacher endure in my memory as a cinematic experience, so my departure does as well—though not with sharp definition nor as a culminating dramatic close. Instead, a dreamlike, narrated flashback montage of random scenes, voices, and faces as I took my final ride to attend a ceremonial farewell event.

FADE IN

EXT: A warm spring evening in May, old Schwinn bicycle leaning against the wall of the garage of the Romans' house on College Avenue

Professor Joe Kirkish, formally dressed, in his early 60s

MEDIUM SHOT: Kirkish mounting bike and heading off on his familiar ride to the nearby West entrance of the Michigan Tech campus.

CUT TO: LONG SHOT LOOKING EAST ON COLLEGE AVENUE: Kirkish turns off side street, onto the avenue on his bike, heads east.

VO (Kirkish): "I pulled my trusty Schwinn (still in service after 30 years) from its nesting place, hopped on, wearing my one good suit, a modest tie, freshly shined shoes, and headed east for Walker Arts and Humanities, to our building's conference room, now modified for my farewell banquet."

CAMERA FOLLOWS KIRKISH slowly bicycling along, as he passes through the campus corridor of mostly new buildings of various heights and parking lots, with DISSOLVES of intermixed historic stone and brick edifices and interior spaces—classrooms, offices, hallways, darkrooms—and faces.

INTERWEAVE AND OVERLAY snippets of conversation with:

Student in Denton House: "How will studying Keats and Shakespeare help get me a job when I leave here?"

President Ray Smith: "I may differ with you on some issues, Joe, but remember, I'm always the boss."

Wife of student in a basic speech class: "Whether he deserved his grade or not, you have to change it or my husband will be drafted and go to his death in Vietnam."

WGGL staffer: "You should get your radio certificate, Joe, so you can join us in sharing time on the air. Don't worry; we'll show you how."

Harley Sachs in The Ghetto: "Joe, welcome into our humble *shule*. Greetings and *mazel tov*."

A student in Fisher (chemistry) building: "Get your humanities requirements in any of Kirkish's classes; he's a tough grader and he's kinda weird, but he's good."

MEDIUM LONG SHOT: students (wearing their clothes backward) cavorting in front of the ROTC building entertaining Kirkish and passersby

VO (Kirkish): "Then, I passed the ROTC building, unchanged except that a parking lot now replaced a grassy space in front. This was the site where I discovered I had a sense of humor when a chaotic, but joyful, group of my Freshman English students staged a 1960s "Happening" in lieu of their final exam ... an early experiment to introduce these science and engineering students to the avant-garde and unlock their own creativity. In odd clothing and makeup, they portrayed a satirical version of life in hell, which concluded with one girl in waitress dress delivering to me—smack in the face—a whipped cream pie, followed immediately by half a dozen of the cast rushing with towels to clean me, my glasses, and clothes. Astonished, all I could do, along with the surprised passersby, was break into hearty laughter. They all received As for their highly irregular efforts."

DISSOLVE TO OVERLAY OF: ghost of stern-faced Dr. Fryxell, "Theater belongs on the stage, Joe, and not a substitute for written performance ..."

BACK TO: Art Young: "Welcome back to academia, Joe; we're a growing department, and with your background in film and photography, we'll expect you to grow with us."

MEDIUM SHOT: Kirkish arriving at Walker Arts and Humanities, parking his bicycle in its familiar place next to the entrance, entering the building and, FOLLOWING HIM, with sound of footsteps as he climbs to the third-floor conference room, now appropriately festooned for a retirement celebration.

PAN ROOM WITH KIRKISH (BACK TO CAMERA) IN FOREGROUND, THEN CLOSE UP OF KIRKISH'S FACE SHOWING surprise at the lavishness, the completely filled room, and the unexpected warm ambiance among colleagues.

VO (Kirkish): "I stepped into the banquet room, met by applause and beaming faces, for the final time as a don in the department. Two hours of a fine meal, reminiscences, and a wine toast. I stifled my built-in discomfort with ceremonial events but accepted the festivity as a sincere sign of academic achievement. Ever the sentimentalist, it was my *Goodbye, Mr. Chips* event, and I left overwhelmed, but eager for my next adventures beyond the horizon."

FADE OUT

※※※

Paris rooftops

PART 4

Emeritus, 1988–99

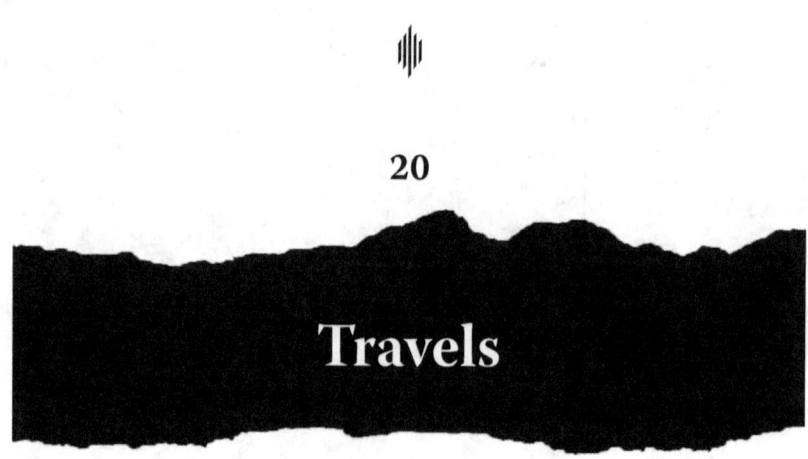

20

Travels

Traveling abroad? For decades I'd been too busy teaching at Tech or working on my dissertation to even consider such a thing. I had listened with envy to people's tales and seen slides and photos (too many!) of their travels to distant places, longing to be able to venture beyond our shores. Now in my late 60s, I had the time, but I wanted more than a "If it's Tuesday, it must be Belgium" tourist experience. I wanted to be immersed in new learning adventures, but also to develop educational slideshows that I could present to local groups (especially children and the elderly) as another form of community service. For me, emeritus meant the freedom to be a teacher at large.

For several years before my official retirement from Michigan Tech in 1988, I taught creative photography as part of the summer Elderhostel travel program on campus; after daily lectures, I would take each visiting group around the Copper Country, cameras in hand, to record its natural beauties, from flora to waterfalls. I became fascinated by these world travelers, heard about the joys of visiting Costa Rica more than once, and decided to take the plunge for a two-week trip in our fall (their spring), 1991. This Central American country, tucked between Nicaragua and Panama, was a perfect place to begin. I knew a bit of Spanish, looked forward to photographing a tropical country, and it was only two short plane hops away.

With one filled duffel bag, a broad-brimmed hat, and some

camera equipment, I was ready for whatever Elderhostel could avail me. It proved far more than I'd ever hoped.

In fact, the novelty of flying out of Miami on a 16-passenger Costa Rican Laksa Airline plane became in itself a hint of the amazingly different little nation I was about to visit. I was about to become Alice as she dove into her rabbit hole. Not only a "first come, first served" system of seating, but there was no enclosure for the pilots! They sat in a cockpit in front of the first seats, in the open, and when a child asked if he could fly the plane, one pilot picked him up, put him on his lap, and let him "steer" to the thrill for the child and amusement for us.

I went up to photograph the situation. A man who resembled a toned-down Liberace in casual clothes, drink in hand, saw me coming and smiled broadly (thinking he was to be the subject), then disappointed, moved aside for me. The resulting photo of the pilot and child became a keeper.

Free drinks made the two-hour flight to San Jose, the capital city, go by quickly. At the gate, Patricia (Pah-TREE-see-ah), our guide for the two weeks, was there to greet us. At first impression she appeared to be a pretty college student, waving her sign that read "Elderhostel" on it—a broad smile that broke into an excited call to us to follow her to a minibus awaiting us near the tarmac. Almost like an old friend, she helped us board the chauffeured mini-bus to our hotel and then got us settled, before she departed with the promise of a surprise a day for the next two weeks. She kept her promise.

From our initial meeting, we found Patricia easy to like; she chatted in perfect English (which she said improved with each new American group's help), had the habit of dropping previews, cautions, and directives along our drives to make us comfortable, but never gave away the direction of each day's tour until we were settled in the minibus and on our way. Acquainting herself with each of us individually and getting to know our likes and dislikes, we became instantly at home with her and looked forward to her lively commentary. Oddly, we learned next to nothing about her, except that she was born in Costa Rica, was in her mid-twenties, well-educated, and carefully trained as an Elderhost. And she obviously enjoyed each new group as if it were her first.

After visiting two major tourist attractions in the city center—the spectacular gold museum filled with Pre-Columbian artifacts and a park with memorials of past presidents—Patricia sprung her first surprise: being a part of an ecotourism urban tree planting project. First, we each planted a small tree in an open field, and then, as we descended from the site, showing us a nearby alligator-infested pool, she finally indicated the tall trees around us as an instant forest in the making. We learned that our saplings would grow, like those trees, at least five feet a year!

A few unexpected things happened that evening, not orchestrated by Patricia. We had front row seats (on folding chairs) in a concert hall for a performance of Finnish music. Imagine my surprise (and his) when the violinist came in front of the orchestra for his opening bow; it was the fellow I failed to photograph on the plane! For a moment we exchanged surprised glances; he smiled and then thrilled us by performing the violin portion of a Sibelius concerto.

Then, after the concert, came my introduction to the underbelly of this tropical paradise. Three of us decided to walk back to the hotel. As we strode down a dark street—enjoying the beautiful night and with the strains of the music still in our ears—all of a sudden, a car pulled up and a man shouted at us: "Don't walk here! It is dangerous!" and drove off, leaving us mystified. (We learned from Patricia that there was good reason for the warning: prostitutes lived surreptitiously there as did small gangs of Nicaraguan youths who mugged anyone daring to invade the territory.)

The events of that first day—Patricia's planned group surprise augmented by my own unexpected encounters—set the tone for two continuous weeks of enchantment. I came to see Patricia as an inscrutable spirit guide who would appear and disappear at just the right moment, always comforting us with each appearance.

The next phase of the trip took us to the west coast, traveling up through the luxuriant Central Highlands with waterfalls cascading down through tropical trees in bloom and crevices on both sides of the road. As we drove higher, we passed small villages and acres of coffee bean bushes, where women were filling their backsacks with the ripe beans. The contrasts mile by mile were like a Disneyland technicolor joy ride, wondering what might be found around each bend in the mountain road. Then, a dramatic contrast, during our descent out of the dense rain forest, we were treated to the breathtaking broad vista of the shimmering Pacific. During our exploration of the pristine Manuel Antonio Beach (and National Park), Patricia ensured that we had daily sensory jolts as we moved back and forth between the ocean and the jungle just at its edge.

After our junket to the Central Pacific coast, we returned to the capital to spend the remainder of the first week exploring the city and its environs. Waiting for me at the hotel was a phone message. It was from Juan, a former Michigan Tech student (whom I had hosted, along with a group of other foreign students, for a weekend at our Lake Superior family cottage); before my departure, I got his address from the Foreign Student office at Tech and sent a postcard to let him know I'd be in the area soon. His message invited me to visit his home on Sunday morning, in time to share a noon Mass with his family! I called him back immediately and made a plan to spend the day with Juan and his family.

At 10:00 a.m. the next day, seeing Juan and receiving his enthusiastic greeting in English, I forgot my initial fears about my limited ability to converse in Spanish. We shook hands the American way, and he walked me to a bus stop where we picked up a rural bus that took us to Cartago, about an hour south. Talking excitedly, he pointed out interesting sights while I shot photos through the window of strange, long-horned cattle in the fields, men on horses corralling them, crops of corn or other grain on broad acres, farm buildings in little clusters. When we reached our destination, Juan guided me to a home with his mother, father, and other members of the family waiting on their porch for us.

Following a round of warm greetings—they in broken English and I in equally awkward Spanish, plenty of hand shaking and bowing, glowing in excessive smiles—plus inside, partaking small cups of aromatic, strong arabica coffee, it was off to Mass. We joined a crowded stream of parishioners walking the dirt road to the imposing Basilica of Our Lady of Angels rising up in the midst of a huge park. No vehicles, just hundreds of people in Sunday best, the mothers carrying babies, the fathers, blankets, and all carrying bundles of food for afterwards.

We deposited our blankets and bundles at a spot in the park, then I followed Juan and a pack of family groups to a side entrance of the cathedral and down into an underground chamber, barely lit with candles surrounding a life-sized figure of the Virgin Mary. People were chanting, either touching or kissing the Virgin's foot, and then without stopping, ascended up into the cavernous nave which was large enough to hold hundreds. With bells ringing, at noon the High Mass—organ, choir, the works—began. Afterwards, the throng poured from the church into the park, where the fun began: a cacophonous outdoor party where all generations were picnicking, relaxing, socializing, and making music. And of course, I took plenty of photographs.

Juan explained that the original church had been built under Spanish colonial rule with local (forced) labor on the site of a miracle involving a black stone statue of the Virgin Mary and Jesus Christ. Cartago had been a colonial center, then abandoned. Native peoples, who had not been permitted to worship there, reclaimed it. When the Black Madonna (*La Negrita*) was declared the patron saint of Costa Rica, it became an important pilgrimage site and, over time, grew into the present large Byzantine-style edifice. Once a year, he explained, they would symbolically celebrate the day the church became theirs, carrying the statue of the Virgin around the church, scattering flower petals and singing to her, then ending with communal feasts in the park. The ritual of the after-Mass feasts remained. "You should be here to see that special day," he said, his eyes shining in remembrance.

Whenever I traveled in the States, I always enjoyed going to Sunday Mass at the local Catholic churches; the styles changed, yet the familiar ceremony of the Mass remained. But here, for the first time, I was at a mystical holy site and witnessing firsthand the cult of Mary within a Latin culture. The experience was thrilling—the singing and praying in Spanish, the people in their Sunday best— but only when I received communion along with the throngs, did I begin to feel part of the electrifying aura, which remains an embedded sensory memory.

Back at their home, while his mother made dinner preparations, Juan took me to his room. He stood in the doorway, showing off what few young men had: a private space of his own, about five by eight feet with a small bed on one side, a home-constructed armoire on the other, and his guitar on a wall hook near the door. He beamed proudly as I complimented his special status.

For dinner, we feasted in the kitchen at a table large enough for the entire family (eight in all) and me. All kinds of spicy dishes, but most memorable was a thick, rich rice pudding covered with tiny leaves that tasted like chocolate. By that time, we had shed our awkwardness; the family asked me questions about America, the school Juan had attended, how we'd met and became friends, and I responded in equally broken Spanglish. We drank some rich sweet wine, Juan's mother put a platter of sweets on the table in front of me, insisting, "*Mas, mas!*" It became a homey get-together.

Juan insisted on bussing back with me, reliving our university friendship, and talking about his current job in Cartago as a computer expert in a small enterprise there. When we arrived at the hotel, he took me warmly in a family embrace, said a pleasant "*Vaya con Dios*, Joe," and left.

I thought nothing could top that beautiful day, but Patricia, up to her magic tricks, had more in mind. After free time to roam the city center she took us (all dressed up at her behest) for a special visit to a wealthy suburb. Our destination was the opulent residence of the former president of Costa Rica! He and his wife received us graciously in their grand salon (filled with gifts from around the world and family portraits), and while we nibbled exquisite tidbits on silver plates, he waxed on about his friendship with President Carter, with whom he planned a peace visit soon to an Asian country.

On the way back to the hotel, Patricia cocked a grin, saying, "I'm sure you were impressed. Well, you ain't seen nuttin' yet." (Her clever mix of perfect English with slang picked up from American B-films was obvious; she knew we were amused by it and used it often.)

What next during the second week? We headed north, first to an orchid garden with trees dangling with dozens of varieties, to a wire enclosed garden where the air around us was filled with butterflies of all sorts and sizes—some larger than hands, fluttering silently and endlessly—then deep into the dense jungle we went.

Our base for three days in the Monteverde Cloud Forest was a compound constructed ten feet off the ground to evade wild creatures that roamed at night below. Lying in the mosquito-netted beds, we actually enjoyed the novelty of falling asleep to the chattering of the monkeys that dominated the forest around us. During the days, we donned high boots and followed expert guides into the jungle to be shown the hidden beauties and dangers in the area. Most impressive was a tiny red frog that excreted a deadly poison when excited and beautiful pear-like fruit that caused the same deadly results if touched.

During a boat ride down the Rio Sarapiquí (near the border with Nicaragua), we had two close wildlife encounters. We got near enough to an alligator to photograph it just before it suddenly leaped at us. But the most unplanned surprise that day was when a howler monkey dropped from branches above us, wrapped itself around my head and shoulders, and simply stared curiously into my face. For a moment of terror, being wrapped by five pressures (four legs and mobile tail), I was speechless; the rest of the group laughed. The guide easily lifted the curious creature from me and tossed it back into the trees above. My thought later: I wish I had a picture of that!

Our final tour before leaving the area was to a commercial pineapple farm and then, most interesting, to a banana plantation, right on the edge of the river. We watched huge branches of bananas being chopped, cleaned, and then packaged, but I felt the temptation to slip away to get a look at the cluster of the employees' small houses nearby. Passing one house, I heard laughter and splashing, peered through the glassless window to find a young girl giving a little boy a sponging as he stood in the kitchen sink. I couldn't resist the moment, brought up my camera, and photographed the sight. A mother appeared behind the sink, saw me, and motioned me to come in. She turned out to be the wife of an office employee and spoke perfect English!

Capping our exploration of this small country's amazing diverse geography were several days in its northern volcanic region. Our introduction was actually through smell: we stepped out of the van, immediately struck by an offensive odor in the air. Patricia instructed us to follow her up a rugged path sided by huge-leafed plants. The sulfuric stench increased; after about a quarter mile, we arrived at the gaping mouth of Volcán Poás, stood close to the rim, and stared down into a broad rough circle of dark material with fumes, flames, and black smoke rising from its center. "We have nine volcanos in the north mountainside," she said. "We will see a larger, more lively one later, but this is the only one we can actually approach safely." We leaned over the brink, took photos, hands cupped over our faces, then departed down the hill to fresh, humid jungle air again.

We continued our journey, landing us eventually (after a boat ride) at a lodge on a bluff with a spectacular view of Volcán Arenal, a massive active volcano. Patricia gave us a short lecture about volcanoes, concluding, "This is the supreme king of volcanos; you will be able to see and hear him even after dark. It will be thrilling to see at night if it decides to put on a show for you, but I hope its 'voice' doesn't keep you awake."

After a delicious, plentiful dinner of indigenous food at the lodge—a mix of fresh exotic fruit, fish, and root vegetables in a tasty brown sauce—we walked down the hill and followed Patricia to the village for her surprise of the day: a little Protestant church built years ago by its American minister, with Father John and his congregation waiting for us. Besides the pastor, there were about 20 parishioners in their simple, Sunday-best clothing sitting on one side of the church in grouped mismatched chairs. We settled a bit awkwardly in the empty chairs opposite. Father John narrated his (and the church's history) in English, then Patricia told us the group wished to serenade us. First they sang a few Spanish hymns, then a Costa Rican patriotic tribute. After the applause, Patricia turned to us and asked, "And now, would you like to reciprocate?" We looked at one another—this disparate group of American strangers—wondering how to respond. Finally, I spoke up: "How about our national anthem?" So we sang like solid Americans, ending to wild applause from these mountain villagers. After that, we mingled, ate some sweets and mild drinks, and left for our first night under the stars in this Central American fantasy atmosphere. The volcano was silent, though.

My curiosity and my camera propelled me off for a solo exploration the next morning. Down in the village, I photographed children (some of whom recognized me from the night before) beneath colorful lines of clothing hanging between their homes, just as they headed off for a trek to their faraway school. Education, I was told earlier, was extremely important in Costa Rica; the military, considered unnecessary, first had been abolished, then the government spent the money on educating everyone instead.

I then spent a few magical hours, once again a child lost in observation, my camera clicking away, in the rainforest where remarkable flora blanketed the ground: some almost microscopic and hidden under leaves, others climbing trees out of sight in the green canopy overhead. Arriving at a more open area, on hands and knees, I followed trails of busy insects carrying leaves many times larger than their bodies in an endless line to some hidden place beyond.

My desire for one last nighttime ramble produced the most mystical moment of this enchanted trip. Before going to sleep, I wandered up a rutted road to get a better view of the now flaming sight across the lake, when suddenly, out of nowhere, I encountered a white horse who appeared silently on the road above me, theatrically illuminated by the flames of Arenal as if in some unearthly pageant! Would the surprises ever cease in that amazing land?

On our return to San Jose, we stayed at a ranch where I had my one embarrassing episode of the trip. Others rode horseback while I borrowed a bike from a young fellow named Luis to photograph the surrounding community. Among the string of small wooden homes along the side of the deeply rutted road, I used my limited Spanish to engage a family in conversation and got several photographs. Instead of charming them by praising in fair Spanish the girl with a child in her arms, though, I insulted one of the women nearby, mistakenly thinking she was the mother! "Oh, no," laughed the girl, "*Es mi hermana!*" Her sister!

I retreated hastily feeling like the ugly American, biked back to the ranch, returned the bicycle to Luis, and decided definitely never to try such an experiment again.

My way to show gratitude for hospitality was to leave a small, matted photo of an exotic landscape ... a winter scene from our Copper Country. So before departing the ranch, I gave two of them to the owner of the place (one for the maid who was so efficient in keeping our cottages clean, the other for Luis for his kindness in lending me the bicycle). As we took final group photos under a huge banyan-type tree, Luis came rushing up to me, grabbed me by the arms and said in broken English, "I wish to thank you; you are my best friend," and rushed back to work. It was a touching way to leave. I might have insulted one person but had made a friend with another.

Even the last day of our trip had drama awaiting us. Something obviously was in the air and around the central square of San Jose: the nation's "colors" covered carts, walls, statuary everywhere; flags dangled over the streets for blocks leading to the square; one could feel the approaching jubilation. For what? As the afternoon grew long, the square was flooded with hundreds of people carrying lanterns to represent the day a native ran with a lantern from above Costa Rica to San Jose, bearing a signed proclamation that as of that day Costa Rica was a free and independent nation. A scene that was touching in itself, but overwhelming when at precisely the minute the proclamation had originally been received, every citizen—in the square, in homes across the country—stopped to sing the national anthem.

And that evening, we surprised Patricia. As our departure drew near, our group had discussed what to do in gratitude for her guidance. I suggested that we give her money to buy a 35mm camera, which she once said she would most like to have; we pooled more than enough money, gave it to her at a farewell dinner, and decided that her show of surprise and delight was worth every bit of it.

One final bonus surprise for me: on the return trip to Miami, I sat next to the current president of Costa Rica! He and his wife arrived, sat in the seats saved for them, directly across the aisle from me. Though they appeared to be just another traveling couple, the pilots and everyone aboard rose, cheered, and shook hands with them. During the short trip, I was able to converse with them in perfect English; they were headed for Boston, where both their son and daughter were pursuing degrees at a university. As we chatted, a thought occurred to me: could I imagine our President Bush engaging with his public the same way at home? What a contrast!

I could not wait to return home, out of the rabbit hole, to present a completed slideshow and now determined to do a new trip abroad every year.

◈ ◈ ◈

After my first Elderhostel trip in Costa Rica, I had a medley of experiences, never as exciting nor as grand as that initial one, yet worth cataloguing as a string of memories now packed away in boxes of color slides on a shelf, waiting to be revived occasionally or shown publicly whenever asked.

Ireland, the land of my dreams, started them off with a group of professional photographers hired to record the Emerald Isle in a centennial book. (My photos were the most used of all, but to my disappointment, I never received a copy of the printed book.) Then with friend and former colleague, Jim MacKillop, who did guided tours there annually and asked me along when his wife was unable to accompany him; and, finally, thanks to a chance meeting with a University of Limerick technical student who encouraged me to return and spend some time with him (and his family and friends), for a more intimate exploration of culture and countryside. It included excursions from the Cliffs of Moher to the Ring of Kerry, and I got to revisit places with which I'd fallen in love.

Where, next? Another photographic assignment to Istanbul with its magnificent mosques and uncommonly shrewd street vendors; romantic, ancient Dubrovnik (the "Pearl of the Adriatic"); and, most gloriously of all, Venice, Italy, which was as charming as all tour guidebooks claim.

My first trip to Paris materialized through the generosity of friends in New York, who offered me their apartment in the heart of Paris for a week. I roamed the beautiful City of Light from morning until late at night for seven days. The trip yielded some beautiful photos, but in the end, I realized how lonely I was and decided in the future, my travel needed to be as part of a group. So, when my niece Rosie, who was married to Dutch-born Alex Hierman, planned a family trip to the Netherlands, plus side visits to Paris, Brussels, England, and concluding with a long drive up to visit more of his relatives in northern Scotland, how could I refuse? My contribution to that extended voyage was the ability to speak French; it came in handy, especially in Paris (where I'd been just a few months earlier). I loved picking up the local lingo in the British Isles (such as a "cuppa," short for a cup of tea, or "Arthur's Seat," a steep hill adjoining Edinburgh).

I never made it to Lebanon and Israel—a planned tour was

canceled because of the dangers. After that, a more complicated series of responsibilities moored me closer to home, though I still wistfully perused the alluring pages of travel brochures. Meanwhile, I found that there were schools, civic and social groups (Rotary Clubs, etc.) always looking for a good travel presentation. I developed mine by avoiding all the mistakes made by amateurs; I arranged the slides like a movie travelogue and narrated from our airport to the destinations and back again, just rapidly enough to keep people engaged. Always the teacher and intrepid photographer, I enjoyed it and so did the audience; word got around, my phone rang off the hook with requests, until years later when digital alternatives had more appeal. Now, since I'm no longer able to do these long trips, I still get vicarious pleasure looking at those slides of favorite faraway places and adventures.

Retirement meant that, at will, I could also visit family and friends scattered across the United States, rather than having to wedge a short stay into a professional junket. Ever curious to see what changed and what didn't at Camp Nebagamon, I tried, too, to put in an appearance at Post Camp as often as possible. It was gratifying that even with the change of ownership when the Steins retired (in 1990), the place continued to attract an impressive mix of alumni (recent and old) and their families. Time after time, I felt welcomed, not as a guest, but as a member of the extended camp family. My visits always included time spent with Nardie and Sally (who continued to summer in their Little House adjacent to the camp property); they were always very special to me, and in a typically Lebanese way, I'd make my visit an opportunity to bring some gifts for them and their children—for me, a case of the giving almost being more appreciated than the getting.

It was during those post-teaching years that I became a regular pilgrim for the Thanksgiving holiday at the Geismers, the CN family I'd met at Post Camp early on and with whom I'd stayed in contact. Since my first visit to their Shaker Heights home in the early '60s, I had done several stopovers with them as part of trips to Detroit or New York—always treated royally, with a concert or theatrical event usually included—and I kept up an active correspondence with Bobbie (we exchanged long letters almost monthly, which I saved).

I especially savored her matter-of-fact descriptions of their hosting famous musicians, such as "Hephzibah and Yehudi (Menuhin) came to the house for a visit when they were here to perform at the Hall, a delightful couple" (she meant eminent sister pianist and brother violinist who'd just returned from a tour of Europe as if they were simply good everyday friends). Or, "George asked if we could hold a little soiree for him and a few of his special guests here; it was a charming evening. You would have enjoyed it." (George being Maestro George Szell of the Cleveland Orchestra). Never "name dropping," just casual references to their ongoing hospitality for distinguished visitors.

My short visits in the '70s and '80s included a glimpse of their children growing into teenagers, marrying, and having their own families. Heartbreaking, though, was Alan's decline from Parkinson's disease and its impact on the family, especially Bobbie. Accustomed to seeing her as a self-assured wife and mother—ever attentive, ever thinking one step ahead—I witnessed her take on a new role as devoted caregiver, allowing me to notice how she'd eventually adjust their home for his inevitable decline.

As Bobbie's and Alan's active outside social life together diminished, hosting events at their home became even more important for her. I knew Thanksgiving was a big family gathering grandly orchestrated, so I was thrilled to be invited to participate. No longer teaching at the university, I could make the long trip south, staying en route in Detroit and Battle Creek with relatives or friends.

I explained it to my family; they were cautious, but still proud that I, born of a common Lebanese family, could be accepted so easily into a Jewish home and by a prominent family. I drew on my Lebanese gift-giving tradition and always came laden with specialty foods from the Copper Country. Once established as a regular guest—even beginning to feel avuncular—I also brought along a cache of my photos to distribute at the end of the Thanksgiving meal. Knowing that the Geismer family and their friends would be looking at the work in their homes was so satisfying, it was my gesture of gratitude for including me as part of the family and for their interest in my photographic career.

The pleasures and appreciation, I found, were mutual and only grew from one annual Thanksgiving week to the next.

From the moment I received Bobbie's party invitation, I would look forward to the trip. Often I would be the first to arrive and spend hours, perched on a stool watching her, wearing one of her signature smocks, at work in her orderly, spotless kitchen. She presided as the chief cook of meal after meal, with Meg and Mollie pitching in under her demanding direction. She performed, in the kitchen as she did in everything involving her family, with astonishing rightness.

**Bobbie Geismer displaying the family
heirloom Thanksgiving dessert**

Besides a sumptuous, formal Thanksgiving dinner—usually 15–20 guests—attending a concert, a play, and a visit to the Cleveland Museum of Art always lay in store during that week. I could easily slip into my culture vulture persona, but even in my slightly transparent disguise, found it difficult to soak up so much beauty and culture in a week's time—and be accepted into it as, not just a guest of the Geismer family, but one of them. The beauty of that accepting warmth never left me in or out of their presence.

My trips also came to include all kinds of photographic excursions, starting with the walled garden behind the house. I also enjoyed wandering the neighborhood, accompanied by daughters and granddaughters eager to get pointers with their cameras. And one time, with the family consent, I wandered their house from top to bottom, especially drawn to the mysteries of its raw storage and utility rooms (including in the ghostly basement, the largest furnace I had ever seen).

A new ritual was added to my annual visit in 1992: after Alan's death, accompanying Bobbie to the family mausoleum. A very different experience than witnessing Professor Roman's pained routine—she had become the proud and dutiful caretaker of the resting place of several generations. I would watch her brief ritual, all done in silence: unlocking the heavy bronze door, paying quiet homage to Alan, placing a small bouquet of flowers (salvaged from the Thanksgiving table) in front of the vault, checking the pebbles left on the ledges, and finally sweeping up inside and out with a little broom she kept there, while allowing her thoughts to permeate. And then, memories restored and left with a turn of the key, she would smile and ask me where I'd like to have a restaurant meal with her. Of course, she picked a fashionable restaurant (and allowed me to pay for the meal as her "date")—grateful to prolong my time in her lively and mothering presence before heading back north.

When Bobbie turned 80 in 2000, the family decided to do a special celebration over the Thanksgiving holiday: a chamber concert led by renowned clarinetist Franklin Cohen (yes, another friend of Bobbie's). The highlight of the program was Mozart's Clarinet Quintet, truly sublime because of the music and the setting. It was held in the intimate Reinberger Hall at Severance Hall and followed by a formal reception—a singular event for a very singular woman (with 70 of us gathered to honor her).

There she was: her perfectly coiffed white hair wreathing her face almost halo-like, her elegant suit offset by an unusual, finely crafted gold necklace, her charm ever radiating. On my return to Houghton, I memorialized this gala afternoon in my next monthly column in the *Daily Mining Gazette*, as I wrote, "Echoes from that afternoon still reverberate for me, and they will for a long, long time. And for Bobbie and her family, perhaps even longer."

It was not the last time I would see her, but eventually, the trip became too much for me, and fortunately, there were still the letters and phone calls to keep the bond alive. Once, after remarking how much I appreciated the Brahms' Double Concerto, she followed up with a surprise package in the mail—the finest version of the piece ever recorded. Bobbie ever thoughtful.

21

Encores and New Creative Ventures

Unexpectedly, a trip to Seattle in the early '90s to visit my niece Paula was the impetus to pursue a new photographic project: clotheslines. My fascination with them had started during my bohemian days in New York in the 1950s, living in a cold-water, walk-up flat with a view from my bedroom window which overlooked a double row of the rear of apartment buildings. Strung on a criss-cross series of lines on pulleys across the alley that ran for blocks was an endless flurry of laundry, hung with the most amazing variety in sheets and clothes. I learned to identify the owners of the clothes just by observing their styles, sizes, colors, and quality. I never thought of photographing them at the time, but it became a game, getting to know my unseen neighbors, deciphering their identities by what they would hang, and how, on their individual lines.

Photographing clotheslines never entered my mind while at the university; actually, I rarely saw any there (one exception was at the McGintys). But when I returned to teach at Michigan Tech, beginning with classes in introductory writing and speech, and finding the students unable to come up with subject matter for their assignments, I recalled those wonderful clotheslines outside my Manhattan window and decided to experiment: "Go out, find a clothesline, sit in front of it for half an hour, then return to write (or prepare a speech) on what you experienced." They would leave the classroom in a mix of confusion and despair. Most of them would return elated with the results.

I never took the subject seriously until that Seattle visit, when I learned that hanging clothes in the suburbs was forbidden. The same, I learned, was also true in most of the country's suburbs, and even in small towns, where the sight of clothes drying in the sun was deemed unsightly, or where people with indoor dryers felt they no longer needed to take the time nor effort to wait for good weather to hang out the wash. Clotheslines were a vanishing sight! While the rest of the world still used the outdoor system, here the lines were disappearing in America.

Copper Country clothesline

So, I decided to photograph them before they became history. In our Copper Country, where long lines were held up by rugged wooden stalks with a "Y" at one end and where there was little concern for public offense, I sought out lines that looked interesting to me. Actually, they all looked interesting, because regardless what was hung out, from bedding to clothing to towels and carpeting (and even washable children's shoes, toys, and stuffed animals), these displays were apt for interesting photographs. I also noticed, as I drove the highway through small villages to our cottage or back, a plethora of lines were always visible on both sides of the road. I'd pull over, open my window, and snap. Eventually, I drove down country roads for no other reason than to find photogenic lines, sometimes (when no one was in sight) getting out and shooting closer. When I felt a clothesline demanded more inspection, I'd knock at the door, talk to the resident, explain, and nearly always was granted grinning approval.

Even the arrangement of the setup of the lines varied. For example, in central Wisconsin towns, where tree branches are less useful, U-shaped parallel tubes have lines strung between them. Trips abroad provided opportunities to compare or contrast with our lines. Besides the rows of fences carelessly decorated with washings in Costa Rica, I discovered plastic bags drying on Italian lines, spider-webbed lines in crowded spaces in the Netherlands, and lines hidden behind stone walls in the English countryside.

Some of the results looked more than just amusing; with the right angle, the right light, the right movement in the wind, and the right background and foreground (sometimes with a willing owner in the process of hanging them out), I gathered enough pictures to create and exhibit a show in a local gallery. The remarkably positive reaction, including a group of children brought in from school, who excitedly described details of both the clothing and the people who might have worn them, encouraged the next step: having them published, first locally in the daily paper, then beyond, in the *Milwaukee Journal*, and then even in fashionable photo magazines.

All this built notoriety, which helped give me status when I needed to ask permission to shoot. People would respond with, "Oh, yes, I've heard of you;" some would ask, on second thought, "Would you like me to take down the underwear?" I assured them that it wasn't necessary. In fact, to some I became "the guy who photographs underwear on the lines."

The photos sold well at summer art shows in Michigan and Wisconsin, meeting with intrigue, amusement, and nostalgia. One experience confirmed how geographically specific clotheslines are. At an art fair in Detroit one year, a woman walked up, looked at a clothesline photo, and asked, "Did you take this in Laurium, in the Upper Peninsula?" I responded, "Yes, how could you tell?" "Oh," she replied, "I used to live there, and that's the way we always hung our lines up there."

I'm glad I captured this everyday phenomenon before it became a distant memory, like clocks with hands, typewriters, and phones with dials. Doing the shooting felt like a fun, endless game (although I was once bitten in the thigh by one vicious Husky while dodging a second one that succeeded in only ripping my pant leg). And I know I've opened some eyes and expanded photographic horizons: I still receive shots of clotheslines taken by friends, locally or in foreign countries, with brief explanations.

❖ ❖ ❖

My work, besides being included in occasional faculty shows while I was teaching at Tech, had been presented a few times in small solo exhibits in the library. At the opening at one of these, I happened to be standing behind two people seriously savoring the exhibit. One looked at my name, then asked, "Who is this guy?" with the response from the other: "Don't you know? That's Joe Kirkish; he's the finest photographer of the Copper Country." For the first time, I felt I had assumed the mantle of my mentor Ray Forster (the Calumet postmaster and photographer).

A milestone for my creative photography was being included in *Made in Michigan*, a prestigious, juried exhibit at the Kresge Art Museum in Lansing the summer I retired (1988). In fact, an older dye transfer portrait on acetate (titled *Creature in Red*), was singled out in a review, comparing it to the haunted vision of British painter Francis Bacon! Then, for almost 10 years, my work was shown in several exhibits at Clare Spitler Works of Art, a well-regarded gallery in Ann Arbor. (Clare was one of the ubiquitous urban gallery owners around the country who had opened up a basement space for contemporary art work to show and sell; she was, to me, among the best I've known.)

To my surprise, in 1995, the first time I entered the annual Marshfield Art Fair, an Upper Midwest event in Wisconsin attracting major artists and big crowds, I won "Best in Show." Getting regional recognition was a new feather in my cap, and, along with sales of work from gallery and art/craft shows, it helped drive my experimentation with a new medium: laser printing. I started looking for simpler (and less expensive) methods to create my own reproductions. Introduced one day to a print shop in Calumet where a new Xerox machine could turn out remarkably fine prints, I first paid the owner to do the printing, but then he was willing to show me how to manipulate the inks and let me play on my own.

Early experiment with overlay portraiture

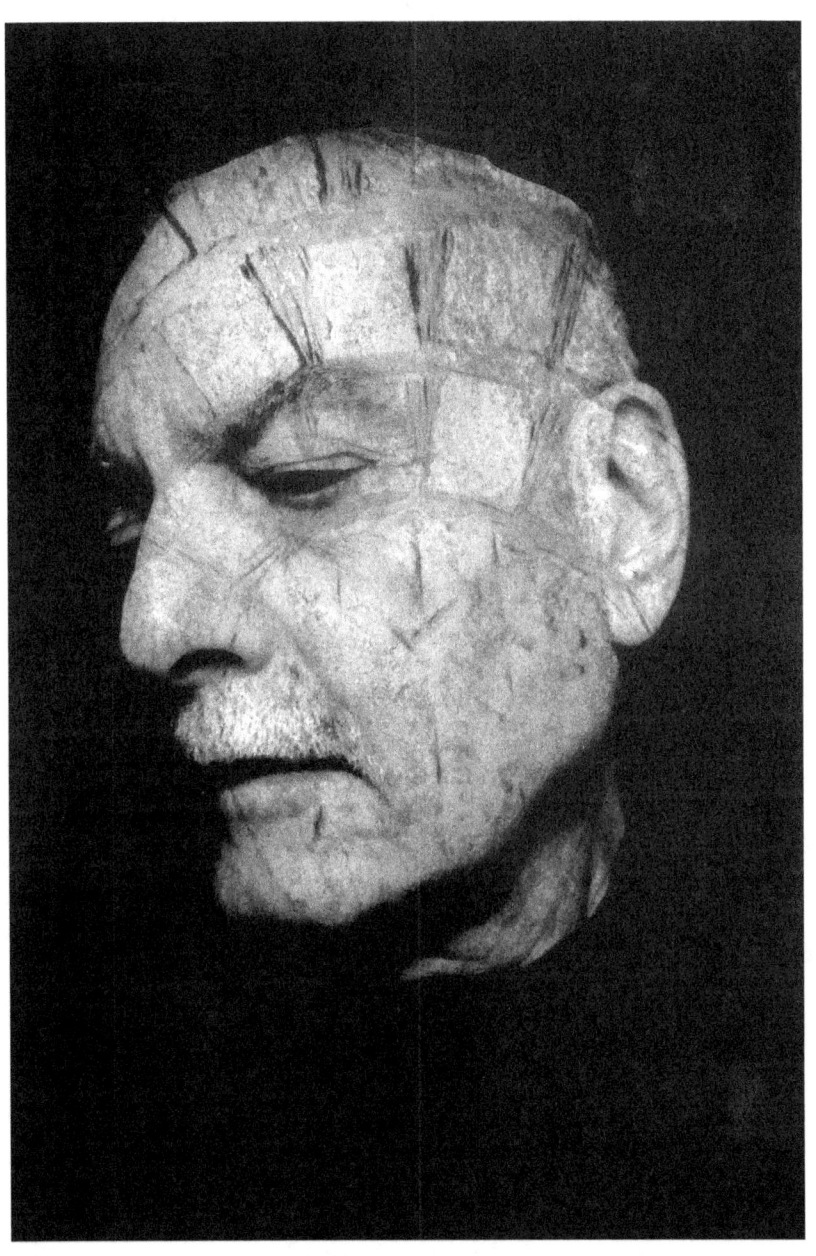

Overlay self-portrait

Quickly, I realized the possibilities of transforming 3 × 5 prints into images up to 11 × 17. I could print with a mix of different colors, change the tones, lighten or darken them, and then began pushing the boundaries with double overlays—make one print, then overlay it on another by running the first print through a second or third time. I filled a small box with cut up 3 × 5s, divided into two kinds: portraits and textures (shots of gravel, leaves, wooden planks, etc.). I would spend a few delightful hours every week and would pay the owner at the end of the month. Puzzled by my experiments, he feared I was wasting too much time and money (I reassured him that since I neither smoked nor drank, I could indulge).

I was not the only one excited by the results: the prints sold well at the art shows and frequently won awards for the best of them. And, unsolicited expressions of pleasure from the public were doubly gratifying—that I had an audience and that the time and travel involved in being an exhibitor were worth the effort.

❖ ❖ ❖

Throughout the '90s, my status as a professor emeritus occasionally pulled me back into teaching photography classes at Tech, but it was now off campus where my teaching interests lay. More and more, I could see my stature waning in the Humanities Department.

Being free from the grading process was such a relief and I eagerly sought out any kind of teaching opportunity. I produced weekly film reviews for the MTU alumni page (often drawing responses from the far corners of the world). I carefully planned my introductions to the monthly films for Club Indigo to highlight one cinematic device after another which prompted one of the regular attendees to admit, "I feel I've learned enough over time to deserve academic credit for what you've taught me." And one presentation could lead to another: a former Tech student from my film courses, who went on to teach at a small college in Nebraska, invited me to lecture for a week on "Religion in Films;" then, at the behest of Father Larry Van Damme, the priest at St. Albert's the Great (the newer local Catholic church at Michigan Tech), I distilled the essence of that week into one lengthy evening for both faculty and students together.

Anytime I was approached, on or off campus, for any subject

with which I felt comfortable, was grist for the mill. I savored each opportunity, as I discovered I could adjust each presentation to suit the age, educational or religious background. It became an endless pleasure, never realizing what importance or value resulted, until in 1998 I found myself honored as "Distinguished Teacher of the Year" by the MTU Alumni. I used the award ceremony to lecture on how everything I knew or did evolved from my parents, clergy, professors, and, most importantly, all the written knowledge that was there forever to continue the learning process.

I enjoyed every minute of proving the value of knowledge absorption—and still do. Why? Because a long time ago I realized that I was not the brightest person in the world, but applying knowledge acquired, I managed quite well among my academic peers. Simple as that.

Ever conscious of the creative life in my community and ever willing to step in when it appeared I might be of help, I was pleased to accept the invitation in 1994 to become a member of the board of directors for the Calumet Theatre. Soon, Club Indigo, a monthly event, would structure my retirement, and in fact, for more than two decades.

A little background: in the late 1800s, the city was in its heyday during the great copper boom, and a group of boosters decided that Calumet should have a grand building to house touring entertainers. The result was that on March 20, 1900, a large theater in Renaissance Revival style opened to a full house of 900 people to watch a light operetta and continued to entertain with the likes of the John Philip Sousa band, theatrical productions, and entertainers from overseas, including the great Polish actress Madame Modjeska (who returned later as a ghost to haunt the theater—honest, I was present at one appearance). Hard times 20 years later encouraged showing movies, and then, in the late '50s into the early '70s, it was used as a venue for summer stock performers from Michigan State University.

Eventually in the late '80s, a group began the restoration of this grand historic theater, inside and out, but only occasionally staged events. My immediate introduction was to complain to the board that this facility was underused; to build a following, we were going to have to re-accustom people to attending all kinds of cultural and social events there. What we needed was a "combo event," something that would cost little yet bring in audiences on a standard monthly basis.

My plan: I could borrow a 16mm movie projector from Tech, bring a film from the shelves I'd been stacking for my film classes, and show it with a themed buffet in the ballroom before each screening (e.g., a French film, a French buffet, etc.). There were several fine restaurants in the area, but we could begin with an excellent chef at a fledgling co-op venture. With the right food as enticement (the chef was good at anything) and an intriguing movie, voila! All for $9 ($5 to the chef), the rest to cover costs for the theater. It was a win-win situation for the chef, the theater, and people looking for weekend entertainment.

The board bought it. I created posters to announce the new monthly Club Indigo (a name that had been used for events presented there), put information in the *Gazette* (a favor from the the publisher), and we were on our way with a showing of the ever popular *Casablanca*.

It would be nice to say it was a resounding success, but, alas, the idea had to be fine-tuned before it brought in large audiences: plenty of publicity describing the film and the food in detail, on-the-air talks by me to sell it. Critical, above all, was selecting the right film—nothing new, just catchy classics by Fellini, Bergman, Kurosawa, and others who, with some introduction, could seduce people to try a whole new world of movie entertainment.

The meals did the drawing at first—good price, fine food— then, selling the values of the films selected. It was difficult; this was a community dedicated to Westerns, Clint Eastwood, and Marilyn Monroe. I turned the event into a modified classroom, and little by little, I began to introduce more recent foreign films.

Procedure: the afternoon of the event, pick up the projector, bring it to the theater and have it set up, not in a booth, but smack in the middle of the orchestra seating. The screen was old, yellowing, but usable, and at the proper distance and with a good bulb, it worked out fine. I'd put on a reel after a few minutes' introduction (background of the film, the director, the stars, etc.) and then show the reel.

Club Indigo poster

To avoid the deadly two-minute pauses while changing reels, I'd make references to normally unnoticed things just seen—camera usage in a particularly unique moment, timing in action, some personal info on the stars—anything to keep the audience interested and treat them to things they never noticed before, when watching just for plot.

It worked. We finally had money for two projectors, the gift of a full-sized screen, and the refurbishing of the projection booth—all huge improvements, bringing in larger audiences from word of mouth and my high-energy pre-publicity. Members of Mu Beta Psi also pitched in as ushers. After each meal, the guests would move from the ballroom into the theater proper, and at the right time, I'd enter the stage in front of the curtain (with an applause that grew over time to my pleasure—and embarrassment) and give my ten-minute lecture, always focusing on something vital to make each film of the night special.

Only a few realized that it required 40–50 hours a month and that I needed to be on hand well before patrons arrived to make spot decisions if things went awry. But the shows went on and rarely did the audience realize when crises occurred (which often felt like a "back to the future" moment from theatrical productions during my college and graduate school years). Year after year my reputation as the instigator of something that livened up the Calumet Theatre brought fame, if not fortune.

22

Another Inheritance

My father's death—several months before my retirement—entailed a new family responsibility: ownership of the cottage. This bequest was not a surprise, because of the long-standing financial arrangement I'd made. What was unexpected were the tensions it created.

As my parents aged, they would spend weeks, not months, at the cottage at Copper Harbor. (They eventually moved from Florida to Battle Creek, to be close to my sister Cis.) Every spring, I would get the place ready for their arrival in late June; I would always surprise them with some little gift such as a microwave oven, a toaster, a radio, but leave untouched the piles of dated *National Geographic* and other magazines. And at last, I was able to take a few intimate portraits of them during their precious days at the cottage; I particularly cherish one of my father sitting on a chair in front of the lake and its huge rocks that formed a kind of bay in front of him, lost in reverie.

Several weeks after their return to Battle Creek, I received a phone call from my father in a hospital there. The voice on the phone was weak, wishing me love. I knew when I rung off that I'd never see him again; he died that night. With foul weather preventing me from driving the 500-plus miles to Battle Creek, I never had the chance to bring our lives to an appropriate closure, but the phone call seemed enough.

Each year, while he was still alive and afterwards, my sisters and I worked out a vacation schedule at the cottage during the summer and fall seasons. (My brother, Jim, and his family, though they enjoyed visiting there, sunbathing, and appreciating its natural quietude, could never bring themselves to stay longer than an afternoon.) Our shared arrangement worked for a while, but complications set in as both Babe's and Cis's families grew in size—and the younger generation regarded it as a place to use, not a special family home.

Azar and Anjool Kirkish with children Joe, Babe, Cis, and Jimmy on Brockway Mountain Drive, 1971

Kirkish clan on Brockway Mountain Drive, 1971

In willing the cottage and property to me as the eldest son, my father had included the proviso that I continue welcoming the rest of the clan as he and my mother had done. I tried to uphold that provision, but once the children became college students at Tech, they frequently violated rules and sneaked up there on weekends for parties I was sure my parents would not have approved. Tempers flared among the families as I attempted to control the miscreants; some accepted new rules, others cried foul and refused to return. It's an old story of combined inheritances, and unfortunately, one that caused a permanent rift.

For me, ownership of the cottage meant its preservation as the rustic retreat my parents had built more than 50 years before. It was a place that had acquired an almost sacred feeling; Dad had often stated that tradition meant keeping it within the family and that each visit would generate situations, recollections, and special occasions to become unwritten "tradition." In Lebanese pattern as well, the eldest in the family had to uphold the traditions.

Of course, maintenance of an aging lakeside dwelling was a constant. Fortunately, I could call on members of the Phi Tau Fraternity to troubleshoot and fix the array of mechanical, masonry, and carpentry problems that arose; it seemed all I had to do was ask and a team of brilliant tinkerers would arrive! I also continued to host their annual fall retreat there, which I enjoyed, except for the inevitable beer drinking and rowdiness that came the last evening.

Phi Tau retreat at the cottage

From the earliest days, my parents had annually hosted local nuns and priests at the cottage for day trips or overnight stays. (Still hanging proudly on the wall, along with a mounted deer head, is a photo of two priests with my father—all in hunter's garb—after their successful fall weekend expedition.) So, in the late '90s, I was delighted when I got a call from Fr. Van Damme, wondering if it were possible for him to spend a Friday night at the cottage, because he was to marry a Copper Harbor couple the following morning. Possible? I couldn't believe the good fortune to have a priest there, not just for a visit, but an overnight! I felt blessed.

Fr. Van Damme insisted on driving; we arrived in time for a glorious sunset and a good night's rest. In the morning, from my little room upstairs, I could hear him making morning sounds in the guest room below, came down to find him rushing out the door in baggy swimsuit and towel for a brisk dunk in the great lake. He returned up to the cottage, dripping wet, toweling himself along the way—a sight so beautiful to be worthy of a photograph. I shot from the front porch, just as he looked up in surprise.

"Are you hungry, Father?" I asked as he came in, drying himself off. "Famished," he answered, "but I'll hold off until after the service. I hope you've enough food for a healthy eater." As he drove away, I removed two mammoth Finnish pasties from the freezer and popped them into the microwave and awaited the good priest's return. We sat together at one end of the long, log-hewed table, enjoying the meal; Father, who was an athletic giant of a person, helped himself to twice my portion. He insisted on cleaning up with me; we washed the dishes together in the kitchen, then packed up for the return home. At the porch door, he turned me around, held me by the shoulders in a firm grip, and solemnly blessed me and the house. I couldn't have asked for more! Later he drove us back to town carrying on a friendly conversation for the 43 miles. I was in bliss.

In his eight years in Houghton, he was as much a friend as a cleric. He never did repeat the request, but a few times, when he brought his "chapel rats" to a nearby Copper Harbor cottage for an overnight retreat, he would show up with them for a bonfire and marshmallows on the beach ... not as blissful as that one earlier visit but still left me feeling graced by their presence. Eventually, he left our parish for a larger one but corresponded often to remind us of his exceptional presence. It may seem impossible, but some of that presence seemed to permeate the cottage and beach for years after his absence.

❖ ❖ ❖

Much as I enjoyed having a stream of guests at the cottage, I also savored time alone there. I would unlock the door, walk into that familiar space with an immediate rush of memories that automatically set the tone and eclipsed the busy world I'd left 43 miles behind me. No phone to interrupt, just a radio to keep me company—able to pick up good news programs or an abundance of classical music from around the world. (Fun once in a while to test my bilingual capabilities with stations from across the lake, just 90 miles north.)

Then, always with camera at the ready, down the pebble incline to the shore as if I'd never been there before. And, indeed, that's true, because one of the delights is the lake's ever-changing surface due to the weather, to a new sunset and sunrise each day, to the seasons. On occasion, my time there would include a dramatic nocturnal viewing of Northern Lights (watched with enchantment from a window in my bedroom).

Those walks, taking me up on the rocks for a clearer view of the lake (so vast one can actually see the horizon's curvature from west to east), were always a breathtaking experience. Forays into the wild forest to the left, right, or across the highway into the densest woods of all, pulled me into the mysterious natural world, so easy to get lost in a matter of minutes. Indeed, one spring when I ventured too far in search of morels, I realized I was in unfamiliar territory ... and without a compass. The sun disappeared behind the clouds, no sound of car traffic, and so there was nothing to guide me. I sank to a log, clutching the basket, closed my eyes—and prayed!

Then, the warmth of the sun fell on my eyes; I looked up to watch for its location and used a trick learned from old timers: I picked out three trees in a line in the possible direction set by the sun, lifted the basket to my arms, and headed in their direction. As I passed one, I selected another beyond, then another, until—heart still thumping—I ran in the direction of the sound of distant waves. In less than 10 minutes, I reached familiar signs and, in joyful relief, crossed the highway down to the cottage and leaped the steps into it. I never made the same mistake of venturing without a compass again.

A favorite morning jaunt (after photographing a sunrise on the beach and a hearty breakfast) was a quarter-mile walk to photograph the daily changes of wild flora along both sides of the road ending at the large, magnificent log cabin B&B for a fresh cup of coffee with its owners, Ole and Ruth, and their startled guests at breakfast. The fun would begin: introduced simply as neighbor Joe, then, a tremendous variety of getting-to-know-you conversations, usually concluding with a farewell invitation to come to visit the cottage and pick pebbles. Many did. I'd return, but not before shooting photos of the latest crop of gorgeous, rare roses bred by Ruth with her green thumb.

Being at the cottage was therapeutic on many levels. On an annual visit to my doctor one year, I was instructed to take vitamin D, which I seemed to lack after each long winter. "Take the capsule if you must but, far better, get enriched by brief doses of sunbathing, a bit at a time with as much skin exposure as possible."

Aha! Another delight to add to my sunrise photos! Not yet completely dressed, loaded up with blanket and pillow, I'd settle down on the pebbled beach—my cap covering my closed eyes, lost in the ubiquitous sound of lapping waves—and sometimes doze off for half an hour or so. Never did I imagine being interrupted, and yet, one morning, I heard the crunching pebbles from afar, pushed up my cap, and saw a woman with two teen girls coming in my direction! They kept approaching, the mother with head down, searching the shore for coveted agates, the girls giggling at the sight of someone lying almost naked directly in their path.

What to do? Embarrassment changed to resentment for having been overtaken by unwanted visitors. I stood up, rearranged my underwear for decent coverage, ripped blanket and pillow from the pebbles and, with my hat clamped angrily down over my eyes, stomped up to the cottage. I never looked back but, to prevent repetition from other unwanted guests, changed my routine. After that I crossed the highway, found a pleasant open space among flora and fauna, and in secluded private performed my instructed duty, observed only by wild critters from all around; it was a delightful new addition to how I spent my time alone at the cottage.

23

The Return of Lord Krishna and the Birth of Pastor Joe

A ll my life, anything old had captivated me: the leaves on trees, for example, were all alike until they fell to the ground and took on individual looks. Same with people. Also, as a young child being a part of a multigenerational household, I found grandparents and elderly relatives absolutely fascinating—the way they shriveled with age (which I thought to be charming), taking on the looks of hand-sewn dolls—sedate, slow in responses, unobtrusive, yet rich with stories real and invented.

Little did I dream I'd ever manage to squeeze a few hours each week to read in senior care facilities. My ongoing activities with Little Brothers had opened my eyes to the isolation of many older community members; then, my mother's entry into a puritanical assisted living facility triggered a whole new dimension to my volunteer work. The only room available was at Still Waters Elders Home, a V-shaped, unpretentious one-floored building surrounded by carefully cultivated trees and flora on the edge of Calumet, about a 20-minute drive from home. Though not far from the Calumet Theatre (where I had just gotten involved), it was eons away in religious aspects. (The Apostolics, who comprised most of the staff and about two-thirds of the residents, were gentle, stoic, rarely talkative except in Finnish, with a religious resolve that made the Amish liberal by comparison.)

It took great force from both my sisters to settle my mother into Still Waters; we were told that was not unusual, that she would settle in on her own in time. So, both Babe (my younger sister) and I, being close by, took turns visiting her. It took some getting used to, but Mom, in her own diminished capacity, adjusted easily.

She would welcome us each time as—what?—friends of the family? My visits, three times a week, were spent with her in her plain but pleasant room (a few pieces of furniture and two narrow beds spaced apart) made homey with two of her painted forest scenes on the walls, a familiar comforter on one bed and a box of ancient family photographs on the other. Her daily chore was to dump the photos on the bed, separate them out by families, then, each evening, toss them all back into the box again. She was content to do so; it passed the time pleasantly.

My visits fell into a routine: drive up through all changes in weather, meet my mother sitting in a common room with other ladies—sometimes in their private world, sometimes chatting away. I'd burst in among them, raise the tempo with idle tales about the outside world, plop down and, with equally idle anecdotes, perk up their interest. Then I'd sit with my mother in her room and read to her (her passion for books never forgotten). I would open the book, holding it between us to let her follow along with the words being read. Every so often, she'd slap my hand and say, "Too fast!" so I'd slow down to a more comfortable pace and she would settle, again, into her semi-studied gaze.

One day it occurred to me that it might be nice to move to a small library room where we could invite others to join us. Soon, I had an audience of about 10–15 listeners, so I changed the venue: I would meet them in the room, pep them up with my "outside world" anecdotes, acknowledge each of them as I got to know them, and then sit in a little love seat with my mother in a chair close to me. She no longer followed my finger, would rest her eyes, and respond in tiny changes of expression befitting the material. And as long as I kept the subjects in a safe scale of religious dramas, historical tales, or biographies of famous men in history, it worked out well (though I had to read ahead to modify salacious worlds like "hell" or "damn").

Most of my groups were women, but then there was Eddie, a slow-witted, doughy fellow, who squeezed himself for male companionship next to me in the love seat—tiny, lumpy hands folded in his lap or brushing flakes of a sweet roll from his rumpled shirt, staring vacantly down as I read, occasionally breaking into a chuckle I never could fathom. He beamed as I'd refer to him as my "Buddy Eddie," then as I read, he would slowly slip heavily and soundly asleep onto my lap to awaken when the dinner bell ended our session. (A member of the staff told me I'd become his only friend, and bashfully he once gave me a small, badly over-colored painting of a bowl of fruit and glowed from my praise and thanks. It hangs still in my kitchen as a memory of him.)

Then I would walk my mother into the dining room for an unappetizing, tasteless, and greasy meal. The self-styled cook was able to turn out an acceptable standard Finnish menu but never ventured into the dining room and simply treated the residents as table numbers. I'd sit with my mother just long enough to help her finish the meal, and then take my leave.

One might think Still Waters was a dull place where routine dominated, but there were unexpected events I'll never forget, like the time one of the residents fell between the wall and his immovable bed. I heard him crying out for help, apparently unheard by anyone but me. It took an attendant, an emergency officer, and me to gently maneuver the poor fellow out and send him to the hospital for attention.

A woman down the hall often had troubles getting her top undergarment on or off; she would stand in the doorway, pulling and pushing around her impressive chest, shouting at the top of her lungs for someone to help. Again, rather than go to her aid, I called in a female attendant to help.

They were my leaves, none really alike, with personalities I came to recognize. There was Alice, cheerful despite a body wracked by arthritis. I would greet her with, "How's your boyfriend today?"—a game I'd play with her regarding her "Arthur-ritis." Grace was a sweetie, so proud of the cheap jewelry she wore, so I'd admire each necklace or bracelet. With each visit I'd notice jewelry increasing, until she would meet me overly bedecked, waiting for me to notice each piece as she glowed with the attention. And Henry, who would smile when I'd greet him with a hearty, "Hi, Hank!"

My heart went out to them. I began to volunteer whenever possible, do whatever I could to entertain them: showed movies or slideshows of my travels (always with enthusiasm, adding to the pleasure of the event), told a wide variety of stories about my life that always brought "oohs" and laughter as I'd blend fact with ridiculous fiction, and even read short stories and poetry to them.

One night I brought a portable movie projector to show *Lilies of the Field*, a film with a religious theme that starred Sidney Poitier as the hero. I set up the projector among the audience of about 60 residents, and suddenly one elderly man caused pandemonium by asking who would want to see a movie with a (expletive) Black person in it. We had to conclude as quickly as possible.

But the most memorable, unexpected incident occurred during a blizzard, when the entire group of residents gathered in a modified chapel for their weekly prayer and sermon, normally given by a minister admired by all of them for the strength and volume of his delivery. An attendant rushed to me as I was leaving for home. "You can't go. They're all waiting for the reverend and he can't get out of his snowed-in garage!" So? "You'll have to take over, you're a teacher, must be something you could do for all those people waiting in there."

A pending catastrophe! Without a second thought, I took off my coat and rushed into a room filled with people patiently waiting for their message for the day. I walked to the ambo, picked up the Bible, opened it to a red-ribboned page and, in a solemn voice, intoned: "We have just recently celebrated one of the holiest days of the year—Easter. It's over now, and we seem to have forgotten all about it. So why don't we go back to that precious weekend and recall it." I read passages that covered Good Friday to the close of Easter Sunday, not doing a very good job at the bombastic delivery they knew.

Finally over, I closed the Bible, made some concluding statement, but no one left. One lady said, simply, "We always sing at the end." Me? "One off-key note" Kirkish? I turned to a woman waiting at the pump organ and nodded. She played a familiar Easter hymn and the group joined in, singing in at least a dozen parts while I mouthed it. Over, they rose and headed for the dining room for lunch. As they left, one of the women said rather loudly to her partner, "That's Joe Kirkish. He's a Catholic. But he did pretty good, didn't he?"

It wasn't until my next visit that I discovered half the staff had been gathered out of sight, eavesdropping. After that, I was jokingly referred to as Pastor Joe. Even now, I still don't know what to make of my first sojourn into the life of the religious messenger....

◆ ◆ ◆

One night, after showing a 16mm movie, I walked my mother back to her room (by that time she was perfectly comfortable with a walker) when suddenly she collapsed. Her legs gave out from under her and plunged her into a series of painful experiences, which made her anxious and uncomfortable if unattended. My sisters and I decided to move her to another facility, where she could be better accommodated. That was the first of a few short stays at other residences for the aged, until she was accepted at a nursing home. Babe and I continued alternating our visits, which amounted to just sitting with her, watching her life shrink away.

Finally, I would lie next to her and talk her back briefly into the real world. She'd been quite proficient in French once, so I'd smile and say, "*un*"; she'd follow up after a pause with "*deux*" and I'd return with "*trois*" until we'd get into the twenties and she'd fall asleep.

But she slowly slipped away, until one day a nurse confessed to me that this would be her end. Her arms began turning blue up to her shoulders; I faced the fact that it was so. Another nurse took over, leaving me outside the door, until it opened to carry her lifeless body on a gurney to an undertaker waiting in the wings. It was an eerie sight, seeming totally unreal all the way even through to the burial.

By that time, I realized, to my relief, that I'd finally spent very tender moments with her, feeling at last a genuine mother/son relationship that I had longed for from childhood. For a while, after my father's death, she tried to engage me in serious rows as the eldest man in the family, which would always end in a truce each time—a roller coaster of fights, shouts, silences, and eventually a sort of giving in together. So, after decades of mixed turmoil, feelings of sympathy and even something akin to love closed that chapter of my life.

⫶ ⫶ ⫶

PART 5

Elder,
2000–

Esrey Park, Lake Superior

24

Zigzagging through Aging

The dawn of a new millennium and a new century, anticipated by so many of my peers, was a nonevent for me. Reaching 75 that year, similarly, had little meaning. If anything, it redoubled my determination to remain youthful—to maintain an open eye, an open mind, and an open heart.

I had devoted the years following high school to escaping the fate of being a small-town grocer's son; I had spent the rest of my adulthood thriving on serendipity and seizing opportunities or zigzagging when obstacles arose—all the time, clinging to my independence. Now my challenge was to apply those lessons to aging. I wanted to follow the sage words of businessman, humanitarian, and poet Samuel Ullman (1840–1924), who wrote in his late life the poem, "Youth": "Nobody grows old merely by a number of years. / We grow old by deserting our ideals. / Years may wrinkle the skin, but to give up enthusiasm wrinkles the soul ..."

So, I continued to fill my days (and nights) with my volunteer work in Houghton and the surrounding communities. I was on call to Little Brothers as a driver and doing readings at several local senior care facilities. After my mother's death, I had found new precious "leaves" like Myrtle at Our Lady of Mercy Home, who would seclude herself in her room, sitting in her wheelchair, clutching a worn purse (which, I learned from a nurse, contained nothing but a container of chewing tobacco). She would wait eagerly for me to take her for a wheelchair ride down the halls. "Fast or slow?" I'd ask, with an immediate demand: "Go FAST." Off we'd go, beep-beeping around corners as she whooped with delight. I'd grown fond of that coarse, often profane woman, and when she died, I visited her at the funeral home and at the request of her family, took a photo of her clutching her purse in the coffin. It nearly broke my heart.

My circle of aging friends continued to grow through a phone call from Isobel, a resident at The Bluffs, newly built in 2000 as an upscale continuing care facility on a hillside above Houghton that had filled almost overnight, mainly with former Tech faculty and their relatives. Isobel, a sophisticated, no-nonsense woman who'd played classical piano and taught lessons until moving to The Bluffs, was fed up with a lack of sophisticated entertainment. She insisted I fill the vacuum.

I approached the manager of The Bluffs a year after it opened, who approved my offer with open arms. Three times a week I'd show up, meeting with the group around the fireplace in the third-floor ballroom. I always began with some personal anecdote to warm them up, then to the book for an hour, ending in time for the evening meal and, before long, by invitation, follow them to the main-floor dining room and become their dinner guest. I truly enjoyed

Joe sharing a meal with a blind resident at The Bluffs

being a part of these evening meals, both for the company and the information exchanged. Through my socializing, I witnessed with amusement and fascination the interesting relationships developing between residents, where there was a ratio of at least three men to each woman. Also, conversations at The Bluffs led me to check out the medical services of the VA; I had been reluctant to take advantage of this benefit, given my lackluster time in the Air Corps decades ago, but soon I became a grateful convert for a growing mix of health issues.

I knew many of the residents from my life at Tech, got to know many more, then, sadly but expectedly, lose them one by one as their time on earth had been spent. It became a custom I adjusted to but not without a touch of regret. I became such an integral part of The Bluffs, I would often be asked by the staff, "Hey, Joe, when are you going to sign up for a room?" with my usual reply, "Not until I absolutely have to."

I continued to write my weekly column, "In the Catbird's Seat," for the *Daily Mining Gazette*. Unlike so many small-town newspapers that either were bought up by larger news organizations or put out of business by the proliferation of online services, it has survived but with frequent turnover of publishers. When I first started writing the column back in the early '60s, the paper had a clear Republican slant that aligned with the Copper Country's conservative bent. In the ensuing years, there were subtle shifts in editorial direction when a change of ownership occurred; a few times, in fact, the column had been dropped but then reinstated due to popular demand.

When it became necessary to shrink the paper, the column shrank as well, slightly longer but only once a month. The title changed to "Over 60," to appeal to the majority of readers but also to anyone else interested. It has kept my writing skills tuned up and enabled me to expand the column from 600 to 900 words, which is a nice trade-off.

As always, I pay constant attention to the state of contemporary life and accumulate a stack of broadly useful information for future use. Friends (nearby and faraway) continue to help, sending pithy or humorous articles (print and online) for me to riff on. Each commentary is spiked with tidbits of rare information and literary references—something to stretch the mind and stir the imagination, that's my goal, always my underlying motivation. Sometimes I get immediate feedback, sometimes delayed (usually, through encountering a community member who comments on a posting I've done). Though the rewards are not the same as seeing the light bulb go on in a student's mind in a classroom, it does reassure me that my efforts to sow curiosity and thought in our northern hinterlands have some impact.

❖❖❖

Of all my community-focused activities, the growth in the audience for the monthly Club Indigo programs was especially satisfying, and I was able to screen more "art house" films such as masterpieces that rarely graced commercial theaters. Bergman's *The Seventh Seal* hit home with our audience for its vigor and questioning of mysticism, as did Fellini's Italian representation of a highly personal recollection of his war-torn city in *Roma, Open City*. Some still remind me of the showing of films like Kurosawa's brilliant depiction of thousands of ancient soldiers in battle in *Seven Samurai*. The key to success was my brief lecture before each film, and the combination of interesting food and a bargain ticket, helped by aggressive promotion of the films through radio interviews.

I became "Mr. Club Indigo"—curator, event coordinator, publicist, maître d', emcee—all in one! Like many of the *auteur* filmmakers whose work I showed, I wanted to be totally in charge of the production, which entailed endless troubleshooting problems large and small. One of the most unnerving, behind-the-scenes episodes happened the evening when I screened the spectacular Chinese film, *Crouching Tiger, Hidden Dragon*: curious people getting tickets beforehand (including many Chinese faculty and students from Tech) ... and no food. A phone call from the Chinese restaurant demanded money before giving us the meals. Quick work: assure them we'd be there with a van to pick up the food and pay them, a van located, drove 15 miles from Houghton to the theater in time to set up for the already arriving guests. Enough to cause ulcers!

Since this was a one-person job, the efforts grew with the audiences and didn't include the fact that we were now getting films from professional distribution companies which entailed another series of rental considerations. I was continually exhausted, and yet, getting the feedback from enthusiastic regulars and hearing the applause after each film always kept me going.

Things changed when the theater manager took over the dining component. The catered food showed less and less spark; regulars complained. Finally, when an unknown caterer served deviled eggs for the meal before the screening of *Tampopo*, a recent Japanese film about a family-run noodle shop, that ended my 23-year run. Another case of a wonderful climb to success slowly destroyed by incidents beyond my control.

Ironically, in the fall of that year (2017), I was honored for my 40-year contribution as a promoter of the cinematic arts in the region at a special event at the annual 41 North Film Festival at Tech. Always eager for the chance to see and discuss new films, I had been one of the regulars at this showcase of contemporary films since its inauguration in 2004. Erin Smith (who taught digital media in the Humanities Department) was the organizer of the event; as with my Club Indigo initiative, she had single-handedly built her festival from a tiny audience of aficionados in a gymnasium into a popular event held in the Rozsa Center for the Performing Arts' auditorium. We had a friendly relationship of mutual admiration, and in 2016, she had decided that at the event in 2017, she wanted to celebrate my efforts.

As the time drew near, all I knew was that I was going to receive a City Lights award before the showing of French filmmaker Agnes Varda's film *Faces Places*, be asked to say a few words, and that there would be a reception. Well publicized, the event drew a crowd of more than 300 people from both Tech and the community at large! (As I found out later, longtime friends Tom Co and Faith Morrison, Tech faculty members who were also ardent film fans, partnered secretly with Erin to pull off the event.) The tribute before the screening went well though I was surprised to find myself tense under a spotlight and with a portable microphone in hand. During the box dinner afterwards held in the Rozsa's huge dining room, when I was expected to reply to the accolades already bestowed, I went comfortably—even exuberantly—to my pitch regarding the special values in non-Hollywood showings. The applause suggested I was successful in selling the filmic alternatives, but it was disappointing to observe lots of empty seats at other festival screenings, an indicator that there still is only limited interest in our community for independent films.

Joe being honored for decades of service by Mu Beta Psi

❖ ❖ ❖

The film festival and periodic lunches with Erin kept me apprised of the evolution of cinema studies at Tech since my departure. Within the Humanities Department, my role of emeritus hardly created a ripple of attention; with the addition of newer, younger members and married couples dominating the scene, it didn't take long for me to feel less comfortable among them. As my cubbyhole mailbox thinned down to advertisements, I felt all but invisible. When I began to recognize fewer and fewer names among the mailboxes, I took it as a signal and discontinued the habit of stopping by for "old times' sake." And when new office employees no longer recognized me, I closed that chapter of my life and turned in another direction, back to familiar grounds in the community at large.

After my emeritus teaching work ended (in 1999), I kept in regular touch with Tech students by staying involved with the fraternities. Gradually I realized, though, I was less and less an asset to the two groups and they regarded me more as a loyal supporter than as an effective advisor. So, in 2007, after 50 years, I bowed out.

I renamed the Phi Tau Room "Marty's Room," since only now and then was I hosting Tech students. It was through Marty's periodic visits as the fraternity's new self-appointed alumni advisor that I kept tabs on their current activities. During his visits, split between time with me and our routine photo trips to the cottage, he kept me updated with each new group as they came and went. He even saw to it that they were on call to help me—handy when I needed one of them for house repairs or to keep my computer functioning properly.

Besides attending Phi Tau reunions (arranged by Marty), I have found another way to feel connected to the fraternity alumni—in fact, both sustaining fond memories and providing me with another teaching outlet. In my former role as an instructor in the humanities, I had instituted a remedial exercise to build students' vocabulary; little did I envision that it would develop into "Word of the Day" (WOTD), a daily email now shared with a far-flung network of former Tech alumni and friends.

What started me on this further education mission was an incident at a Tech graduation ceremony. A former student in cap and gown grabbed me by both shoulders and proceeded to tell me what a wonderful teacher I was. "But one thing," he added, "you always used too many big words in your lectures. Why?"

"Give me an example," I asked, disappointed since I'd simplified my former vocabulary at least by half to meet our students part way. "Yeah," he replied, "you just said 'intimidate.'"

"Intimidate? You don't know what that means?" I was shocked. This straight-A fellow (majoring in physics) answered, "Yeah, never heard of it." A glaring example of a common word that should be familiar to anyone with a college degree. Had we or earlier schooling failed in our duty to properly educate?

Ever eager to remedy an insufficiency, I decided that I would take it upon myself to do a daily posting to former students. The process was simple: feature either a rarely used or esoteric word found in my newspaper/magazine readings, then set it up in this manner:

> WOTD for (date): oeuvre – *urv* – a grouping of creative work by one artist. Example:
> 'According to the online publication *Hyperallergic*, a major Greek artist gets his first US show as a broad survey of his intimate oeuvre, on view in Chicago through July 31.'

Through the two fraternities, I culled lists of former members to circulate my postings; requests quickly multiplied from their relatives or friends to be included. From an early handful of graduating students, the WOTD has grown into nearly 300 subscribers all over the world, with frequent comments from foreign students who especially appreciate adding to their previously limited study of our language and those poorly trained in previous basic classes as well as my *literati* friends who discover they often misunderstood the exact meaning of esoteric words. There still are a few recipients who follow up regularly—one who responds with a pun, another who makes an intelligent addition to my brief material. (I'm disappointed when a posting does not generate comments, but that's rare.) An avid film buff inspired an addition, when she wrote one time: "Joe, I'm familiar with most of your words; how about selecting one of your favorite films as a recommendation to rent for the weekends?" Producing a weekly bonus film tip on Thursday or Friday adds to my pleasure, and it seems, for my readers, as well.

There were some surprises, too, that thrust me back briefly into life on the Tech campus. From time to time, I would get a phone call asking to purchase a photo as a gift for a retiring faculty or staff member. I was particularly excited when I was commissioned to create an abstract backdrop for a production of *Carmina Burana* at the Rozsa auditorium in 2001; I produced a slide series of abstract images that worked so well that it stirred shocked murmurs and resulted in further requests for use in other situations (including the backdrop for an original short opera) and even some sales.

Most unexpected was receiving the prestigious Clair M. Donovan award for Outstanding Service in 2002; I felt thrilled and humbled to join a pantheon of exceptional Tech faculty, staff, and students who had made such a difference to the university. At the formal banquet, I was given the opportunity to talk not about my artwork, but to reveal how the cause for the award was simply the compilation of the influences of my life, beginning with my Lebanese heritage. Although several family members were present, I wished my parents could have been there to see how they fit into the continuum. (Once, back in the 1980s, they had attended a campus ceremony in which I had received a national award for my service to the Phi Tau fraternity and heard me pay public tribute to the values they had instilled in me.)

By this time in my life, I had learned to accept that "all good things end," and thus the necessity of moving on to the next unknown. I was active on the summer art show circuit in Michigan and Wisconsin for several years, but two things ended my participation: the advent of digital photography that made everyone feel like an artist, flooding the market and making my art prints much less salable (except for the "pretty pictures" of the Copper Country); the tiring nine-hour days required to be an exhibitor, plus the process of putting up and taking down the booth by myself, left me exhausted each time. I never stopped photographing; the impulse to examine the world through a camera lens is as strong as ever!

Similarly, the pleasure of traveling abroad and visiting friends and family around the country gradually waned. With more free time, I had been able to visit relatives in Arizona, California, and Seattle at least once a year. Great fun! But I began to feel jinxed by the airlines, because I always had to face the inevitable complications—getting window seats (a bonus opportunity to shoot the country from above) and troubles with connecting flights. It seemed that every trip had a glitch, either leaving me stranded or losing a bag (including, one time, a correctly-addressed, well-packaged portfolio that I finally got back after days of phone calls to four different flight sources). Though the anticipation of adventure had been so exciting in the early years of my retirement, I came to dread what was in store, and the stress produced a variety of new anxiety-related ailments.

Around the time I turned 80, I decided as well that I could only manage short day trips and had to forego visits to places that had become so special, especially Camp Nebagamon and Cleveland. Instead, I tried to get people to visit me at the cottage, and I did continue to host people from all over the world and from many parts of my earlier life. Spending time with the Walters (and whichever children or grandchildren were there) while up at Copper Harbor also made me feel as if I had traveled afar.

25

Long Exposure

For years I had been observing the signs of climate change, especially through my photography around Lake Superior, where cloud formations became less defined, moved more rapidly and lower in the sky. Others seemed to ignore this phenomenon but looking through stacks of similar sky shots made it perfectly obvious to me: these were telltales of significant, destructive atmospheric patterns.

The Father's Day flood of 2018 turned my life upside down. My life had begun during a blizzard, and I'd endured many examples of bad weather since but never anything like a prolonged 11-day rainstorm (no doubt, an example of the impact of climate change). It caused historic flooding and landslides around Houghton and Hancock, and my basement filled with muck, up to the knees, daily. Only the goodwill of the fraternity next door, who sent at least two fellows every day and night with sump pumps and shovels, helped rescue me.

At 93, for the first time in my life, I felt deeply desperate—even suicidal. It happened on Day 9 of the flood, when I was awakened from a deep sleep by another roar of sludge flowing in. Barefoot and in PJs, I rushed down to find what I'd dreaded: the flood pouring in from every possible entry, already knee-high, with no sign of letting up. I sat on the top step, staring for the ninth time (and with no sign that it would <u>ever</u> let up), and I began to lean forward, fully prepared to drop into the dirty water and end an impossible disaster once and for all. At that very moment, as I leaned forward to drop, the outside door opened and two fellows from next door rushed in, pushing me aside to repeat the pump work all over again. It was only hours later that the flood subsided and I realized what I'd almost done.

Finally, two days later, the stationary rain clouds moved on, and the massive cleanup began. Always wanting to be a giver, I now had to accept the necessity of being a taker and soon discovered, to my surprise, the relief in being helped by other givers. It was a marathon (for me and everyone else): scraping out the muck, ridding a basement of stoves, washers, furnaces—all ruined—and in a rush to restore things before winter set in.

As I struggled through the daze of the recovery process, a beefy, middle-aged fellow with a businesslike assistant was going from house to house to assess the losses. Soon after came a phone call: the recently organized Portage Health Foundation would like to see me. Puzzled, I found their offices, met with a group of them, including Executive Director Kevin Store (the man who had led the inspection team) and his assistant among them. They planned to buy everything needed to restore the basement's losses, repair the damaged walls inside and out, and in general return the house to its normal state.

I was stunned. Kevin returned home with me; we sat in the dining room, discussing all the details of the restoration process. All the while he seemed to want to say more, finally asked (looking at a stack of solicitation letters from charities near and far sitting on the far end of the table) how I managed my gift giving. I explained that since I had begun teaching, every year I had set aside money to donate to international humanitarian organizations and local community service groups but always agonized over how much to give and to whom. That prompted a lecture about the little-known fact that a sizable portion of these donations would likely support high administrative costs of these charities, not go to their clients. I was shocked, even floored at the thought of my hard-earned money being siphoned off. What to do? He drew out a sheet with many names and addresses on it—organizations that the foundation supported and that served members of the community. His primary concerns were the plight of hundreds of children "at risk" and dozens of battered women living in destitute situations in the area.

I was aware of the problems of seniors in our locale through my work with Little Brothers and my weekly reading at the senior care facilities, but until I talked to Kevin, I was unaware of the breadth of health and social welfare problems in the place that I thought I knew so well. I checked my "charity bank account," found a substantial amount in it, and decided to entrust it to him.

His compassion, hands-on leadership, and holistic vision about individual and community health impressed me, as did his background—a Finnish kid who had grown up in one of the many declining copper towns and wanted to make a difference in his home territory. We quickly developed a rapport, and with his guidance, I've enthusiastically expanded my yearly contributions.

I mentioned to him one day about my lifelong desire to become a philanthropist (one of my childhood passions was spending hours reading aloud the dictionary and "philanthropist" had been one of my favorite words), but I had never thought of my generosity as meriting that designation. "Joe," he said with a grin, "being our top donor to the organization, you ARE a philanthropist." That was one of the happiest days of my life, thrilled to realize that without fanfare but with an ongoing secret delight, I was helping people in my own backyard change the course of their lives for the better.

My house was put back together over several months; healing from the trauma of the flood, however, took more than a year. With the help of counseling at the VA, my bout with PTSD has subsided, but the sight and sound of violent wind and rain still make me nervous.

◆ ◆ ◆

The flood was a setback that interrupted my established patterns, but in time, I was able to resume much of my daily, weekly, and seasonal activities. Then, at 95, came the next challenge: surviving the 2020–21 pandemic. Feeling vulnerable, caged and lonely in my house, and realizing that age had finally overtaken me, I needed to funnel my energy into some creative outlet.

What to do? Working on a memoir seemed an appropriate way to pass the time. Since my youth, I had done photographic self-portraits—mostly as visual or technical experiments—but this project needed a different approach: true self-study, the literary equivalent of a long exposure shoot which would illuminate the enduring and ephemeral elements of a life filled with unexpected adventures.

As part of this retrospective process, I've spent time pondering several recurring questions that I've been asked but up until now, never probed deeply. To complement the recollections of the previous sections, here are my reflections from 14 months of an unplanned but productive retreat.

The most commonly asked question: "Why did you return and then remain in Houghton all those years?"

While working on this memoir, I found part of the reason when I read that *Tempo 24/7*, the online lifestyle magazine branch of *24/7 Wall St.*, ranked Houghton #9 on its list of the "23 Most Charming Towns in America." When I studied the descriptions and the photos of all the ones chosen, I realized how similar all these towns looked, their blocks of 19th and early 20th century buildings well preserved, as if time had passed them gently by.

In fact, the center of Houghton looks much as it did in my youth (the multistory building that housed the Kirkish brothers' enterprise is little changed and still bears the remnant of the original sign). But it is an island surrounded by formerly open spaces now being turned into new clusters of homes, malls, and other commercial complexes as if to ignore the "old downtown" look in favor of aggressive development in its parameter.

The article struck a chord for me about my enduring attraction to my hometown, especially the parts that remained untouched: it was where I felt comfortable—a country hick who adapted easily to other environs and who gained a certain sophistication from the experience, yet who felt most at ease in his original surroundings. As one Finn was supposed to have said after a brief exploration of life in the lower peninsula, "To hell with Dee-troit; I go back to Michigan."

Looking closer at a few seemingly unimportant incidents here might also help to explain my ongoing attachment:

- Sarah Williamson, unmarried, living unobtrusively in her small apartment in an aging quadraplex building, now in her 80s, called our WGGL station to apply for one of the AM-FM radios we were selling at cost ($30 for $90 models) simply to attract local listeners; our student technician personally delivered it, plugged it in for her, and showed her how simple it was to tune into our station and at what volume. It wasn't long before he heard from her in her sweet, simple voice requesting help; for example, when she said it refused to turn on, he would oblige and solve the problem easily (a chair had pulled the plug from the wall). She was ever grateful. He never failed her for that and similar other technical problems beyond her aging mind. Only in Houghton....

- The time I'd made one of my friendly visits to Temple Jacob for a special familial ceremony celebrated communally. The rabbi searched among the men present to create a minion in the ritual procession around the aisles carrying the Torah scrolls; there was one person short. The rabbi turned to me and asked if I would fill in. I did, in my borrowed *yarmulke* and hefting the heavy scroll seven times around the temple, I, a Roman Catholic, was more than happy to oblige.

- One evening I had landed in a peculiar situation, called 911, explained my problem: I'd just made a meal in my pressure cooker, but could not open it. What to do? In less than five minutes, the chief of police arrived, manipulated the cooker with a screwdriver, and in seconds, Mr. Joe Kirkish had his meal.

But there are some other important factors, too, why I didn't uproot. Because through decades of lecturing in front of classes large and small as well as gaining mastery in the use of a microphone and camera, I became fearless in time, and yet for some reason, I always felt insecure and inadequate. Not having a mate, the familiarity of place and fellow citizens became even more important for my well-being.

What's more, living here also allowed me easily to move back and forth between the intense academic environment of the university and the ever-changing wonders of the natural world beyond it, especially around Lake Superior. From my sojourns in cramped cities (large and small) came my understanding of the importance of being near water and vast open natural spaces to feed my soul and my creativity.

Did I sacrifice opportunities in staying here? Possibly, but I've created, developed, and contributed so much to the area that, without actually realizing it, I became a "big frog in a little pond." For me that feels good. It's hard to explain, but to walk into shops or on the streets, it's heartwarming to be greeted with, "Hi, Joe," even when I don't recognize who they are.

Yet, I must admit, too, that I have a love/hate relationship with my Copper Country. Yes, I'm at heart a naif who acquired a certain amount of worldliness, but my experiences have brought me to understand there is a Yooper mindset here that is real, and that small town life is rife with compromises in a hardly hidden climate of intolerance and cultural, social, and political divides that have grown, especially politically, of late.

It hasn't been easy to face the fact that, for example, contrary to knowledge of what gas guzzlers are doing to the world, there is skyrocketing proliferation of trucks and other polluting adult "toys." I have tried to make peace with growing numbers of community members who seem prone in their ignorance to be stubbornly, vehemently obstinate, and even paranoidal toward serious social or political issues, much like their ultraconservative compatriots elsewhere. They reinforce the Yooper stereotype. Not easy for a teacher to find such otherwise wonderful people around me, accept them as neighbors and, at times, even humbly try to spread a little helpful knowledge when possible.

The other big downside for me to life in the Copper Country: the harsh winters, which I'd originally liked as a child for the pleasures of playing in the snow, came to represent endless bitter months. Though I delight in the regular changes of the seasons, each winter, more and more, I feel exiled to a period of Siberian existence. Moreover, the serious impact of climate change on our weather systems (especially longer, more powerful events like the 11-day flood) leaves me anxious about further threats to our well-being. Am I the only person to recognize the impending doom of trucks and other gas-guzzling toys?

So why did I remain here? Simply because, after nearly a century of observation, I realize that there is no perfect spot on earth, no Shangri-La, no place better than what I've become used to right here. I have adopted a "make do" attitude. My roots are here and my comfort in knowing that I've found my niche is just fine.

Over the years, I've often thought of the words of Professor Roman's niece, who'd left a privileged aristocratic life in Poland to join a nunnery in Rome and who wrote me to say: "I am not happy with my choice, but I am content, and that makes all the difference."

Amen, Zofia.

◆◆◆

What purpose has religion played in my life? My answer to that question is a corollary of why I remained in Copper Country.

Put simply, the religious education I received at St. Ignatius (church and school) and reinforced by my parents at home gave me a lifelong moral and spiritual framework which has served me well through the twists and turns of my life. At the same time, my fascination with the beliefs and practices in other religions has not only made me deeply aware of common denominators and differences but, also, without realizing it, strengthened my own Roman Catholic faith. Yes, I'm a believer in a Superior Being, in the importance of the Ten Commandments as guides to a good life (i.e., recognition of right and wrong), and the ultimate judgment for our cumulative deeds. And since I'm human and make mistakes along the way, I have my church's teachings to help me over those humps as well.

Naive? Sophomoric? Deluded? Perhaps, at one time or another, but always with the guidance of great visionaries—St. Augustine, Teilhard de Chardin, the Gospels—enough to keep me contented ... most of the time.

That also explains why daily devotion and weekly attendance at church is so meaningful. All the precepts and familiarity of ritual are an automatic source of comfort, and from childhood, a feeling of grounding, a pattern of relying on something in the church's teaching. To say nothing of the clergy themselves: I have been instructed and inspired by the priests at St. Ignatius and St. Al's in Houghton—all truly holy men who did not abuse their position, as has happened in some communities. For me, those scandalized priests are sad exceptions and don't align with my experience of devoted religious leaders.

Another big question I've grappled with: Did I miss out by living alone the majority of my life?

When I saw the 1952 screen adaptation of Carson McCullers's play, *The Member of the Wedding*, it left a permanent imprint on me. The story focuses on a young, lonely girl who always wanted to change her life from being a "me" to becoming a "we." I never forgot it, I guess, because I strongly identified with her desire.

Growing up in the 1930s, I had been a big fan of the Andy Hardy movies, and the portrayal of the cohesive Hardy family overseen by the kind and wise Judge Hardy planted in me an idealized picture of family relationships. As a kid, with Lebanese families around us, sleeping, eating, and playing together, our family seemed more of a cultural unit. I even thought of aunts and uncles as part of the "we" that we grew up with. While in our limited way, our family of six were to some extent a natural caring, if not a truly loving, "we," I became more aware of the emotional distance between my parents and me once I left home.

Camp Nebagamon gave me a totally different view of family relationships. I discussed it one evening with Muggs, commenting on my admiration of obvious signs of love as, for example, when a father openly hugged and kissed his son, with tears in his eyes as they parted after the father's brief visit to camp. Muggs berated me, said I was wrong in assuming too much by that loving gesture, that it was just a difference in his open display of affection in contrast to a more reserved one from between my father and me. Perhaps, I thought, but still recalling my father's simple handshake, rather than the typical Lebanese-style hug when relatives reunited, at my return from the Air Corps, it could hardly match that boy's father's intensity of affection.

The result? Quite without realizing it, I gravitated to families of my aspirations—more the Judge Hardy families than mine—and eventually wound up with many such surrogate parents. I reveled, too, in the honorary role of uncle that I came to assume (as a child, we always referred to any adult relatives as "aunts" or "uncles" with older Lebanese visitors to our home). The "we" that I adopted in such cases has always been genuinely sincere and it continues to this day, each time I find myself still drawn in the same manner, in a yearning to become a "we."

Why did I never marry? How many angels can dance on the head of a pin? That's the number of reasons I look back upon, when I passed the usual age to marry—always assuming the "right" girl would come along. Too picky? Too aware of possible changes after marriage? Too late in selecting a right person after she'd finally gone searching elsewhere? Ask any person left behind the same question and you'll get one or more reasons similar to mine, including some unpleasant disappointments as the right girl became the wrong girl. Or, one time when the "perfect girl" came along and, just as we knew it, was taken away when the family moved out of town.

A thousand reasons to hide the actual truth: how I was marked by the tensions and unhappiness of my parents' marriage and many others living around us—marriages that came about with innocent high hopes only to result in disastrous lifelong disappointments and bitter compromises … in contrast to the rare true partnerships of people like the Steins, the Romans, the Walters, and a few others.

At various intervals, I reread the results of the Rorschach test I took years ago as a graduate student, but in this dimension of my life, the conclusions about my personality traits provided no insight or explanation. Ultimately I ignored the "why" of staying single and simply learned to accept remaining a "me."

❖ ❖ ❖

"Joe, you're an odd duck. You have thousands of acquaintances all around you, but do you have any real friends?" This is the question an astute university colleague once posed to me, and one that has lay dormant in my consciousness.

Years of casual friendships, due to my itinerant existence from my brief military service through my bohemian days in New York, became a series of sometimes warm relationships but never lasting ones. To fill the breach, as my university friend had observed, it became a search for quantity over quality, temporary friendships that only rarely narrowed down to that desired, long-lasting soul mate, the kind I read about, saw in movies, or in my imagination. My friendship with Tallie Handler in New York was as close as I came—two oddballs in sync—but then, we drifted apart when I returned to Houghton and she disappeared without explanation. (I still don't know what happened to her.) I adjusted, adapted to new friendships but always hesitant to get "too close." Safety in numbers seemed to serve. As I progressed through my 20s into my 30s and watched good friends slip into the next natural state of life—marriage—I could feel an island growing around me, isolating myself from my peers.

A good friend/priest once said to me in my late 20s, "Joe, you're obviously quite comfortable with the status quo right now, but someday, years later perhaps, you'll miss a natural close relationship." I never believed him, ever satisfied with decades of what I considered copious friendships among students and peers during my academic career, plus my camaraderie with local church and synagogue members.

Once I departed from the groves of academe, I clung to my independence with plenty of things to accommodate myself (travel, photography, the cottage, volunteering, etc.). Friends and family began to drift away, and then when I passed not so gently into my 90s and alone, I began to feel suddenly left behind and invisible. I first realized it one day when I was making a shopping purchase. Normally, the clerk would automatically write my name and even address without asking; I was obviously known. Until that fated day when the young clerk looked up at me and asked, "Could you spell that out for me?"

A blow to the ego! True, I'd been living off the past and now began paying the price for it. Finally, the priest's words came to haunt me, especially now as I was approaching the century mark and facing mental, physical, and social deficits that have changed my existence. I had so many longtime friends and dear relatives scattered everywhere, but the absence of close friends nearby and local family members headed down roads of their own, gave me the sinking feeling that I was going to finish out my life as a stranger in my own community. I also felt overwhelmed by the demands of my large century-old home, the cottage, and my incompetence in an increasingly digital society.

Then an amazing thing happened to veer me in a new direction and renew my spirit. Not all at once, I found unexpected "payback" from decades of wide-ranging contributions to the community in the form of a band of angels: local men and women popping up, one or two at a time, introducing themselves, and taking over just as I thought no one ever noticed. Chief among them:

Fred, who discovered me through his wife (who used to live across the street). He dropped by one summer day, behind the wheel of his flaming red roadster, top down, displaying a glowing tan across his exposed portly body; he honked the horn and asked if I'd care to have lunch with him. So began a lively and wonderful relationship: a weekly visit by Fred and Joe to one of the many fine restaurants in the area and then the question: "Where would you care to go to take pictures?"

Kevin, who stepped into my life after the horrors of the 11-day deluge, became a friend (bonding particularly as first-born sons in our families) and Mr. Fixit just as I needed one.

Michelle, whom I've known from our church parish and as an occasional companion for various events, but also as the mental health guide for American veterans, doubling as graceful, positive friend and counselor when needed.

Rick, an Episcopal priest, now retired with his wife, Sherrie, also a retired priest, who live just a few miles away from the cottage, who provides not only clerical advice, but useful guidance on building repair and maintenance. We've spent hours in friendly, intellectual discussions while he hovered over me and the cottage through all four seasons.

Terry, a former Phi Tau and now a respected local physician, has always been special over the years, and who now hovers over me as my own personal medical guide.

Two others from afar have parachuted in at key moments to keep me going. Out of the distant past, Bernie, a former Tech student from China, who lives in Seattle and returns to the area with his family because his son is now enrolled at Tech. It has been heartwarming, after 35 years, to have them move into my life, through constant emails or on summer visits, always generous as long-lasting Chinese friends, loaded with foreign goodies and help around the house.

And, of course, there was always Marty, our relationship only strengthening through the years despite our separation by over 500 miles; we managed to bridge the gap with a familial love and guidance by the sheer length and strength of what had begun as a surrogate father/son relationship half a century ago.

Others came into my life as new friends, each in his/her own manner, enfolding me with their caring, all the way through the miseries of fighting the pandemic that plagued all of us. Despite the fear of contagion, we managed to thrive, to increase in true friendships. Payback continues still; my life has been enhanced as never I could've imagined. Astonishingly, I am still a big (if ancient) frog in this welcoming little pond.

❖❖❖

Not Mandrake the Magician, not a priest, but who am I?

It has taken me more than a year to produce as complete a response as possible to this ultimate question. From reading my memoir, you have some idea of a final reply. Actually, like anyone else, I'm a multifaceted, complicated human being. Bear with me as I do my best to synthesize what the process of long exposure has yielded.

I am a composite from four sources: first, from my parents who, for better or worse, instilled in me the values and characteristics of their Lebanese origins; from our Roman Catholic faith which sustained me when I didn't have all the answers; then, from study and teaching of literature and film; and, finally, from great philosophers and thinkers, such as Aristotle, St. Augustine, Pierre de Chardin, Sigmund Freud, John Henry Newman, and contemporary sages like Muggs and Abraham Kaplan who went above and beyond their professions to grant me their personal insights.

But I am a strange composite, a conundrum to many. Throughout my life I've experienced cases of mistaken identity—most commonly, people believing I'm gay or Jewish. But odd incidents have translated into false impressions: I'm a mystic, a con man, a starving artist, a cultural snob, a cross dresser, even a lush (I once greeted a student, who came to my house in the early morning, holding a beer can—a liquid remedy recommended by my doctor that I preferred to consume first thing—who then broadcast his experience around campus).

What is true is that I've been driven by the need to belong, always feeling most alive when I'm feeling needed. Consequently, I've become a chameleon—changing, camouflaging to blend in—to result in this response: "I really don't know." And, yet, I am content not being bound into a fixed identity. As Walt Whitman wrote in his poem "Song of Myself," "Do I contradict myself? / Very well then, I contradict myself. / (I am large, I contain multitudes.)"

Examining my life with my mind's camera, focusing sharply at times and then out of focus at others, what appears in the view-finder is rarely a constant scene as I chose to be giving or taking, to be good or bad, to grow or lag behind. But I never chose to stagnate nor drift. I trust I made decisions that, in aggregate, reciprocate all I could in gratitude to having been surrounded by people of such wildly varying backgrounds as I experienced life's vicissitudes, hoping, ultimately, to wind up on the plus side, more thankful for the blessings bestowed on me than regretful for what errors I've made along the way. I still earnestly hope so.

In the process of reversing the open-shutter lens on myself, I've revisited forgotten encounters and personalities, examined motivations, been forced to reconsider long-held notions, and had some important epiphanies. Yes, many wonderful and some regrettable episodes, but all adding up to a life of learning, contemplation, inspiration, and self-expression—not over with yet, still capable of contributing. What? Not sure.

Memento

LIST OF ILLUSTRATIONS

(Photography by Joe Kirkish, unless otherwise noted)

Front cover
Lake Superior sunset from the cottage at Copper Harbor

Preface
vi   Self-portrait, 2006

Foreword
xii   Meg by University Circle Lagoon, 1969

Part 1 Roots, 1925–43
1   Portage Lake Bridge with view of Houghton (courtesy Michigan Technological University Archives and Copper Country Historical Collections)
4   Joe's grandmother, Shafeeha Brady, with daughters Anjool and Nabeeha (personal archive)
7   Joe with his parents, Anjool and Azar Kirkish, 1925 (personal archive)
24   Azar Kirkish with Joe, Babe, and Cis (personal archive)
33   Early self-portrait

Part 2 My Educational Odyssey, 1943–56
34   Brooklyn Bridge
42   Joe with Army pals in California, 1945 (personal archive)
55   Joe directing a play at Central Michigan University (personal archive)
63   Joe performing a magic show (personal archive)
64   Joe shooting a Univ. of Wisconsin actress at the Wisconsin Dells (personal archive)
69   Mrs. Ayoub
78   Camp Nebagamon basement darkroom (photo by Bill Rosenthal)
83   A Priscilla Beach Theatre production (personal archive)
94   Boys jumping into the icy East River; Manhattan street scene; Tallie Handler on the Brooklyn Bridge; "5th Avenue High Fashion"; Boardwalk at Coney Island

97   Don Redlich

110 Campers plunging into Lake Nebagamon (courtesy Camp Nebagamon)

113 Muggs Lorber (courtesy Camp Nebagamon)

117 Joe on a Brooklyn photo shoot (photo by Tallie Handler)

Part 3 Careers in and beyond the Copper Country, 1956–88

118 Portage Lake Lift Bridge

133 Tamburitzan dancer, Lake Nebagamon

154 Joe and Harvey the Rabbit with Janie and Ted Stein (personal archive)

154 John Kander, 1961

156 Family Camp, 1961

169 President Smith (in white) in a copper mine

171 First WGGL studio in Sperr Hall (courtesy Michigan Technological University Archives and Copper Country Historical Collections)

191 Abraham Kaplan

194 Edward Teller

216 Kirkish family cottage at Copper Harbor

216 Reidar Hahn and Keith Meisel "show and tell" photo session (personal archive)

221 Professor Roman

231 Marty Schendel

237 Larry Richardson—"Dancer Posing As If Touched by Sunlight"

Part 4 Emeritus , 1988–1999

244 Paris rooftops

259 Bobbie Geismer displaying the family heirloom Thanksgiving dessert

263 Copper Country clothesline

266 Early experiment with overlay portraiture

277 Overlay self-portrait

271 Club Indigo poster (personal archive)

274 Joe's parents with Babe, Cis, Jimmy, and Joe on Brockway Mountain Drive, 1971

274 Kirkish clan on Brockway Mountain Drive, 1971

275 Phi Tau retreat at the cottage (photo by Marty Schendel)

Part 5 Elder , 2000–

284 Esrey Park, Lake Superior
287 Joe sharing a meal with a blind resident at The Bluffs (photo by Marty Schendel)
291 Joe being honored by Mu Beta Psi (personal archive)
309 Memento

Back cover

Joe Kirkish at Brockway Mountain Drive (photo by Marty Schendel)

ACKNOWLEDGMENTS

The author gratefully acknowledges the assistance of Susan Burack, Rosie Hierman, and Gene Purdum in filling in various memory gaps. I am deeply indebted to Marty Schendel and Meg Ostrum for the hours they devoted to assembling and preparing the photographs for this publication, along with Lisa Kankanala, Adam Kaplan, Paula Kirkish, Louis Levin, Tom Leytham, and Allison Neely, whose help I also enlisted for this task. Thanks are due as well to the staff of Mission Point Press for their professionalism throughout the production process.

ABOUT THE AUTHOR

An early passion for drama, photography, and film, along with a deep desire to serve his community, spawned multiple, interwoven careers for immigrant son and Copper Country native Joe Kirkish. Besides teaching from 1956 to 1988 in the Humanities Department at Michigan Technological University, Kirkish also founded WGGL (the FM campus station that became one of the charter NPR stations). For over sixty years, he has been a columnist for Houghton's *Daily Mining Gazette.* He was the 2002 recipient of Michigan Tech's prestigious Clair M. Donovan award for his extracurricular services to the university and community, and his sustained efforts to promote the cinematic arts earned him the 2017 City Light Award from Tech's 41 North Film Festival.

Kirkish's career as a photographer also spans many decades. Beginning in his teens, he did freelance work, first for the *Gazette* and eventually for college and daily newspapers throughout the region. In addition, he developed the photography program at Camp Nebagamon (Wisconsin), which houses a collection of his work shot there from 1952 to 1967. His fine art photography has been featured in major magazines (including *Popular Photography, US Camera,* and *Modern Photography*), and he has exhibited at art galleries, museums, and art fairs in Michigan and beyond, garnering numerous awards.

www.ingramcontent.com/pod-product-compliance
Lightning Source LLC
Chambersburg PA
CBHW070906120626
46546CB00001B/150